3|10

3000 800066 21030
St. Louis Community College

D0152264

Meramec Library
St. Louis Community College
11333 Big Bend Blvd.
Kirkwood, MO 63122-5799
314-984-7797

WITHDRAWN

Violence against Women in Families and Relationships

Volume 4
The Media and Cultural Attitudes

Edited by
Evan Stark and Eve S. Buzawa

Praeger Perspectives

Praeger

An Imprint of ABC-CLIO, LLC

A B C · C L I O

Santa Barbara, California • Denver, Colorado • Oxford, England

Copyright 2009 by Evan Stark and Eve S. Buzawa

All rights reserved. No part of this publication may be reproduced, stored in a retrieval system, or transmitted, in any form or by any means, electronic, mechanical, photocopying, recording, or otherwise, except for the inclusion of brief quotations in a review, without prior permission in writing from the publisher.

Library of Congress Cataloging-in-Publication Data
Violence against women in families and relationships /
edited by Evan Stark and Eve S. Buzawa.
   v. ; cm.
   Includes index.
   Contents: vol. 1. Victimization and the community response —
vol. 2. The family context — vol. 3. Criminal justice and the law —
vol. 4. The media and cultural attitudes.
   ISBN 978-0-275-99846-2 (set : alk. paper) — ISBN 978-0-275-99848-6
(vol. 1) — ISBN 978-0-275-99850-9 (vol. 2) — ISBN 978-0-275-99852-3
(vol. 3) — ISBN 978-0-275-99854-7 (vol. 4) — ISBN 978-0-275-99847-9 (ebook)
   1. Abused women. 2. Family violence. I. Stark, Evan.
II. Buzawa, Eva Schlesinger.
   HV6626.V56   2009
   362.82'92—dc22   2009006262

13 12 11 10 9   1 2 3 4 5

This book is also available on the World Wide Web as an eBook.
Visit www.abc-clio.com for details.

ABC-CLIO, LLC
130 Cremona Drive, P.O. Box 1911
Santa Barbara, California 93116-1911

This book is printed on acid-free paper ∞

Manufactured in the United States of America

Contents

Set Introduction

Evan Stark and Eve S. Buzawa

The first call for shelter in the United States was made to Women's Advocates in St. Paul, Minnesota one afternoon in May 1972. The story of this group of courageous women opens *Violence against Women in Families and Relationships*. As recalled by Sharon Vaughan, a founder of the program and a pioneer in the battered-women's movement:

> The call was ... from Emergency Social Services. A worker said a woman was at the St. Paul Greyhound bus station with a two-year-old child. To get a job, she had traveled 150 miles from Superior, Wisconsin, with two dollars in her pocket. What were we expected to do? Where would they stay after two days at the Grand Hotel? One of the advocates borrowed a high chair and stroller and we took them to the apartment that was our office. These were the first residents we sheltered. The two-year-old destroyed the office in one night because all the papers were stacked on low shelves held up by bricks. His mother didn't talk about being battered; she said she wanted to go to secretarial school to make a life for her and her son. She tried to get a place to live, but no one would rent to her without a deposit, which she didn't have.... After a couple of weeks, she went back to Superior, and every Christmas for several years sent a card thanking Women's Advocates for being there and enclosed $2.00, the amount she had when she came to town.

This recollection captures several major themes highlighted in volume 1: the importance of women reaching out to other women, the reinforcing effects of poverty and domestic violence, and the extent to which those who escape abuse are intent on reconnecting with their hopes and dreams for a better life.

The shelter started in St. Paul was one stimulus for a domestic violence revolution that quickly circled the globe, stirring women from all walks of life, of all races, religions, and ages, and in thousands of neighborhoods, to challenge men's age-old prerogative to do with them as they willed. Even as these grassroots movements offered victims options for safety and empowerment that were never before available, they called on their governments to do the same. Importantly, these calls elicited an unprecedented response, almost certainly because women had become a formidable political and economic force. In its scope and significance, the domestic violence revolution is a watershed event in our lifetime.

On the ground, the domestic violence revolution consists of four critical components: the proliferation of community-based services for battered women; a growing sensitivity to how domestic violence affects families and particularly the children who are exposed to this violence; the criminalization of domestic violence and the corresponding mobilization of a range of state resources to protect abused women and their children and to arrest, sanction, or counsel perpetrators; and challenges to the normative values that have allowed men to exercise illegitimate forms of power and control in relationships and families. Although huge obstacles remain to changing cultural mores, these challenges now extend to the popular media, which shape how tens of millions of children and adults interpret the world around them.

Violence against Women in Families and Relationships takes stock of the seismic changes instigated by the domestic violence revolution, devoting separate volumes to its major components: community-based services (Volume 1), the family (Volume 2), the criminal justice response (Volume 3), and popular culture and the media (Volume 4). In addition to describing what happened, two overriding questions link these volumes. How is our world different today than when the domestic violence revolution began? Are abused women and their children better off because of these changes? We also identify the remaining obstacles to eliminating sexual injustice in relationships and families, ask what can be done to remove these obstacles, and identify a host of innovative programs designed to do this. The major conceptual contribution of these volumes is to provide an understanding of abuse that extends far beyond physical violence to the broad range of tactics actually used to coerce and control women and children in relationships.

THE DOMESTIC VIOLENCE REVOLUTION

Our goal is to provide a map of the scope and significance of the domestic violence revolution.

Since the opening and diffusion of shelters, the policies and the legal landscape affecting victims of partner abuse have changed dramatically. Reforms include billions of dollars in federal support for intervention, removing discretion in deciding whether to arrest those who assault their partners, a range of new protections for victims, the burgeoning of a vast network of researchers, specialized and integrated domestic violence courts and prosecutorial approaches (called "dedi-cated" or "evidence based"), one-stop justice centers, and putting part-ner abuse center stage in decisions about custody and visitation. In the past, battered women who retaliated against abusive partners hid their abuse, fearing it would provide a motive for their crimes. Today, women accused of crimes against abusive partners can use a "battered woman's defense" and call on a new class of experts to support their claims of victimization. The constitutional rationale for these reforms in the United States is straightforward: under the Equal Protection Clause of the Fourteenth Amendment, women assaulted by present or former partners are entitled to the same rights and protections as those who are assaulted by strangers. In other countries, domestic violence has been identified as violation of basic human rights.

The helping professions have also undergone radical changes in response to the domestic violence revolution. Medicine, nursing, public health, psychology, psychiatry, social work, and child welfare have intro-duced a range of innovative programs to identify and respond more appropriately to the adult and child victims of abuse. Forty years ago, when Anne Flitcraft asked the director of the emergency medical services at Yale–New Haven Hospital if she could study "battered women" for her medical school thesis, he was puzzled. "What's a battered woman?" he asked. Today, in part as a result of pioneering research by Dr. Flitcraft and hundreds of other scholars, training in the health, mental health, legal, and social service professions would be remiss if it did not include specialized units on domestic violence. Every major health care organization has made domestic violence a priority. Hundreds of hospitals in the United States have protocols requiring that medical personnel identify and refer victims of abuse. In hundreds of communities, once perpetrators are arrested, they are offered counseling as an alternative to jail through "batterer interven-tion programs." Moreover, several thousand localities now host collabora-tive efforts to reduce or prevent abuse in which community-based services such as shelters join with courts, law enforcement, local businesses, child protection agencies, and a range of health, education, and service organi-zations. In dozens of communities, small and large businesses alike have taken initiatives to extend protections from abusive partners to employees or supported broader community-based initiatives.

Never before has such an array of resources and interventions been brought to bear on abuse or oppression in relationships and families. By any conventional standard, the domestic violence revolution has been an incredible success. Politicians across a broad spectrum have embraced its core imagery of male violence and female victimization. As telling is an increasing sensitivity to the portrayal of abused women by the mass media and a growing awareness of how mainstream mes-sages conveyed by sports, popular music, and other cultural media con-tribute to abusive behavior by males.

Hundreds of thousands of men, women, and children owe the fact that they are alive to the availability of shelters, to criminal justice and legal reforms, and to equally important shifts in research, health services, and popular culture. Just recently, historically speaking, a man's use of coercion to chastise or discipline his female partner or his children was widely considered a right inherited with his sex. This is no longer so.

In 1977, during one of the many incidents when Mickey Hughes assaulted his wife Francine, their 12-year-old daughter Christy called police. He threatened to kill Francine with police present. This seemed like "idle talk," an officer testified at Francine's trial for murder. "He hadn't killed her before; he wouldn't do so now." A few hours after they left, Francine set fire to the bed in which her husband was sleeping and he was fatally burned.

Things have changed dramatically since 1977. Mickey was never arrested, though he had raped Francine on several occasions and assaulted her dozens of times. Not until 1979, as the result of lawsuits in Oakland, California, and New York, were police required to replace their "arrest-avoidance" strategy, respond quickly to domestic violence calls, and presumptively arrest whenever they had probable cause to believe a felonious assault had occurred or when a misdemeanor assault was committed in their presence. Marital rape was still not a crime in 1977, and in New York and a number of other states was not even considered grounds for divorce. In several states, Francine could have gotten an injunction, though police had no role in enforcing these orders, and only if she was married, and only pursuant to a divorce.

Farrah Fawcett portrayed Francine in a TV film version of this story, *The Burning Bed*. In the mid-1990s, when her boyfriend slammed Fawcett to the ground and choked her after an argument at a restaurant, he was arrested, tried, and convicted. By this time, the marriage-rape exemption was largely abolished, police in most areas were mandated to arrest perpetrators whom they believed had committed a domestic violence crime, and courts in most countries were routinely providing a range of protections for abuse victims. On the two occasions that Francine left Mickey to return to her parents, he stalked and harassed her without consequence. Today, stalking is a crime and harassment is widely recognized as a facet of abuse. Aside from her family, Francine had no recourse, no shelter to enter, and no support services. A woman faced with a burning-bed situation today would mount a "battered woman's defense" rather than plead "temporary insanity," as Francine did. The forces of law and order that protected a man's right to "physically correct" his wife in 1977 now target this bastion of male authority for destruction.

Perhaps the most significant change that resulted from the domestic violence revolution involves the portrayal of male violence against women in the media, particularly in film and on TV, the ultimate family medium. As women made unprecedented gains in economic, political, and cultural status after 1960, the hazards that men pose to their wives and girlfriends became a moral compass for the integrity of relationships generally. From Johannesburg to Caracas, from Jerusalem to Dayton, Ohio, young girls understand that no male has the right to lay his hands on them if they do not want him to do so. Well into the 1980s, violence continued to be glamorized as the penultimate test of manhood (the ultimate test remains sexual conquest), as illustrated by the popularity of gangsta rap and *James Bond* and *Rambo* films. But male violence has increasingly been forced to share the stage with images of women as equally capable of using force and of abusive men as purposeful, obsessive, and cruel rather than romantic. Julia Roberts' portrayal of a housewife who kills an abusive husband who is stalking her in *Sleeping with the Enemy* (1991) contrasts sharply with Eleanor Parker's role in the 1955 film *The Man with the Golden Arm* as a wife who sets out to heal her husband (played by Frank Sinatra) while enduring his physical abuse, betrayal, heroin addiction, and mental torment.

Partner violence against women is no longer "just life." And yet, anyone with reasonable sympathies and a passing acquaintance with abuse or current interventions will have a range of questions about the impact of even the most dramatic reforms.

VICTIMIZATION AND THE COMMUNITY RESPONSE

Volume 1 reviews the development, operations, and effectiveness of battered women's programs; the progress of intervention in health; and the interplay of domestic violence with race, poverty, sexual identity, and the changing economic landscape of communities caused by globalization. The core questions addressed in this volume are as follows: what do battered women's programs actually do? Has the "success" of the shelter movement led it to compromise its original ideals? Is the support that advocates provide sufficient to help victims regain their footing? To what extent does help "help"? Or does it actually make things worse by blaming victims for their abuse? Does the medical system need to look beyond physical violence to improve its response? What special problems face lesbian victims of abuse? What unique dynamics are put into play in the experience of abuse by the disadvantages associated with poverty, racism, or deindustrialization? How must intervention change to accommodate these dynamics? Where do we go from here?

THE FAMILY CONTEXT

Volume 2 looks at the ways in which domestic violence shapes family dynamics in general and affects children in particular and at the two major systems responsible for managing these effects: the child welfare system and the family court. How are children threatened by domestic violence and coercive control? Domestic violence is the most common background factor for child abuse and neglect, and it is typically the same man who is abusing the mother who is the source of harm to children. After much prodding, the child welfare system began to address domestic violence. But its first steps were missteps. Instead of protecting mothers and their children, the child welfare system punished them for being beaten. Why did this happen, and what can be done to correct this problem? Family courts have also been pressured to consider domestic violence in custody and divorce cases. But are they doing so? How can the family court reconcile concerns for the safety of women and their children in abusive relationships with the widespread belief that children must have access to both parents after divorce? To what extent are each of the systems confronted by victims of battering and their children sending contradictory messages that do as much to confuse and further entrap them as to provide for their safety? What reforms are needed to set child welfare and family court systems on the right track? And what about the offending fathers? How do they extend their abusive strategies during custody disputes? And what about the movement for "father's rights"? Is it a positive or negative force in this process? Can offending men learn to father more appropriately? How does working with them on fathering affect how they understand and treat the women in their lives? What is at the root of the problems with these systems? Are we dealing primarily with individual bias or something more systemic? How would broadening our understanding of abuse to include the multiple ways in which men subjugate their partners enhance the child welfare or family court response?

CRIMINAL JUSTICE AND THE LAW

From the start, the domestic violence revolution in the United States called on the state to mobilize its justice resources to protect victims and hold offenders accountable for their acts, usually through some combination of arrest, incarceration, and/or reeducation. Volume 3 reviews the revolutionary changes in policy, criminal law, and policing affected by the domestic violence revolution. Severe violence against wives had been against the law for centuries. But it was only in the 1980s, as states passed domestic violence laws and made arrest mandatory in abuse cases, that police, prosecutors, and the criminal courts treated it as a crime. How are these reforms working? Has the domestic violence revolution relied too heavily on criminal justice? Have the changes in policing, prosecution, and criminal law gone too far or not far enough? Are abusive men changed by arrest? Does counseling for batterers work, and, if so, with what kinds of men? How should we understand and respond to partner violence by women or to families in which both partners are abusive?

THE MEDIA AND CULTURAL ATTITUDES

However much the domestic violence revolution may have reformed the helping and justice professions, these changes are unlikely to endure unless the underlying cultural supports for domestic violence are displaced. Prevailing cultural norms reproduce the sex stereotypes that underlie sexual inequality even as women win formal legal equality and make unprecedented gains in education, income, and political participation. Volume 4 maps how these stereotypes are represented and challenged in a range of cultural media, including newspapers, film, women's magazines, video games, and rap. After explaining how the core narratives in a culture shape experience, the chapters in this volume consider what the stories told about sexual violence in these media suggest about how and why violence against women happens; who or what causes it; whether it is the by-product of specific social factors, malevolence, or just "bad luck" for instance; and how it can be ended. How these stories are constructed is as important as what they say. This volume considers the transformative potential of the media, including theater, as well as the role they play in reinforcing the status quo. The closing chapter considers whether community values have, in fact, changed over the course of the domestic violence revolution.

WHAT YOU'LL FIND HERE

An estimated 13,000 books and monographs about domestic violence have appeared since the early 1970s. Digesting and translating this published material are obviously beyond our capacity. Nevertheless, we started this project by scouring this literature for the major trends and cutting-edge ideas about abuse. Next, we reached out to both established scholars as well as to younger researchers doing cutting-edge work. We asked these writers to do three things: tell us *what* has changed; tell us *how* these changes have affected families, particularly the women, children, and men most immediately involved; and speculate about *what is next*. Where are we likely to go, and where *should* we go from here? We welcomed criticism of existing approaches. We are not pushing a particular cause. But if there are new approaches, innovative practices, or changes in policy that would help set things right, we wanted readers to know about them. And we insisted they write for educated readers who have little or no prior knowledge of the subject, not always an easy thing for scholars whose main audiences tend to consist of academics like themselves. The model we suggested was a feature article for the Sunday newspaper. Think of yourself as the

expert you are, we told them. This meant limiting notes to direct quotations and controversial statistics. We gave the contributors the option
of directing readers to further information likely to be available on the
Web or at a public library. Frankly, this charge posed an editorial challenge we had not anticipated.

One might think that summarizing the wealth of research on violence in families would be sufficient. Not so. One of the most insidious
characteristics of the type of oppression we address in personal life is
that it typically occurs "behind closed doors" and proceeds in ways
that are often hidden from outsiders, often including close friends,
neighbors, coworkers, and helping professionals. Researchers too have
little direct access to victims or offenders and typically meet them or
hear their stories only after they call police, come to court, or enter a
shelter. Since whether victims report what is happening to them is
largely a function of the opportunity to do so as well as the fear of possible consequences, millions of battered women and their children have
no contact with police, shelters, courts, hospitals, or child welfare and
so never appear in the public spaces where data are collected. Telephone surveys pick up some of this hidden abuse. But the questions
asked on surveys are too broad to capture its meaning, contexts, dynamics, or far-reaching consequences. We were less interested in gener-
alities about abuse than in the nuances, the particulars. We are not
after sensationalism. But we wanted readers to know battered women
as people, to walk in their shoes to some extent, as well as read *about*
them. Another problem is that researchers can ask questions only about
things they already know are present. A key theme in these volumes is
that the images of violence and physical injury that have dominated
our understanding of abuse miss an underlying reality of coercion and
control in these relationships that can be as devastating as assault and
is almost always more salient for victims. The harms caused by these
coercive and controlling tactics are rarely recognized, let alone documented, even among those who are able to get help. The fact that so
many of those affected are poor or from disadvantaged groups also
contributes to their invisibility.

To unlock the knowledge contained in what Yale University political
scientist James Scott calls the "hidden transcripts" of these lives, it is
necessary to listen directly to the voices of women and children who
experience battering as well as to their abusive partners. This means
allowing them to tell their stories as they were lived rather than as fil-
tered through the preconceptions we all bring to the field, ourselves
included. In addition to chapters that summarize what is known about
particular aspects of interpersonal violence, therefore, we have called on
practitioners who work or have worked directly with victims, perpetrators, and their children in a variety of settings. A number of the practitioners herein have helped to design or implement imaginative

programs. We include authors who have started or worked in shelters, facilitated batterer intervention programs, trained child welfare workers, and directed a state coalition for battered women. We have several chapters by lawyers who have represented battered women and their children in family and criminal courts and other chapters by forensic psychologists and social workers. Several of our authors have translated their research into practice. In a chapter in volume 4, anthropology professor Elaine J. Lawless describes a theater project she started with a colleague and some students at the University of Missouri. Professor Lawless had conducted fieldwork for a book at a battered women's shelter in her community. Feeling dissatisfied with a purely academic presentation of her "findings," she helped students perform the stories she had collected as monologues to stimulate a broad, community-wide discussion about abuse. The presentations not only gave audiences a picture of the abuse going on around them but also opened up a space in which student actors and audience members could tell their own stories about abuse, some of which became part of subsequent "performances," creating a community of witnesses that enhanced the overall safety of women and children in that neighborhood.

A basic premise of the shelter movement is that those who are battered by their partners are the only real "experts" on their experience and that their expertise is the centerpiece of any real knowledge about how abuse unfolds. We have tried to respect this view by interspersing the informational chapters with chapters that rely heavily on women's stories or explain why "storying" domestic violence is so important. If we have succeeded, the topical chapters should dovetail with lived experiences of abuse. Like the Missouri theater project, we hope these volumes help stimulate a broad-ranging conversation and new ways of seeing, listening to, and interpreting what is happening in our midst.

These volumes also have an international dimension, though it is unfortunately limited to English-speaking countries. We include writers from England, Canada, Scotland, and Australia. The authors of these chapters have done groundbreaking work in their particular areas for which there was often no parallel in the United States. For example, the report on child homicides prepared by Hilary Saunders on behalf of Women's Aid Federation England (WAFE) is a stunning model of advocacy that has elicited family court reforms that are long overdue in the United States. But the international focus also reflects the fact that both the grassroots women's movements in these countries and the systemic changes they elicited have grown from a continuing interchange between researchers and practitioners in these nations.

In each of the respects outlined above, this set of volumes is unique—in its breadth, its mix of researchers and practitioners, the emphasis on victim voices, the attempt to weigh changes in popular culture, its international scope, and its focus on what lies ahead.

But our approach will not satisfy everyone.

Most of us initially got involved in the domestic violence field because we hoped to call attention to and ameliorate the injustices suffered by millions of women and children who were being subjugated in their relationships, mainly (but not only) by male partners, and because we found the response to this suffering by the courts, police, hospitals, and other institutions woefully inadequate. From this vantage, behavior is seen as abusive and as meriting public concern if it involves coercive and/or controlling behavior whose primary intent and/or consequence is to hurt, threaten, frighten, or control a partner. Notice the broad understanding of abuse.

From the day we welcomed the first victims to our shelters, our strongest feelings of sympathy and anger were elicited by the physical scars caused by their partner's violence. Even though many women insisted that the "violence wasn't the worst part," hinting at a yet-to-be-identified range of tactics used by their partners that they found even more hurtful than physical abuse, it was the woman's bruised face or broken bones that held our attention as well as the media's.

We now know that abuse is limited to physical and psychological abuse in only a minority of cases, somewhere between 20 and 40 percent. In the rest, the vast majority, forms of coercion such as violence, threats, or stalking are combined with a pattern of control that can include tactics to isolate victims; restrict their access to money, food, transportation, medical care, or other basic necessities; and microregulate their everyday activities, such as how they dress, cook, clean, talk on the phone or relate to their children. This pattern, known as coercive control, is referred to repeatedly throughout the volumes and is the major focus of chapters by Stark (volume 2), Lischick (volume 2), and Turkheimer (volume 3). Because the aim of coercive control is to limit a victim's resources as well as their opportunities to escape, it greatly heightens women's risk of being seriously injured or killed as well as of developing a range of medical, behavioral, and mental health problems. But the major consequence of being subjected to this strategy over time is that victims become entrapped. Their autonomy is compromised, and their basic liberties protected by the U.S. Constitution are abrogated, such as the right to free speech, their freedom of movement, and their right to make decisions about their bodies. Many of the rights that are violated by coercive control are so tightly woven into the fabric of everyday life that they are rarely protected explicitly (such as the right to cook, clean, dress, or toilet as they wish) and have to be inferred as rights by our general right to pursue our lives as we please. While women frequently assault male and female partners, coercive control appears to be largely committed by men against female partners. Of the estimated 15 million U.S. women who are battered, somewhere between 8 and 12 million are victims of coercive control.

If our major focus is on the use of violence in these relationships despite our broad definition and on the provision of safety, this is because of the appalling consequence of violence for the women who seek help and because most research and almost all interventions are designed in response to domestic violence, not coercive control. But even here, it is not violence per se that concerns us, but coercion used in the context of inequality, coercion that exploits and strengthens existing disadvantages.

Our framework will make at least two groups unhappy. A significant minority of researchers in the domestic violence field morally opposes the use of violence in any form in families or relationships and believe that trying to distinguish the use of force by its motive, context, or consequence or by the relative standing of its victims expresses a personal bias. To this group, couples who use force during fights among relative equals are as wrong to do so as is the man whose violence is unilaterally designed to quash his partner's autonomy. So committed are many in this group to a vision of families and intimate relationships as nonviolent spaces of cooperation that they oppose a vigorous police response in any but the most extreme cases, favoring couples counseling and other forms of conflict resolution instead. This group also holds that women's use of force with their partners is as significant a matter of public concern as men's use of force, even though the probability of injury is far greater to victimized women in these situations; women are far more likely to report being threatened or controlled by abuse than men and they are far more likely to seek or require outside help. Another group will also be unhappy with us. This group opposes vigorous state intervention in abuse less because of its devotion to the family than because they worry that inviting the state into people's personal lives will ultimately do more harm than good, no matter the rationale. This group is willing to accept a wide range of controlling and physically hurtful behavior in relationships to preserve privacy.

We are concerned with preserving and protecting physical integrity at all levels of relationships. But we hope this set helps shift attention from the sheer physical violations caused by abuse to the ways in which coercion and control are used to deny persons their rights and liberties in personal life. However imperfectly they may do so, we believe that governments have an obligation to address these harms and with the same commitment they bring to stemming harms in public life.

Many of those who pick up these volumes will undoubtedly do so because they have experienced abuse in their own lives or known someone who has. As several of the authors eloquently report, the forms of violence, intimidation, isolation, humiliation, and "control" that excite much of the help sought by women who have been battered by partners are closer in their dynamic to hostage taking than to what we normally think of as assault. Except, of course, these victims are "hostages at home"; they have been prisoners in their personal lives. It is easy to be depressed by the statistics and descriptions presented in these pages or to become cynical about the willingness of humans to inflict cruelty even on those they supposedly care for.

But we ask readers to also consider this: that the women who populate these pages have survived to tell their own stories. And many women and children subjected to abuse have done more than merely survive, as Hilary Abrahams illustrates in volume 1 in her record of women who have left shelter: "I sometimes feel like a spring flower." Some elements of women's stories may elicit pity; other details we provide about abuse may provoke anger, even outrage, as they should. Clearly, no community can be truly whole or free so long as one group is allowed to use the means of coercion and control to subjugate others, whether sex or some other factor is the basis for this practice. Once we know such crimes are occurring in our midst, we cannot turn away. But in addition to our protection and concern, the women in these volumes deserve our respect and admiration because of the courage, strength of character, and resolve required to survive the forms of oppression they faced.

We have recently completed a presidential race in which one of the candidates was justly celebrated for his ordeal as a POW (prisoner of war) during the Vietnam War. To those of us who have worked in this field, it is absolutely clear that resisting, standing up to, or even just surviving coercive control is often comparable to the heroism exhibited by returning POWs. If only as a token, we offer these volumes in lieu of a public monument to those who have survived the horrors of personal life. And there is a larger lesson too. Once we appreciate what the women here have accomplished, we see that each of us may be capable of remaking the world we are given, even against what may seem at first impossible odds.

The final justification for this set is that our society has invested billions of dollars and hundreds of millions of human service hours in managing the domestic violence in our midst. Apart from the unprecedented commitment of resources to protect women and children and hold perpetrators accountable are the enormous costs of not effectively addressing abuse in families and relationships. We have made a huge investment in ending an age-old form of injustice. Readers deserve an accounting.

Introduction to Volume 4

Evan Stark

The well-known journalist Charles Merz once remarked that it is doubtful whether anything really unifies the country like its murders. There is a kernel of truth in this observation. A good deal of what we know or think we know about our own lives and the lives of others in our communities comes via the media. Moreover, the "human interest" appeal of stories about violence in relationships probably does more to make exposure to the mass media a habit than anything but the coverage of sports.

If the "culture" we consume shapes how we understand and respond to violence in our relationships, so too does any hope of eliminating partner violence rest on changing the "culture of violence" that surrounds us. Only a small proportion of lawbreakers is ever arrested or sent to jail. So, in addition to changing the institutional structures that support sexual inequality in relationships, preventing domestic violence requires a broad shift in tolerance for abusive behavior, starting with how the media portray the causes and dynamics of domestic violence and whom they hold accountable for ending it. Challenging the culture of violence entails not merely bringing new faces onto the screen or giving voice to those who have been silenced, but rewriting "the story" told about abuse to highlight the suffering and courage of those who are victimized rather than their culpability and the sole responsibility of those who inflict this suffering.

Volume 4 maps the cultural terrain in which we hope to make inroads and suggests ways to move forward. Despite its importance, there has been little written about how the domestic violence revolution has affected media portrayals of partner abuse let alone about how it has changed popular attitudes or the sorts of stories we tell about perpetrators or victims of violence.

The main focus of this volume is on the media. Chapters on popular magazines, news stories, video games, and rap music approach their subjects literally, dissecting the explicit content of story lines and portrayals. But *how* the media convey their meanings can be as important to understanding their impact as *what* they convey substantively. The influence of print media such as magazines or newspapers is mediated because we can step back and think about what we read, weigh conflicting arguments, or fact-check on the Web. But visual media such as film or TV can have a more visceral impact that is more difficult to gauge. For instance, films invite an immediate level of psychological involvement that is conducive to a dream-like assimilation of images, and so to unconscious, unreflective, or transgressive forms of identification. In this sense, to play off a point made by the media guru Marshall McLuhan, the medium is both more and less than "the message." Whether the Internet, rap, or video games operate in ways that are more akin to film than magazines is open to debate. In any case, efforts to self-consciously use media to change attitudes have to consider the form in which education is presented as well as the proclivities of particular target audiences.

IMAGERY IN HISTORICAL CONTEXT

Like other businesses, the media survive by competing successfully in the marketplace. This means that their messages must be tailored to popular tastes to some extent. This is true even of media like film that live off direct patronage rather than advertising. Violence sells. So does sex. When the two are packaged together, the entertainment appeal is hard to match. A key question here is whether, in making sexual violence palatable to a mass audience, the media "story" illuminates or obfuscates the realities of abuse experienced by women and children.

Sexual violence has been a recurrent theme in the high arts for centuries. But only with the development of modern media as vehicles for marketing to mass audiences in the first half of the twentieth century did popular magazines, film, radio, popular music, and then television strive to tell stories about "love gone wrong" with which ordinary people could identify, and to project these stories into our private lives and homes.

ALL IN THE FAMILY

The chapters in this volume concentrate on the last few decades, a period when, thanks in large part to the movement for women's liberation, women made unprecedented gains in education, as well as in economic and political life. Not surprisingly, their status in the media improved in tandem, with women increasingly occupying a range of roles that had been exclusively reserved for men. Part of the growing media sensitivity to women's lives and careers outside the home was a heightened awareness of the importance of violence in their lives.

Although the sheer number of women portrayed as professionals, corporate executives, politicians, or violent protagonists is new, independent women made an appearance in the media long before *Thelma and Louise* (1991). Women who are footloose, aggressive, and clever like Clara Bow had key roles in the films of the 1920s and in comic strips like *Blondie*, whose madcap antics as a flapper captured that era's spirit of female economic independence. In the 1930s, actresses such as Katharine Hepburn, Rosalind Russell, and Joan Crawford portrayed women for whom career and ambition came before domesticity. But Blondie's marriage to Dagwood in 1933 reflected a general trend during the Depression for assertive personalities to redirect their energies to make things work at home and to endure hard times, including physical abuse, the character trait that defined Ma Joad in John Steinbeck's classic *Grapes of Wrath*.

According to myth, Rosie replaced her rivet gun with a vacuum to make room for her returning husband after World War II. In fact, women's labor market participation slowed during the 1940s and 1950s, but did not decline, and then took off in the 1960s. Ironically, this reality was masked by the pro-natalist ideology disseminated by media portrayals of women only as wives and homemakers during the 1940s and 1950s, portrayals that openly discouraged their efforts to translate economic independence into autonomy in personal life. As illustrated by Kim Hunter's portrayal of Stella in the 1951 film version of *A Streetcar Named Desire*, wives were expected to accept and even tame the savagery in their husband's heart, including their violence.

Prior to the 1970s, the family and social science literature is silent about domestic violence. Instead, the loveless barrage of passivity, rage, violence, and control we now identify as coercive control was dismissed as "marital discord," sharply distinguished from criminal violence, and set alongside the many other "normal" problems housewives were expected to manage, albeit with the assistance of the emerging corps of therapists or marriage counselors if need be.

A similarly imagined disconnect between anger, conflict, and literal violence was epitomized in the 1950s sitcom *The Honeymooners*, in which Ralph Kramden's raised fist famously stops just short of Alice's face when he threatens to send her "to the moon." We laugh at this pretext of self-control because we see the vulnerability of men like Ralph through the eyes of TV wives who face their husbands fearlessly, reassuring the female audience that the threatened blows will never materialize, using a combination of humor, insults, manipulation, and emotional distance to manage.

The outbursts and implied terror were slightly muted in the comic bravado of Archie Bunker in the 1970s. *All in the Family* is an intergenerational conversation about how to treat women that takes place largely among men. Archie's wife, Edith, is a carryover from stoic sufferers like Ma Joad and lacks even the hint of hysteria evident in Kim Hunter's portrayal of Stella. But Archie's anger is an update: elicited by the claims of women, blacks, gays, and other emerging minorities for rights and recognition, his immediate target is his "meathead" son-in-law who refuses to adapt an autocratic pose with his own wife. Archie expresses the dilemma posed to traditional manhood by a new woman who works and has a mind (if a small one) of her own. The meathead talks the talk of the new man, complete with racial tolerance and sexual equality. But he is also indolent, dependent, and passive to his fate, suggesting that the cost of abandoning the search-and-destroy Rambo philosophy of life Archie advocates is the loss of manhood. The show suggests that the choice men face is to change with the times or become trapped in a loser's personality like Ralph Kramden and Archie himself. Many of the abusive men in my clinical practice described a similar dilemma. They waxed nostalgic for their fathers' "control" over their mothers, but despised themselves when they acted "like them."

Homer Simpson is the Archie Bunker of the 1990s. Homer presents a similar composite of bluster, pettiness, ignorance, and rage that is transparent to everyone except himself, but without overt race, sex, and class biases. In an early episode of *The Simpsons*, a therapist asks the family to pictorially represent the image they associate with anger in their household. Mother, son, daughter, and baby draw Homer, while Homer draws a fighter plane. In marked contrast to ever-loyal Edith, Homer's wife Marge joins the rest of the Simpson clan in a defensive alliance against him. Where it was common for men to identify with Ralph or Archie as well as with their propensity to scapegoat, only the most paranoid person can identify with Homer's isolation and rage.

An older generation can still watch reruns of *The Honeymooners* and *All in the Family*. But by the 1990s, domestic terrorism was no longer funny. Paralleling the burgeoning field of domestic violence research, the media focus shifted from the comic machismo of the father/husband to the realistic pain of the victim. In *Public Enemy* (1931), the prototypical film about male violence, director William Wellman shot James Cagney squashing a grapefruit in his girlfriend's face from the gangster's standpoint, openly inviting his audience to identify with the aggressor. By contrast, in an episode of an evening medical drama in the mid-1990s, *Chicago Hope*, a young black woman is hospitalized after being beaten by her white boyfriend. The camera moves from a close-up of the woman's battered and swollen face to a physician (the woman's brother) and nurse—regulars on the show—who are formulating a strategy to protect the girl against the bully. More exacting is the portrayal a few years later on NBC's *ER*, one of the most widely viewed dramatic shows ever. After a battered woman is admitted to the hospital, a social worker pressures an attending physician to call the police, which he does reluctantly, not wanting to be drawn into "private troubles." When the doctor returns to the hospital room, a policeman is present, which the physician assumes is in response to his call. In a chilling moment, the officer puts his arm around the woman, and leaves with his wife. The emotive dynamic in the Cagney film is inverted: we identify with the epiphany experienced by the stunned physician, thereby admitting—and so penetrating—our own naiveté about abuse. The seminal female image for the 1990s is Julia Roberts's portrayal of a battered woman in *Sleeping with the Enemy* (1991). In place of Eleanor Parker's codependent pursuit of Frank Sinatra in *Man with a Golden Arm* (1955), it is Roberts's husband who pursues and is eventually killed by her; the Roberts character is portrayed as victimized and heroic, a marked contrast to Depression-era films in which women with similar stealth are portrayed as selfish and sinister.

The mass media remain misogynist in many respects. Violence continues to be glamorized as the penultimate test of manhood (the ultimate test remains sexual conquest), as illustrated by the continued popularity of the James Bond, Rocky, and Rambo films. But male violence has increasingly been forced to share the stage with images of women as equally capable of using force and of abusive men as purposeful, obsessive, and cruel. Domestic violence, a problem that had been officially invisible, even to social science, is now regularly featured in every medium. By the 1980s, domestic violence had displaced sexual infidelity, divorce, and terminal illness as the social problem of choice on daytime soaps and evening drama. Acknowledging the reality of sexual violence was a step forward. As the chapters in this volume suggest, however, how this violence is depicted remains deeply problematic.

TELLING STORIES

In the media, as in cultural conversation more broadly, domestic violence always appears "packaged" in stories. In Chapter 1, sociologist Donileen Loseke explains the importance of stories or narratives in our lives, highlighting the extent to which they are a pervasive form of social expression not limited to the media, help make complex realities salient to policy makers and other target audiences, and help the rest of us make sense of an increasingly diverse world. She then contrasts the stories about abuse told by the early battered women's movement with the then-dominant family narrative which made no mention of violence—except in the lives of "the poor"—or else conflated it with other forms of a husband's authority to which wives were expected to defer. The movement story of abuse was effective in persuading state actors to intervene, in part because of the stark contrast it drew between the extreme violence used by male partners and the relative innocence and passivity of wives. Designed largely for external consumption, this public story of abuse was as alien to women's actual experiences as the patriarchal myth it was devised to replace. Loseke shows that much of the complexity and uniqueness of women's lived experience is lost when they try to make public stories of abuse their own, causing a significant subgroup to resist identifying themselves with the shelter movement or as "battered." The solution she proposes is to broaden the public story of abuse based on listening to the actual stories victimized women tell.

The second chapter also shows that public stories are not always what they seem. Focusing on film violence, Karen Boyle opens by arguing that copy-cat explanations that blame media violence for violent behavior inadvertently shift responsibility away from perpetrators and the other multiple sources that normalize violence against women in our culture. Film critics who conclude that movies are "sexist" solely because of how men treat women on-screen miss a critical aspect of the cinematic experience, how film *as film* privileges "the male gaze" by encouraging all members of the audience, including women, to derive pleasure from identifying with the male protagonist driving the action forward and objectifying the relatively passive female who is acted upon. Boyle suggests that the setting of film viewing, of seeing without being seen for instance, simulates voyeurism, allowing audience members a sense of power and control over the characters being viewed even when they are not literally sexualized or victimized. Using *Halloween* (Carpenter, 1978) as an example, she shows that even ostensibly sexist slasher films may elicit a paradoxical, even an antisexist response in male audience members, in this case by fostering identification with an invisible stalker who turns out to be a deformed child or by exposing the violent underbelly of family life much as the campaigns to publicize domestic violence or child sexual abuse were trying to do. She offers equally intriguing analyses of "thrillers" like *Silence of the Lambs* (Demme, 1991) and rape/revenge films, arguing that the reactions elicited can subvert the explicit sexist story line as well as reinforce it; reveal the patterned and structured nature of male violence (in *Silence of the Lambs*); the gendered nature of rape; or play off the absurdity of rape myths. She extends her critique to the portrayal of men's violence against other men in film, showing how their violent action allows male characters as well as audience members to disavow their erotic attachment to other men, contrasting the portrayal of men's violence, which just *is,* to the endless scrutiny of women's violence and its link to their sexual assertiveness.

Lori Post, Patricia Smith, and Emily Meyer also highlight the formal and structural dimensions of the media they examine, in this case journalism, as well as the content of news stories about intimate partner homicide. Drawing on qualitative as well as quantitative research, they show how a concern with "newsworthiness" leads reporters to abstract the fatal event from its social context, including the abusive history in the relationship, and then to draw on a range of framing techniques (such as selected interviews and the inclusion of extraneous information) to portray the situation as unusual (hence as newsworthy), the perpetrator as either abnormal to start or as driven crazy, and the victim as at least partially to blame for her death. These features are suggested, for example, when a killing following a simple disagreement is taken out of the context of a long prior history of threats and abuse and selective quotes from neighbors are added to suggest what a kind, decent fellow the murderer was before he "broke." Which homicides are covered is as critical in shaping public perception as descriptions of how and why they occurred. From the universe of homicides, coverage is disproportionately given to those that involve "worthy" (that is, white and affluent) female victims killed in large cities by a stranger, the group that is *least* likely to be victimized in real life. Systematic bias in reporting intimate partner homicides reinforces common myths about domestic violence, in effect contributing to levels of misinformation and misunderstanding that can actually jeopardize potential victims in the community. Proposals for change include "participatory communication," a collaborative relationship between advocates and news organizations that is illustrated by an initiative in Rhode Island.

The next three chapters analyze the types of stories told about sexual violence in popular magazines and video games.

In chapters 4 and 5, Kathryn Phillips Thill and Karen E. Dill and sociologist Nancy Berns analyze the stories told about sexual violence in popular magazines.

Thill and Dill bring a psychological perspective to their study of magazines, starting with the three principal needs readers seek to gratify through reading: diversion, information gathering, and, perhaps most importantly, a desire to build personal identity, a need that can link readers to the characters in stories in ways that open them to new ways of understanding themselves and others. Magazines can be subdivided based on which of these needs comprises their primary appeal, with those driven by information trailing far behind those that emphasize "infotainment" in circulation. While the latter group cannot be expected to emphasize the depressing realities confronting abused women, a number of popular women's magazines such as *Redbook* or *Good Housekeeping* cover problem areas that may be taboo in other media, helping young women in particular get their moorings. The authors track coverage of domestic violence in popular magazines between 1974 and 2004, examining the extent of coverage, the nature of coverage in different seg-ments of the market, changes in the language used, and the extent to which published pieces transcend the "fluff" and "it happened to me" narrative formats. Although they identify successful examples that com-bine accurate information with diversion and suggest ways magazines might model coverage of domestic violence on the coverage of alcohol-ism or other "depressing" problems, they remain skeptical about the possibility that market-driven media will transcend the currently domi-nant fantasy that "Mr. Right" will replace "Mr. Wrong."

Nancy Berns examines magazine and other media stories from a sociological perspective in Chapter 5, comparing the dominant narra-tive to fairy tales, but with a twist. Instead of a "white knight" or prince rescuing the victim, she must rescue herself in domestic violence folklore, a process known as "victim empowerment." In this approach, domestic violence is portrayed as a private problem, the abusive part-ner plays a minor role, violence is introduced mainly to move the story along, and the victim alone takes on the challenge of escaping abuse. Berns identifies the structure of the empowerment story and then ana-lyzes the facet of this frame required for the happy ending, when the victim takes personal responsibility for ending the abuse either by going to counseling or just leaving, presumably inspiring women in similar situations to do the same, becoming what the feminist historian Linda Gordon calls "heroes of their own lives." Interestingly, the mag-azine editors Berns interviewed see cajoling women to get out, laying responsibility for continued abuse on women who fail to do so promptly, and supplying uplifting examples of women who took con-trol of their predicament as fulfilling a form of service to their readers, presumably in lieu of the real service they might provide by emphasiz-ing perpetrator accountability or the availability of supportive resour-ces. Berns links this focus not merely to the marketing constraints on magazines, but to the prevailing emphasis on victims in the shelter movement as well and extends the analysis of infotainment in the ear-lier piece by showing how it is constructed on talk shows like *The Oprah Winfrey Show* and *Dr. Phil*. While empowerment is compatible with a social justice framework, in the media world, when the concept is detached from its political dimension, that is, from the recognition that an individual's capacity to "take back the power in relationships" is inseparable from her understanding of and access to political and economic power, the result is to foster a dangerous illusion among vic-tims rather than to enlighten. Berns closes with intriguing comments on how to restore "deleted scenes" and "alternative endings" to the pervasive script that highlight the abuser's behavior and the social and cultural contexts which foster sexual violence.

As the first generation of gamers reaches their forties accompanied by a new generation of sophisticated video games, the role of these media in socialization takes on heightened significance. Gaming may not excite the level of psychological involvement elicited by film and the early alarms about its hazards may seem as exaggerated today as the initial warnings about rock and roll. But gaming has a significant feature lacking in most other media: it is interactive, particularly compared to the relatively passive ways in which we consume film or print. As games allow consumers an ever-increasing role in determining the course of action, fostering the illusion of autonomy if not genuine control, and do so amidst virtual communities of peers, video games bind players to behavioral scenarios in ways that other media do not.

In Chapter 6, social psychologist Karen E. Dill joins the debate about whether the antisocial content of video games can be harmful, particularly when, as illustrated in the best-selling game *Grand Theft Auto*, sexist imagery is joined to rape and other forms of violence against women. Dill summarizes compelling research suggesting a direct link between viewing violent content and aggressive, violent, and antisocial behavior, in part because players are "rewarded" for successful violence. An even more important connection may involve the acquisition of sexist attitudes and values from video games, or attitudes that are "violence friendly," including a heightened insensitivity to violence, even among players who think they can clearly distinguish the fantasy world of gaming from the real world. While most writing has emphasized the effects of viewing violent content in the context of stereotypic sex roles on males, researchers have also documented a wide range of negative effects of this content on female players, including depression and lower self-esteem. Dill also reports the results of her own research, showing that exposure to violence in video games increases the propensity for subjects to accept a range of myths about rape—such as that women want to be raped or like it—as well as their negative attitudes toward women generally and does so independently of whether gamers were more aggressive to start. Thus, even where the behavioral correlates are not exact, sexist imagery in gaming reinforces negative attitudes toward equality in the larger political climate in which women seek to be full persons on an equal plane with men.

The sexist content in video games is a carryover from the B-film industry. By contrast, rap, and particularly the subgenre known as "gangsta rap," replaced the relatively restrained sexism of earlier forms of popular music by embracing violent misogyny as an explicit theme typically expressed in overt acts of rape, femicide, and the torture of women. The irony here is that the popularity of gangsta rap in the 1980s and 1990s coincided with the enormous gains in female equality documented throughout these volumes, a shift toward normative condemnation of violence against women, and a decline in violence on the streets of the urban ghettoes in New York and Los Angeles from which rap emerged.

In Chapter 7, Edward Armstrong examines these trends, tracking the emergence of rap from the hip-hop culture of the 1970s, the turn toward misogyny associated with 2 Live Crew and other groups, and the emergence of gangsta rap in Southern California in the late 1980s and early 1990s as a subgenre that directly challenged the East Coast "party music" and embraced misogyny, violence, and violent misogyny. He also describes its demise in 2002–2003 and its replacement with music that emphasized manhood roles rather than criminal violence per se. With the important exception of Detroit-born Eminem, all of the performers of gangsta rap were black. But its audience was predominantly white, and the most violent examples of rap commanded the highest proportions of white listeners. Armstrong examines hundreds of songs, subdividing the contexts in which violence against women is described. While some of the occasions for violence are age-old, such as jealousy, the pretexts are far-ranging and extend from saying the wrong thing, having a bad attitude, or showing disrespect to situations where no reason at all is given from hurting or killing a woman. Women are gang raped or beaten, raped, or killed because of bad personal hygiene, their weight, or how they do their hair. They are beaten or killed for telling a lie or giving the rapper a sexually transmitted disease. Importantly, Eminem's songs are both the most popular and contain the highest proportion of violent misogyny.

Armstrong's analysis is qualified in several important respects. For one thing, although misogynistic violence is central to gangsta rap, it is not typical. Almost 80 percent of the lyrics Armstrong examines do *not* include misogynistic violence. For another thing, just over 2 percent of the lyrics of Dr. Dre and Snoop Dogg, two of the most important performers of the period, involve violence against women. But the outstanding question is whether the "rape culture" advanced by gangsta rap should be treated as art rather than advocacy, fantasy more than fact, whether the artists, the producers, or the largely white audiences should bear the blame for its content, and whether the vehement opposition it evoked was more akin to the moral panics that greeted virtually every new musical genre in our age or a progressive counterpoint to a reactionary medium.

WHERE DO WE GO FROM HERE?

The last two chapters in this volume point the way forward.

In Chapter 8, Elaine J. Lawless, a professor of English and folklore studies at the University of Missouri, describes an imaginative project in which she and a colleague converted field research she had conducted at a local battered women's shelter into a performance strategy to put domestic violence at the center of their community's concern. Lawless starts her work where this set and the battered women's movement itself began, with the stories of victimized women. Like so many of our other authors, she was fascinated not merely by the content of what they said and the suffering they had endured and resisted or escaped, but also in the ways in which storytelling about violence served as a vehicle for them to reframe their lives and even to gain new insights, through the telling of their stories to strangers, into the logic of their decision-making process. Even after publishing a book featuring her fieldwork, Lawless was plagued by the need to do something more with what she had heard. A colleague in theater had started a group in which those with HIV-AIDS shared their stories with community groups as a way to foster understanding of their problem. They decided to adapt the technique to the stories Lawless had collected, starting the Troubling Violence Performance Project to stimulate community discussion and action around abuse.

The chapter describes the evolution of the performance troupe from using students to tell the stories Lawless had collected, to students telling their own stories, to audience members sharing their experiences, to the translation of shared stories into a broad process of community healing. Creating a safe space to talk about abuse and a model of listening and telling stories that can be easily replicated "outs" abuse in the community, reduces the isolation that is a common cause or consequence of abuse, and points toward a shared responsibility for providing safety that is critical if we are to end the problem once and for all.

The strategy devised in Missouri epitomizes a key tenet of anti-violence work, to think globally and act locally. In the final chapter, a team of Australian researchers provides an international perspective on community attitudes toward violence against women using meta-analysis, a technique used to summarize a vast amount of research in a field. Changing community attitudes is a key end-product of culture change and is important not merely as a backdrop to support for needed reforms, but also as a context in which men and women make choices about whether and how to deploy coercion and control, how to respond, and whom to hold accountable when violence occurs. Research has consistently found that men who hold negative attitudes toward women, including rape-supportive beliefs, are more likely to use coercion with partners and other women. Although the institutional response to abuse is ideally driven by legal mandates, in reality, everything from the propensity of police to arrest to the willingness of local clergy to ask parishioners about abuse is shaped to suit community attitudes.

Large majorities in many countries now recognize that violence against women is serious and a criminal offense and not a private matter, though this is not true in all nations, even among women. In Australia, the domestic violence revolution appears to have affected a major change in the willingness to regard violence as a crime. But there are three important caveats to this conclusion: a smaller proportion regards minor violent acts as abusive than did so previously; contrary to fact, significant minorities believe women and men perpetrate violence in equal numbers; and many of the most common controlling behaviors typical of abuse are still not viewed as crimes. These findings bear not only on the challenges we face regarding public education about violence, but also to the mistaken picture of abuse promoted by the advocacy movement, the point made by Loseke in Chapter 1. Any attempt at summary would miss the nuanced information the chapter provides about how violence-supportive attitudes are linked to demographics (age or gender, for example), immigration status, organizational affiliation, employment status, occupation, and community characteristics, including peer associations, and pornography. The chapter also reviews research on the positive potential to change attitudes of social marketing campaigns and law enforcement.

In an appropriate conclusion to the volume, the chapter provides a science-based outline of the strategies most likely to affect major change in violence-supportive attitudes and violent behavior. Suffice it to say that all of the areas on their list are highlighted in chapters in *Violence against Women in Families and Relationships.*

Chapter 8 closes this volume—and so the set—with a sobering reminder. While changing attitudes that accept or justify violence against women is an important aim in our efforts to preserve women's physical safety and individual autonomy, it is not sufficient. The domestic violence revolution has affected major changes in how societies around the world understand and respond to the abuse of women and children in families and relationships. But millions of men continue to coerce and control the women in their lives and communities. Whatever motivates these men as individuals, men abuse women because they *can* and because doing so reinforces male power over women and the privileges this power confers in areas that extend from sex to employment, education, and family responsibilities. Men inherit these privileges simply because they are born biologically male. But the power to sustain and support these privileges is not biological, but rooted in the sexual inequalities that remain pervasive in societies around the globe. Ending violence in families and relationships means replacing the laws, structures, and cultural practices that support these inequalities with laws and institutions that recognize women as full persons with all the rights to dignity, respect, and liberty that this implies.

Chapter 1

Public and Personal Stories of Wife Abuse

Donileen R. Loseke

The historical record makes it unmistakably clear that women have always been victimized by the significant men in their lives. Still, until the mid-1970s there was no public concern about what we now call wife abuse. Many chapters in these volumes detail the considerable work it took—and continues to take—to convince disbelieving people that all too often women are victimized by their male partners, that such abuse is morally intolerable, and that these women deserve sympathy and require public assistance. I am also interested in understanding how wife abuse came to be accepted as a public problem worthy of attention and social resources. My particular focus is on the importance of stories in encouraging public concern and the relationships between these publicly circulating stories and the personal stories of individual women whose experiences might be understood as those of wife abuse.

NARRATIVES AS A TOPIC OF STUDY

The past twenty years have seen incredible academic interest in stories, or what academics call "narratives." There are three explanations of why scholars in a wide variety of academic disciplines are currently interested in narratives. The first is that narratives are important to study because they are a *pervasive* feature of social life. For example, many stories of wife abuse told by individual women are found in works written by and for academics, testimony in public policy hearings often includes stories, and stories figure prominently in court cases. Stories of wife abuse are an aspect of popular culture because they appear in movies, books, television talk shows, and magazines.

Second, academic researchers are interested in narratives because they are *socially consequential*. Although our modern world prizes the importance of logic and scientific evidence, humans at all times and in all places are drawn to stories. As compared to statistics, stories are rich in detail, intrinsically interesting, and emotionally engaging. This is extremely important given that social observers from Aristotle onward have argued that persuasion is most effective when it appeals to minds *and* to hearts, to reason *and* to emotion.[1] Therefore, publicly circulating stories about wife abuse are common because they can be effective in encouraging legislators in particular and the public in general to take wife abuse seriously and because they encourage people to purchase magazines or watch television shows.

Third, academics examine narratives because they are *personally* consequential. In stark contrast to earlier times or to places governed by strict adherence to tradition, modern-day Westerners encounter a constantly changing and incredibly complex world characterized by remarkable differences in how people live and what they value. This leads to many practical problems: How do we understand ourselves and those around us when there is so much change and so many disagreements? Social observers have argued that we often do this by comparing our individual experiences with stories we have heard and read. In this way, publicly circulating narratives of wife abuse can be used by individual women to ask: Is this story of wife abuse *my* story? Am *I* experiencing wife abuse? Am *I* a battered wife? Social service providers also use their understandings of publicly circulating narratives to evaluate the meaning of stories told by their individual clients.

In brief, narrative is an important topic of academic study because stories are pervasive, because they can be persuasive, and because they can offer individuals templates for understanding themselves and others. Critically, the scientific study of narratives does not require a specialized vocabulary or technical understanding because "narrative" is just another name for "story" as commonly understood. Narratives contain characters that have some kind of a relationship with one another; events within narratives contain a "temporal order," meaning that one event can be understood as leading to another; narratives have plots which give meaning and coherence to the narrative characters and events. As with stories, narratives also contain morals, the reasons why they are told. In brief, narratives are simply stories by another name.

I will begin with the topic of public stories, which are socially circulating narratives about types of people engaged in types of activities. When stories are widely circulating, they can become a part of common knowledge. So, for example, most Americans can conjure images of stories of "drug dealing" or "winning the lottery" even if they never have seen a drug deal or won a lottery. Although such publicly circulating stories refer to no particular person and to no specific event, they are the outcomes of countless personal narratives. Public understanding of the story of wife abuse therefore is a general image formed by countless individual stories, each told as a story of wife abuse.

After placing the wife abuse story within its cultural context, I will turn to examining the characteristics of this story as presented in public life and I will ask two questions: First, what are the characteristics of the wife abuse story that encourage audience members to evaluate it as important and believable? Second, how are the stories of *individual* women interpreted as the stories of the *type* of woman known as the battered woman? While I will argue that the public story of wife abuse has done considerable work to inspire social change, it is not the only socially circulating story that can make sense of marital "troubles." Therefore, I will continue by examining characteristics of stories that compete with the wife abuse narrative. Here I will focus on exploring how women in support groups for battered women struggle to make sense of their own experiences and how they only sometimes embrace the story of wife abuse as their own. Finally, given common differences between images in the public story of wife abuse and the practical experiences of individual women, I will consider some perplexing questions about relationships between public stories of wife abuse and further social change to help women who are experiencing violence. Understanding the public story of wife abuse requires starting with its cultural context, the environment within which this story is told and evaluated.

THE CULTURAL CONTEXTS OF THE PUBLIC STORY OF WIFE ABUSE

Our public world contains countless stories of types of experiences and kinds of people. New stories are constantly created but few of them do the important work of encouraging public concern or offering individuals ways to understand their lives. Many stories are interesting to only a few people, so they are limited in their social consequences; many other stories are of general interest but receive decisively mixed audience reception due to incredible diversity in how Americans understand and evaluate the world around us. So, for example, a story evaluated as believable and important by many wealthy elderly Anglo women might not be seen as so believable or important by many poor young minority men; a story assessed as compelling by very religious people might not be so meaningful to those who are not religious, and so on. To understand how the public story of wife abuse received, and continues to receive, general acceptance requires understanding the cultural scene which influences what audience members likely will evaluate as believable and important. This takes us to complex and interlocking cultural understandings of gender, marriage, family, violence, and victims.

I will begin in the early 1970s, when traditional ideas about family were embraced by the overwhelming majority of Americans. "Family" was a densely packed and interrelated series of largely unquestioned assumptions about how families were organized, how they should be organized, and relationships between families and the wider social world. Although they remain to this day, at that time ideas about family were far more tightly and inextricably related to gender, so images of relationships between husbands and wives were all but indistinguishable from cultural ideals of the characteristics, rights, relationships, and responsibilities of men and women.

So, for example, remaining to this day but far stronger in the past, is the belief that men are, and should be, the heads of their families. As many historians have demonstrated, men's authority over their wives was rarely challenged in the past and, when it was challenged, it was enforced by the law. Also, while many Americans continue to believe that women's primary goals and work in life should center on their families, in the early 1970s this belief was far more powerful. Indeed, in that era the cultural image of a "good woman" was of a "good wife" and a "good mother," and there was considerable agreement that an "employed mother" could not be a "good mother." Also, and again remaining to this day although in weaker form, in the early 1970s the ideas that men were the heads of their households and women were keepers of home and children were strongly supported by a lack of economic opportunities for women. In addition, and which now has changed a great deal, there was overwhelming public support for the sanctity of marriage in the 1970s, so preserving marriage even in the face of adversity was evaluated as noble. This also was enforced by law, which made the process of divorce expensive, time-consuming, and complex. Further, and which also has changed a great deal, in the 1970s there were strong beliefs that what went on inside homes should be private. Outsiders tended to ignore evidence of family troubles, and minimal public interventions promoted family preservation, not family dissolution.

Critically, public images of family in the early 1970s did *not* include a notion that violence within marital relationships should be criticized. Partly this was due to the belief that what went on inside homes was not a matter of public concern, partly to the belief that men should be the heads of their families whose rule should not be challenged. But in addition, there were—and remain just as strongly to this day—two more subtle systems of ideas that block public concern about violence of *any* type. First, while many of us wish it otherwise, Americans in general never have been known to condemn all violence. Rather,

Americans tend to evaluate violence on a case-by-case basis.[2] Our densely packed system of ideas about violence yields a classification of a specific act of violence as either "normal/legitimate" or "abusive/ illegitimate." Americans tend to evaluate violence as normal/legitimate and hence morally tolerable when the violent acts do not sound severe (such as pushes, shoves, and/or slaps), when violence does not create injuries, and when it is done for an understandable reason, such as a momentary emotional outburst or self-defense. In stark contrast, abusive/illegitimate is the evaluation of violence that sounds severe (such as beating up, punching, and/or choking), that creates injuries, and that is done for no understandable reason. While Americans continue to evaluate the moral tolerability of violence in these ways, what has changed is that people in the early 1970s simply assumed that violence within marital relationships was normal and therefore not morally troublesome.

A second set of ideas surrounding moral evaluations of violence (of any type) involves appraising characteristics of people experiencing harm: Normal/legitimate violence is not morally troublesome because it does not produce a "victim." While this sounds simple, it actually is quite complex because Americans—then and now—do not accord the status of "victim" to all people experiencing harm. "Victim" rather is a label reserved for those evaluated as *good* people who are *greatly harmed* through *no fault* of their own. People in general are not concerned when those suffering harm are evaluated as somehow morally deficient and/or as responsible for their experiences. Within this system of ideas, women evaluated as acting in ways "justifying" the violence they experience are not victims so, therefore, the violence they endure is not a problem.

In brief, prior to the wife abuse public story, Americans were willing to believe there was abusive violence in the homes of poor people, but they simply assumed that violence inside the homes of those who were not poor consisted of pushes and shoves, that it was an expectable outcome of marital arguments, and that it was mutually created and therefore did not produce a victim. That there could be abusive violence in the homes of middle-class people was, simply stated, unthinkable.

One incident during hearings on domestic violence at the U.S. House of Representatives demonstrates the difficulty facing early wife abuse advocates. Lenore Walker had been testifying that "psychological abuse" should be included in the definition of morally intolerable violence. James H. Scheurer, the chairman of these hearings, chided Dr. Walker when he said:

> In all of your discussions with us you might keep in mind that the government role here has, by definition, to be limited. Government can't necessarily take on the burden of making better or happier people. There are

some things that people have to do for themselves, and there are some problems that people have to work out for themselves, and there are relationships that people work out for themselves, must work out for themselves. Government can hardly structure happiness and government can hardly structure sensitivity or caring, or love, you know.[3]

This, then, was the context within which early wife abuse advocates attempted to convince the public that violence against women by their partners existed, that it was morally intolerable, that women experiencing such violence were good people who were greatly harmed through no fault of their own, and that they therefore deserved public sympathy and support. Critically, this effort was about far more than changing the way the public thought and felt about this violence. Changing hearts and minds were in the service of justifying very real social changes. Abuse advocates wanted shelters for battered women; they wanted police and courts to take this violence seriously; and they wanted changes throughout the social order that would promote greater equality for women. This raises a question: How could stories challenge the dense network of interlocking ideas about gender, about what families were, and about the proper public response to what historically had been evaluated as distinctly private troubles?

THE PUBLIC STORY OF WIFE ABUSE

The public story of wife abuse was, and continues to be, authored by many people, including feminists, academics, public policy makers, journalists, and other media personnel who obviously do not speak in a united voice. The story was—and continues to be—told in books, public policy hearings, movies, magazines, newspapers, television talk shows, and, in our current era, on innumerable Web sites. Here I will focus on examining the plots and characters in the story of wife abuse as told by feminists and by mass media targeted to an audience of women.

Feminists Tell the Story of Wife Abuse

The public story of wife abuse must begin with feminist activists, those who rightly are credited with beginning the social movement on behalf of battered women. These activists tell stories in order to convince others to take wife abuse seriously and to support calls for social change.

I start with one woman's story of wife abuse told in "Letter From a Battered Wife" that opens *Battered Wives* by Del Martin. I chose this story for two reasons. First, Del Martin continues to be widely recognized as one of the most influential women in the early days of the anti-battery movement. She offered testimony at public policy hearings that eventually led to very real changes in social policy surrounding wife abuse and was one of the experts commonly cited by journalists in mass-media publications such as *Vogue* magazine. Second, Martin *explicitly* offers this personal narrative of one woman as a *typical* story of wife abuse, so readers are encouraged to read this as more than an idiosyncratic story of one woman's experiences.

Try to read this story as a person in the 1970s who believes that any violence between marital couples either is just another problem of poor people or is mutual, legitimate, and nonconsequential; try to read it as one who believes that men are the appropriate leaders of their families, that women's purpose and goals in life should center solely on marriage and family, that families should be private, and that marriages should be preserved. The basic question is: How do the specific plots and characters in this story of wife abuse challenge these commonly held beliefs?

I am in my thirties and so is my husband. I have a high school diploma and am presently attending a local college, trying to obtain the additional education I need. My husband is a college graduate and a professional in his field. We are both attractive and, for the most part, respected and well-liked. We have four children and live in a middle-class home with all the comforts we could possibly want. I have everything, except life without fear. For most of my life I have been periodically beaten by my husband. What do I mean by "beaten?" I mean that parts of my body have been hit violently and repeatedly, and that painful bruises, swelling, bleeding wounds, unconsciousness, and combinations of these things have resulted. Beating should be distinguished from all other kinds of physical abuse—including being hit and shoved around. When I say my husband threatens me with abuse I do not mean he warns me that he may lose control. I mean that he shakes a fist against my face or nose, makes punching-bag jabs at my shoulder, or makes similar gestures which may quickly turn into a full-fledged beating. I have had glasses thrown at me. I have been kicked in the abdomen when I was visibly pregnant. I have been kicked off the bed and hit while lying on the floor—again, while I was pregnant. I have been whipped, kicked, and thrown, picked up again and thrown down again. I have been punched and kicked in the head, chest, face, and abdomen more times than I can count. I have been slapped for saying something about politics, for having a different view about religion, for swearing, for crying, for wanting to have intercourse. I have been threatened when I wouldn't do something he told me to do. I have been threatened when he's had a bad day and when he's had a good day.... Now, the first response to this story, which I myself think of, will be "Why didn't you seek help?" I did. Early in our marriage I went to a clergyman who, after a few visits, told me that my husband meant no real harm, that he was just confused and felt insecure. I was encouraged to be more tolerant and understanding. Most important, I was told to forgive him for the beatings just as Christ had forgiven me from the cross. I did that, too. Things continued. Next time I turned to a doctor. I was given little pills to relax me and told to take things a little easier. I was just too nervous. I turned to a friend, and when her husband found out, he accused me of either making things up or exaggerating the situation. She was told to stay away from me. She didn't, but she could no longer really help me.... I turned to a professional family guidance agency. I was told there that my husband needed help and that I should find a way to control the incidents. At the agency I found I had to defend myself against the suspicion that I wanted to be hit, that I invited the beatings ... I did go to two more doctors. One asked me what I had done to provoke my husband. The other asked if we had made up yet. I called the police one time. They not only did not respond to the call, they called several hours later to ask if things had "settled down." I could have been dead by then! I have nowhere to go if it happens again. No one wants to take in a woman with four children. Even if there were someone kind enough to care, no one wants to become involved in what is commonly referred to as a "domestic situation." ... The clergyman, the doctor, the counselor, my friend's husband, the police—all of them have found a way to vindicate my husband. No one has to "provoke" a wife-beater. He will strike out when he's ready and for whatever reason he has at the moment. I may be his excuse, but I have never been the reason. I know that I do not want to be hit. I know, too, that I will be beaten again unless I find a way out for myself and my children. I am terrified for them also.... But staying with my husband means that my children must be subjected to the emotional battering caused when they see their mother's beaten face or hear her screams in the middle of the night. I know that I have to get out. But when you have nowhere to go, you know that you must go on your own and expect no support. I have to be ready for that. I have to be ready to support myself and the children completely and still provide a decent environment for them. I pray that I can do that before I am murdered in my own home.... The greatest tragedy is that I am still praying, and there is not a human person to listen. Being beaten is a terrible thing: it is most terrible of all if you are not equipped to fight back.... My situation is so untenable I would guess that anyone who has not experienced one like it would find it incomprehensible. I find it difficult to believe myself. It must be pointed out that while a husband can beat, slap, or threaten his wife, there are "good days." These days tend to wear away the effects of the beating. They tend to cause the wife to put aside the traumas and look to the good ... A loving woman like myself always hopes that it will not happen again.... Several of the times I have been abused I have been amazed that I have remained alive.... each night I dread the final blow that will kill me and leave my children motherless. I hope I can hang on until I complete my education, get a good job, and become self-sufficient enough to care for my children on my own.[4]

Immediately at the conclusion of this letter, Martin invites her readers to understand this as a *typical* story when she says: "In the preceding story one woman tells her secret. It is a secret shared by many women."[5] Because Martin's book is titled *Battered Wives*, it follows this must be a typical story of wife abuse. If so, what does this woman's story tell us about the plot, the characters, and the morals in the story of wife abuse?

As with many stories, this one begins with setting the scene, and in the first few lines this woman prevents her audience from understanding her story as "just another poor people's problem:" She lives in a middle-class home, her husband is a "college-educated professional," they are "attractive," "well-liked," and "respected" people.

She then introduces the story's plot that, with the exception of one brief mention that "there are good days," centers solely on violence. As a member of our culture, this woman knows that Americans might simply assume that any violence in middle-class homes such as hers will be normal/legitimate. She explicitly counters this assumption by saying that her beatings "should be distinguished from all other kinds of physical abuse including being hit and shoved around." She wants her story to be understood as one of morally intolerable violence and she returns repeatedly to describing the brutalities she has experienced. Yet should there be any doubt that this violence is severe, she includes descriptions of her injuries, including bruises, bleeding wounds, and unconsciousness. Critically, she twice mentions violence while being "visibly pregnant," and Americans evaluate violence—any violence for any reason—toward a pregnant woman as morally intolerable. If this woman's story is typical, we know that wife abuse is about the types of violence Americans evaluate as abusive/illegitimate and therefore morally intolerable.

This woman also anticipates that those reading her story will be prone to withhold their concern if they believe she acts in ways making violence toward her "understandable." She explicitly counters this when she says: "No one has to 'provoke' a wife-beater. He will strike out when he's ready and for whatever reason he has at the moment." But readers do not need to believe her general conclusion because she offers many concrete examples that readers can judge for themselves: She has been beaten after saying something about politics, for having a different view about religion, for wanting to have intercourse, and for crying. It is likely that few Americans would evaluate these as understandable reasons for any violence, much less for the severe violence she has experienced. Hence, if this woman's story is typical, we know that wife abuse is about violence in which women are pure victims—they have been greatly harmed through no fault of their own.

When read against the backdrop of public understandings about families in the 1970s, this story is incredible—it lacks credibility because it is diametrically opposed to the then simply taken-for-granted beliefs about what families were. As such, it raises questions about her: Is she making this up? She anticipates such reactions and agrees they are logical: "My situation is so untenable I would guess that anyone who has not experienced one like it would find it incomprehensible. I find it difficult to believe myself." She also anticipates that her audience will ask another question about her sanity: "The first response to this story, which I myself think of, will be 'Why didn't you seek help?'" This introduces what becomes a major subplot: She repeatedly sought help, but there was no help. In great detail she tells of going to clergy, doctors, a professional family guidance agency, and the police. In each instance she needed to defend herself against suspicions that she wanted to be hit and against suspicions that she had done something to create the violence she experienced. If her story is typical, we know that although wife abuse is about extreme, repeated, and devastatingly consequential violence, the public will not intervene and instead will blame women for the problems they experience.

From the discovery of wife abuse to the present day, the most commonly asked question is "why do women stay?" This is a sensible question: If the abuse is as bad as women say it is, if they do not "like" the abuse, then why do they not just leave? The woman in this story offers an answer to that question. No, she does not like the violence—she is incredibly fearful of it. Yes, she knows she must leave. She knows that she will be beaten again if she does not leave, and she fears that the next beating will kill her. She stays because she has no choice: She has found no help and she does not have the ability to financially support herself and her children. The story closes quite ominously: She only hopes she can remain alive long enough to finish her education and obtain a job so that she can become self-sufficient enough to care for her children. If her story is typical, what we know about wife abuse is that women who remain in these situations are not freely choosing abuse and that their staying does not indicate they find the abuse acceptable. Definitely not. What we know from this story is that a battered woman desperately wants to leave but is trapped—in this case by economic dependence and unresponsive social services.

The story of wife abuse contains characters, so we can ask what we know about them. The two main characters, a battered woman and an abusive man, are both very narrowly drawn: All that we know about either of them is that she is a "loving woman" victim and he is a brute. The story also contains a cast of minor, unnamed characters who are important to the plot. These include her four children who are vital to the story because the woman fears the consequences of their witnessing her abuse and because they keep her trapped. There also are a variety of police officers, doctors, and clergy important to the story because they offer no help.

This particular story can be read as a moral tale about the horrid consequences of the gendered social order that in multiple and interlocking ways confers power on men and makes women powerless. This woman is trapped within her abuse because she does not have the means to support herself and her children and she is trapped by others who are unresponsive to her plight and persist in blaming her for the brutalities she experiences. Most certainly, this woman's story graphically illustrates why there must be social change: Change is needed to save the life of *this* woman; it is needed to save the lives of the many others who share her story.

This particular narrative offers a plausible answer to the question of why the story of wife abuse was evaluated as believable and important by the general public. Even those who tend to neutralize the moral intolerability of violence by arguing that violence is a "natural" and "normal" part of marriage likely would evaluate this *particular* violence as morally intolerable. Even those who are prone to dismiss violence because they believe women create it or deserve it likely would find it difficult to blame this *particular* woman for the extreme violence she experienced over the most trivial of incidents. Even those who believe that the public should not intervene in family life nonetheless might cringe when reading how the public failed to intervene in this *particular* woman's dire situation; even those who believe in the importance of family preservation might well agree that this *particular* woman's relationship should end lest she be killed by her husband. Simply stated, although there are countless individual instances of violence that might be evaluated as normal/legitimate by some people and abusive/illegitimate by others, this story leads to a clear moral evaluation that this *particular* violence is abusive/illegitimate. Critically, because readers are asked to understand this as a typical story of wife abuse, it follows that readers' thoughts and feelings about this woman's story should be generalized to the many women who share it.

I turn to a second feminist telling of the story of wife abuse from *Women and Male Violence* by Susan Schechter. I chose this story for three reasons. First, many characteristics of this narrative and those in "Letter from a Battered Wife" are so similar that these two stories could be combined and still be consistent. Second, narratives are about individual lives and, because lives are unique, each story necessarily will differ in details from all others. In this instance, differences between the next narrative and "Letter from a Battered Wife" enrich the content of the wife abuse plot and offer additional moral tales. Third, I chose this narrative because, as with "Letter from a Battered Wife," it is offered as a *typical* story, a "story that is horrifying because of the regularity with which women repeat it."[6] As you read this, again think about the specific content of the wife abuse story and about how this woman's story challenges the multiple and interconnecting sets of ideas that often serve to morally neutralize violence.

When we were married, if I didn't agree with what he said, I'd get pushed or told, "You're not thinking right; sit down and think about it."

I'd think, "Of course, he's right." ... You know, one Father's Day ... he didn't want to go to my family. He said, "Just tell them you're not going." I said, "I want to go." I got slapped in the face and he said, "Now call them and say we're not going." So, of course, I called. I was very scared. He pushed me and slapped me a lot; I was never badly beaten. Once he ripped two nightgowns off me. He ripped one off and pushed me into the hallway—naked. I got back into the apartment and he ripped off the next. I can't understand why the neighbors never said anything. Usually, it didn't take much to get me in my place. You'd say to yourself, "I don't want this to continue." So I'd say, "I'm sorry; I made a mistake. I didn't mean to say that. You're right." We were together ten years. In the beginning, I was pushed once a year. In the last five years, I was in a constant state of worry. My whole life revolved around him and keeping things quiet. I'd make the kids be quiet. I'd say to people, "Please don't call when he is home." I had no friends. I never wanted anyone in the house because I'd never know what he would say or do.... I thought it was my fault. I was afraid everyone would say, "You didn't do a good job so that's what you get. You weren't a good wife." I believed that if I only did better, it would stop.... No one ever knew. I said "no more" when I got punched and had hair pulled put; there were big clumps in my hands. He threw chairs at me. I remember being on the floor screaming. It was a nightmare.... I was just very alone. There were no movies about battered women. This was my private responsibility. If I had knocked on a neighbor's door for help, it would be like saying, "Listen, I failed." I had the idea that I'm doing this for him. I'm coping; I'm controlling the amount of abuse I'm taking. I must be a good person. The importance I got was what I was doing it for him. When I locked him out, I got support from my family.... They were emotionally helpful. Financially they were great. Shoes and clothes would just appear.... It took a year to get welfare. It's been a challenge to get through. I just wanted to be left alone. But he sometimes still comes around. I call the police if I hear a noise in the hall. I'm still jittery. I think I'll have this all my life. I'm afraid he'll hit me and be out of control. Thinking about it upsets my stomach.[7]

This narrative is both similar to, and different from, "Letter from a Battered Wife." They are similar in that each features two primary characters and the characters are very narrowly drawn. All that we know about each woman is that she is a good person who is an obviously pure victim; all that we know of each man is that he is an evil brute. In addition, the types of violence and their consequences in both stories are such that few audience members likely would evaluate the violence as normal/legitimate. Still further, while the woman in the second narrative achieved independence while the other woman did not, at the end of each story both lived in constant fear of further attacks. In these ways the two narratives are so similar that they could be combined and produce one, consistent story: Both are the story of wife abuse.

While these two narratives tell a consistent story, their details none-theless differ. First, the only developed subplot in "Letter from a Bat-tered Wife" was the woman's constant search for help and her failure to find it. In comparison, the second story contains the subplot of fail-ing to find help as well as another: This woman assumed that the vio-lence was her fault and she tried to be a good wife. Second, the violence in "Letter from a Battered Wife" was solely physical. While the second woman did include physical violence that definitely sounds severe (her hair pulled out, chairs thrown at her), she explicitly denied that she experienced severe physical abuse and rather emphasized psy-chological abuse: She was completely terrified of her husband; his wishes controlled her entire life. Third and finally, while the woman in "Letter from a Battered Wife" never found the help she sought, the woman in the second story eventually found emotional and financial support from her family and, with it, achieved independence.

As in "Letter from a Battered Wife," the second woman's story is a moral tale about the deplorable consequences of typical beliefs about gender, marriage, and family, and it is about the devastating conse-quences of setting up a world in ways that keep women trapped in abusive relationships. The first story dramatized the consequences of economic dependence and an unresponsive social system, and the sec-ond story included those morals and added another about the dire con-sequences of women accepting cultural notions: The second woman's own beliefs in cultural prescriptions that "women are responsible" became an entrapment that looms larger in her story than her eco-nomic dependence. Clearly, both stories are testimonies for the critical need for social change.

These are two examples of feminist tellings of the moral tale of wife abuse. However, no matter how important this feminist telling was, and is, in recruiting activists to work on behalf of battered women, it has a fairly small audience. This takes us to another question: What are the characteristics of the wife abuse story told in places with more gen-eral audiences, such as in mass-media magazines and in television talk shows offered to an audience of women?

Mass Media Tell the Story of Wife Abuse[8]

Stories presented in the mass media are critically important because they have the potential to reach extremely large audiences. This means such stories can be powerful in changing the hearts and minds of the public. We know the wife abuse story remains compelling to general audiences of women for the simple reason that this narrative has been told in both magazines and on television talk shows for many years. But is the story of wife abuse compelling for the same reasons as the story told by feminists? When the media telling is compared to the feminist telling, how is the wife abuse story the same, and how does it differ?

While eventually I will add considerable complexity, I will start simply by examining the personal stories told in three articles. Two of these appeared in *Good Housekeeping* and had the same title: "I Was a Battered Wife"; the third was in *Mademoiselle* and was titled "On Being an Abused Wife and Living in Fear." I chose these articles because the title of each is centered on the central character of the wife abuse story, and because each contains the story of one particular woman without additional comment.

In comparison to stories of wife abuse told by feminists, articles in magazines tend to name characters, and there often is considerable dialogue. In some ways, these magazine conventions make for more compelling narratives because names personalize the story and dialogue adds rich, engaging detail. At the same time, the contents of the wife abuse story can be very similar, whether told by feminists or in the mass media. For example, the problem of wife abuse cannot be dismissed as just another problem of poor people: Karen married Frank, who "had a middle-management position at a financial-consulting firm" and was "the model of gentle behavior";[9] Peg's husband, Jack, was "handsome, intelligent, hardworking, and well respected in our community";[10] everyone thought that Sarah and her husband, Bob, were "the perfect couple."[11] Whether told in magazine articles or by feminists, wife abuse is a compelling story because the plot unfolds in the unexpected setting of middle-class homes.

As with stories told by feminists, the wife abuse story in magazines is *not* about morally tolerable "normal" violence, assumed to be minimal in force and inconsequential in effect. On the contrary, Karen tells of how Frank "struck me with the back of his hand" and "grabbed me by the neck and slammed my head against the wall." After one beating, Peg had "internal bleeding" in her ear and her eye had swollen shut. Sarah talks of "weekly attacks" and being "punched in the mouth or in the stomach." In both feminist and magazine tellings, wife abuse is clearly and most certainly about abusive/illegitimate violence.

Of course, with such extreme violence, few people might wonder what women did to "deserve" it but, as in the feminist telling, the plot of wife abuse in these magazine articles includes explicit attention to portraying victims as innocents. Karen's husband became enraged when they disagreed about a movie they saw, when he came home early one day and Karen was having coffee with a woman who lived in the neighborhood, and when she "hadn't lost the extra weight" after her pregnancy. Peg tells of how "any small thing would set him off—like misplaced car keys, an overdone roast, or just my facial expression which he interpreted as 'insolent.'" Sarah's husband attacked her "because we disagreed on the purpose of a building we passed during a drive, because I expressed an opinion different from my husband's, or when a table doily was wrinkled." Regardless of whether told by feminists or in magazines targeted to general audiences, the story of wife abuse features women as innocent victims.

As with stories told by feminists, stories in magazines also dramatize how women often accept the blame for violence and do everything they can to please their abusive partners. Karen knew her husband was in a "bad mood" one night, so she prepared one of his favorite meals and set the table with candles "hoping to get him back into a good mood." When she saw her husband's anger building, Peg said, "I'd do everything I could to please him, but nothing worked." After beatings, Peg would ask him "What am I doing wrong, honey?" Sarah says, "I tried to keep peace by doing everything the way Bob wanted it done."

While story plots and characters in magazine articles share major similarities with the narrative of wife abuse told by feminists, magazine stories do differ in two interrelated ways from those told by feminists. First, a subplot in both examples of feminist tellings of the wife abuse story was the lack of help offered to women requesting it. In comparison, a subplot in these magazine articles is women's hesitancies about receiving help that *is* offered. Karen's neighbor offered her a place to stay so that she could leave but Karen was "embarrassed" and felt that telling others about her abuse was "betraying her husband." Peg lied to her obstetrician when he asked about her bruises because "by lying, I felt that I was reconfirming my faith in the man I had married." Sarah's pastor recommended she leave her husband but she said she wanted to remain because he was her "security." In brief, the supporting cast of characters in the story of wife abuse as told by feminists includes an array of people who prevent women from receiving help, while the supporting characters in these magazine articles include others who do offer assistance. In a very subtle way, these magazine stories blame women for their failures to take advantage of help that seems readily available.

A second difference between feminist and mass-media tellings of the story of wife abuse is in the endings. In both, the story plot of dangerous abuse done by brutish men on meek women logically leads audience members to hope for a "happy ending" that would feature a woman free from the torment of her abuser. Yet the two stories from feminist tellings of wife abuse did not feature such a happy ending. The "Letter from a Battered Wife" ended with the woman only hoping she could remain alive long enough establish her independence; the second woman did achieve independence but continued to live in perpetual fear of her former husband. In stark contrast, my three examples of stories in mass-media magazines have indisputably clear happy endings: With help, the women achieve independence and happiness. A school psychologist noticed Karen's bruises and gave her information about a shelter. She soon moved to the shelter, where workers helped her with legalities, and her parents paid for a "good divorce lawyer." The story closes with Karen saying, "I found another job, learned to drive, and have saved enough to buy a used car. I never see Frank anymore ... and I have friends." Likewise, a shelter worker visited the hospital where Peg was recuperating from a beating and told Peg about shelter services. Peg soon moved into the shelter, and the story closes a year later when she is working as a salesclerk while finishing a secretarial course. Her final reflections are that the "combined responsibilities of a job, school, and household sometimes can be over- whelming ... [but] compared to what my life was like before, I realize that I am very fortunate to have another chance." Finally, Sarah's pas- tor eventually convinced her to call the shelter, where she found infor- mation and support. She left her husband and now has "gained a lot of self-confidence and that's worth the pain. I'm beginning to like myself now. More importantly, I *am* myself now. And I wouldn't trade that kind of security and the peace of mind that comes with it for all the 'married' security in the world" (emphasis in original).

Such happy endings in media stories of wife abuse can be criticized because they make it seem as if sufficient help is available, so they do not promote the need for more *social* change, a point elaborated in the chapter by Nancy Berns in this volume. Also, when stories end with women characters who are very happy, they deny the potential linger- ing psychological effects from abuse. However, the story of wife abuse told in these magazine articles nonetheless is compatible with the femi- nist telling: When women find help, they *can* become independent; when women become independent, they *can* be happy.

I began this section with a question: How can we understand the success of the publicly circulating story of wife abuse? A plausible an- swer is fairly obvious from the recurring themes in *all* stories so far. Particularly in the 1970s, when this story was first authored, but con- tinuing to the present, there are sets of commonly accepted ideas that encourage Americans to define a great deal of violence as normal/ legitimate because it is evaluated as not severe, as not consequential, as understandable, and as not creating a victim. The stories of all women thus far clearly and most certainly and without a doubt construct the violence of wife abuse as abusive/illegitimate: It is obviously extreme and consequential, and women are obviously virtuous victims terror- ized by their partners. It is an effective image that encourages people to take wife abuse seriously, to intervene in family life, to offer battered women sympathy and assistance. Such narratives of morally pure women in life-threatening circumstances can be understood as encour- aging a change in public hearts and minds. This is one type of work that narratives can achieve in social life.

Widely circulating narratives about wife abuse also might be used by those trying to make sense of their own experiences. Hence, women enduring violence can read or hear stories of wife abuse and ask: Is this what *I* am experiencing? Am *I* a battered wife? This leads to a series of questions about relationships between personal experiences and publicly circulating stories.

PERSONAL EXPERIENCES AND PUBLIC STORIES OF WIFE ABUSE IN THE PUBLIC REALM

So far, I have illustrated the commonalities of personal stories told as those of the social problem of wife abuse. I want to turn now to a technical question: How are personal experiences linked with the public story of wife abuse? There seem to be three primary ways in which media stories establish relationships between unique personal experiences and public stories of types of experiences.

First, the media can directly alert audience members that the story they are about to read or hear should be taken as one of wife abuse. Consider, for example, a segment from *The Oprah Winfrey Show* titled "A Mother Burned Alive by Her Husband."[12] The violence experienced by the guest was incredibly extreme—her former husband had poured gasoline all over her and set her afire, leading her to endure seventeen surgeries while remaining physically deformed and debilitated. Oprah nonetheless encouraged her audience to understand this as a typical story of wife abuse when she said this woman's story was "classic, classic." Magazine articles containing one story likewise can be accompanied by information explicitly telling readers that the article they are reading should be understood as a typical story of wife abuse. For example, a story in *Glamour* titled "When Love Turns Violent" is one woman's story introduced with the following: "In 1990, an estimated 1,500 women will be killed by angry husbands or boyfriends. This is the story of one who escaped."[13] Another article in *McCall's*, "How Battered Wives Can Learn to Leave," begins with alerting readers that this is "how one battered wife finally escaped her violent marriage."[14] In each instance, information accompanying an article transforms it from a story of one woman to a type of story known as wife abuse.

Second, women who tell their stories in magazine articles can directly connect their own experiences to the type of experience known as wife abuse. I will demonstrate this with a woman's story in *Vogue* titled "He Beat Me: Battered Wife Tells Why She Took it for Seven Years."[15] This woman's story contains the plots and characters I already have discussed: Her violent husband was a resident in psychiatry, she elaborates at length on her experiences of extreme, consequential, and repeated violence; it is undeniably clear that her actions did not cause her victimization, and others did not help her. What is of particular interest is how from time to time she pauses her story to make explicit links between her own experiences and those of the type known as wife abuse. At one point she ponders why she did not recognize that her husband was violent before they married:

> One explanation surfaced when I was doing research for the legal proceedings of my divorce. Researcher Richard Gelles wrote in his book *The Violent Home: A Study of Physical Aggression Between Husband and Wife,* "From our interviews, we are still convinced that in most cases, a marriage license also functions as a hitting license."

A bit later in her story she tries to make sense of her awful experiences in divorce court. She informs her readers that

> I have since discovered that an abused wife has status in society similar to a rape victim. Supposedly, the raped woman is "seductive," seeking violent intercourse. In much the same logic, the abused wife "provokes" her husband's violent behavior. This thesis was reinforced by my husband's attorney, a woman, in brutal questioning during legal proceedings.

As the story continues, she links her own economic situation to what is known about wife abuse:

> Wife abuse knows no economic or social barriers. As a middle-class woman, I found it impossible to phone the police or to discuss the problems with friends.

Finally, she concludes her story by explicitly defining the characteristics of a type of woman, a battered woman, and identifies herself as such a kind of woman who needs help: "We battered wives are basically a frightened, insecure group who need an outstretched hand."

As another example of how individual women can make links between their own experiences and the public story of wife abuse, consider a segment of *The Oprah Winfrey Show* titled "A Suburban Mother's Nightmare Captured on Tape." This woman reflects on the importance of a program on wife abuse she had seen in the past:

> I had seen a show of yours ... and a woman was on and I don't remember the show.... And I remember watching the show. And he had done this to me. But I watched the show and I said, hmmm ... I wonder if that's what he's doing to me? No.... And so I watched that and I thought, no. And, and I look back at it now and, and I never forgot it. It was something that would continually, that particular thing, over the years, it would come back up in my mind.[16]

Academic observers have argued that when people experience trouble of any type, they actively search for ways to make sense of it. In making sense of her experiences and in preparing for her divorce, one woman did research and used what is known about the public problem of wife abuse as a way to make sense of her own experiences; another woman directly compared her experiences to a show she had seen on television. In the end, both women embraced the wife abuse story as their own.

Third and finally, articles in mass-media magazines connect particular experiences and typical stories by citing experts. The following is from an article in *Ladies' Home Journal* titled "The Secret Problem that Destroys Marriages." At one point, the article includes a paragraph on Rachel, who talks of how she fell in love with Hank because he seemed to be so "in control of his life." Yet Hank was emotionally abusive and controlling, and Rachel started to believe he was very insecure. This short segment of a story is followed by:

> "Insecurity about one's self-worth makes an individual especially prone to denigrate others," says Mildred Daley Pagelow, PhD, who teaches a course in marriage and family living at California State University at Fullerton and is the author of *Family Violence*. "No matter how high a man goes in the world, there will always be others who have more power or who are capable of stripping him of power. This causes men like Hank to develop an enormous need to control," says Jeanne Weigum [master's in social work and a marriage counselor with the Center for Rational Living in St. Paul, Minnesota].[17]

Rachel's story continues in the next paragraph, now pursuing the theme that Hank complained so much about the long hours she spent in her teaching job that she quit and became a low-paid secretary, which made Hank very happy. This is followed by:

> "Men like Hank don't want a woman 'on top,' no matter how much her success would enrich the men themselves,' says Letty Cottin Pogrebin, author of *Family Politics*. 'Thus, many women like Rachel are in jobs below their educational level and earning ability."

Experts cited in this magazine article use the details of a particular woman's story to exemplify the typical story of wife abuse. In this way, the behavior and characteristics of one man, Hank, come to symbolize the behavior of all "men like Hank," and the particular experiences of one woman, Rachel, become the experiences of "many women like Rachel." It is important to notice that unlike the previous stories in which women themselves accepted the story of wife abuse as their own, we do *not* know whether or not Rachel accepted the wife abuse story as her own. But that does not matter: The prominent display of experts' credentials makes their understandings the "official" story of Rachel's life.

Not all experts have formal academic credentials. Indeed, perhaps the most respected expert of our times on all matters of social

relationships is Oprah Winfrey. Consider this segment from her show titled "A Mother Burned Alive by Her Husband." This interaction comes
at a point in the conversation when they were discussing how Ms. Cade's
husband was very romantic in the beginning of their relationship.
Ms. Cade started explaining how she was, by nature, a very trusting person. Notice how the story of what this woman's husband did to her is
used by Oprah to tell a tale of what "they"—abusive men—do.

Ms. Cade: I would like to think people are nice and have values.
Winfrey: You know, this is what is so interesting about men who abuse,
           if they—you know, a lot of them are very romantic in the be-
           ginning.
Ms. Cade: They are.
Winfrey: It's like—it's like—it's a part of the seduction that they're very
           romantic in the beginning.
Ms. Cade: Mm—hmm.[18]

A bit later in the conversation the guest was explaining that she
thought her husband loved her, and Oprah used her remarks to make
connections between this one woman and "millions" of others.

Ms Cade: I made it what I wanted it to be. I would like to think people
          are good. And I . . . I try to see good in everyone.
Winfrey: But you know what, I want to tell you this, that that's one of
          the most powerful things you could ever say, because that is
          what millions of people do in relationships all the time. They
          don't look at the reality and they pretend that it is what they
          want it to be. They stay because of what they want it to be,
          instead of looking at what it really is.
Ms. Cade: Mm—hmmm.

After using this woman's experiences to talk about how "they"
don't look at reality, Oprah concludes the segment by returning to this
woman who becomes a "living example" of what happens when "you
don't pay attention to the signs" of wife abuse.

Winfrey: And so I'm really proud of you for being here to share your
          story, because I think you are a living example of what hap-
          pens when you don't pay attention to the signs. And I know
          that's why you wanted to be here.

Magazine articles and segments of television talk shows demonstrate
how the personal stories of individual women can be used to exemplify the public story of wife abuse. Readers can be explicitly told how

to understand stories, women themselves can make connections between their own experiences and the general narrative, and experts can categorize the stories of particular women as those of wife abuse.

The practical reason why this is important is because when stories such as wife abuse circulate widely they can be available to those who are trying to make sense of their own experiences. Women having troubles can read books or magazines and can watch television and compare their own experiences with those of other women. At times, the media can be quite explicit in encouraging the audience to do this. After a commercial break, for example, Oprah Winfrey told her audience "... it is my fervent hope and prayer that every woman who is watching you right now who is in a similar situation where there is a potential for disaster (to know) you're not alone." Another show featuring one woman's story began: "This is a show for every woman who's ever been abused";[19] yet another show featuring a woman's story began: "If you have ever been screamed at or called names, you've been humiliated or hit by your husband or boyfriend, do not turn off your television."[20] Audience members in each of these instances are explicitly encouraged to consider the possibility that their own stories are the story of wife abuse.

Oprah is not alone in encouraging her audience members to consider the wife abuse story as their own. It is fairly common for magazine articles to contain sidebars giving women instructions for what to look for in order to understand their own story as one of wife abuse. These often are in the form of easy checklists such as "Will he hit you again?" (*Essence*), "Is your daughter at risk?" (*Ladies' Home Journal*), "Are you abused?" (*Essence*), and "Five signs your boyfriend may turn violent" (*Mademoiselle*).[21]

Thus far, I have been focusing on stories of wife abuse told in the public realm; it is important to note that these are provided for particular reasons: Feminists offer stories as support for their calls for social change on behalf of battered women in particular as well as women in general, while the media offer stories that will be interesting to their audiences and thus will sell magazines or increase program viewership. As such, we can assume these stories are manufactured: Writers decide which stories they will put in their books and include those portions of stories that best exemplify the points being made; media personnel choose stories and then might edit them so that they are more compelling stories than the ones actually told.

I want to change focus and move from what now seems a relative predictability of the plots and characters in the public story of wife abuse to the messiness of lived experience. Although I have given examples of how individual women and experts can use their understandings of the story of wife abuse to make sense of individual lives, this is anything but an automatic process. My next questions are: When does it make sense in daily life to use the story of wife abuse in order to understand individual experiences? How do women make sense of their experiences with violence?

PUBLIC STORIES OF WIFE ABUSE AND PERSONAL EXPERIENCES[22]

I will begin with the obvious: The wife abuse story has undoubtedly saved the lives of countless women. While victims continue to encounter a social world that tends to disbelieve their stories of violence, while they continue to encounter unhelpful social service providers, it remains that before the story of wife abuse, such disbelief and unhelpfulness were far more prevalent than now. Likewise, while the American public continues to question the extent to which women "cause" their own victimization, women's complicity was simply assumed before the public story of wife abuse. Furthermore, the more the wife abuse story circulates socially, the more it is available for women to use in order to define their own experiences as those of abuse, and the more women do this, the more likely they will seek help which can be lifesaving.

Now I will add considerable complexity: While the wife abuse story has been successful in helping to create and sustain public concern, it most certainly did not eliminate other publicly circulating stories that can be used to make sense of violence. What this means is that when people try to make sense of their own experiences or the experiences of others, they will find many socially circulating stories that *might* pertain to the situation at hand. The first question is about relationships between the messiness of lived experience and the clarity of the public story of wife abuse: How must experiences and people be understood in order for them to be seen as individual instances of the public story of wife abuse?

First, troubled relationships often contain many problems—perceptions that the partner is unfaithful, alcoholic, or irresponsible; troubles with in-laws; disagreements about children; or perhaps just a vague feeling that "we are growing apart." However, recall that a characteristic of the public story of wife abuse is that its plot is centered solely on violence. Classifying violence as wife abuse therefore requires evaluating violence as a problem rather than as a consequence of other problems, such as alcoholism or frustration over losing a job. Furthermore, categorizing a relationship as one of wife abuse requires evaluating violence as the *central* problem rather than as merely one of several troubles.

Second, recall that the violence in the public story of wife abuse is of a particular type: It sounds extreme *and* it yields severe physical and/or emotional consequences *and* it recurs *and* it is done for no understandable reason. Violence in lived experience is not always so easily categorized. It might be experienced as only more or less extreme, it might yield consequences that are evaluated as only more or less troublesome, it might happen repeatedly but very infrequently, the complicated situations surrounding individual events of violence might make some incidents understandable, even if not preferable, and so on. Although violence in public stories of wife abuse most clearly and certainly is abusive/illegitimate and therefore morally intolerable, violence in real life can be experienced on continuums of moral intolerability.

Third, the battered woman and the abusive man characters in the wife abuse story are one-dimensional figures. She is known only as a morally exemplar virtuous victim, while he is known only as a vicious villain. Yet we all know there are few saints in real life and that even the most despicable person usually has redeeming qualities. Understanding experiences as those of wife abuse requires assigning the status of victim and villain when evidence for those appraisals might not be so clear.

Given the complexity and indeterminacy of lived experience, it is not surprising that the public story of wife abuse has not eliminated other publicly circulating narratives that potentially also make sense of women's experiences with violence. As primary examples, the wife abuse story competes with the narratives of "marital troubles" and "mutual combat." While the wife abuse story constructs violence as the central plot, the marital troubles and mutual combat narratives often include several equally troublesome problems. Also, as compared to the wife abuse story, violence in the marital troubles and mutual combat stories is framed as a consequence of larger problems. Critically, characters are not assigned victim or villain statuses in the marital troubles or mutual combat narratives. There also are images of women and men that compete with the victim and villain characters in the story of wife abuse: The battered woman character competes with the "shrewish wife" who creates the violence she experiences; the abusive man competes with the "former abused child," or the "mentally ill" or "alcoholic" husband whose violence is understood as a consequence of illness, rather than the result of his malicious intent to control. My point here is that there are many well-known stories about marital troubles in general and violence in particular that circulate in our social world and might serve as resources for making sense of lived experience.

In the public realm, the wife abuse story continues to compete with these other stories. For example, although I have demonstrated the wife abuse story appearing in magazines with target audiences of women, these same magazines just as commonly contain stories that are more clearly those of marital troubles or mutual combat rather than of wife abuse. In an article in *Ladies' Home Journal*, Jill talks about how she and her husband, Trevor, were arguing. He tried to walk away but she "went after him." When he then turned around and pushed her, she called him a "big ape and a bully and a coward."[23] In another article, Ellen complained that her husband, Joel, got angry at her and slapped her when she wouldn't stop talking. Ellen admits that she does tend to talk a lot. A counselor commenting on the story said that Ellen's "incessant talking" was a problem and that she was not aware of how this, her excessive shopping, and her typical failure to keep appointments "clearly provoked" her husband. Women in such stories are not as clearly and most certainly instances of the battered woman character. Likewise, their husbands are not the wife abuser character who is an unrepentant brute. Joel says that "smacking Ellen was reprehensible" and he was "disgusted" with himself.[24] Trevor left Jill after the violence because he was "shocked—and overwhelmingly ashamed" that he had been violent.

How individuals make sense of their lives is of vital importance because stories contain explicit agendas for how lives should be lived and changed. Understanding a life in terms of the mutual combat or the marital troubles story can lead to couples counseling to repair relationships. Problems understood as created by a "shrewish" wife or an "alcoholic" husband point toward counseling to help individuals. The wife abuse story, of course, contains a different agenda for action: Because this violence is dangerous, and because the men are unrepentant, the women must end their relationships. At stake is not only how women should think of themselves, but also what actions they should take.

THE COMPLEXITIES OF WOMEN'S EXPERIENCES WITH VIOLENCE[25]

I want to continue with some examples of how individual women who are experiencing what might be considered wife abuse talk about their lives. My examples are from support groups for battered women who are not living in shelters. I will start with the expected: Upon initially entering support groups, many women already tell their own stories as those of wife abuse. Consider, for example, the following interaction between Deborah, a woman who had attended several group meetings, and Melanie, a woman attending her first group. Melanie had sat on the couch during the entire session, saying nothing. From time to time the group leader had asked her if she wanted to speak, but Melanie continued to shake her head, no. After going around the room with each woman talking about her week, Deborah turns to Melanie:

Deborah: Can I ask you a question (Melanie nods, yes)? Are you still with the guy? (Melanie nods, yes.) That's why you can't talk about it. Do you want to leave? (Melanie shrugs her shoulders.) Are you married to him? (Melanie shakes her head, no.) Does he hit you?

Melanie: Only once in a while. He'll be OK for a few months then ... something will happen and he'll ... it's like a Dr. Jekyll and Mr. Hyde thing. It can be anything that sets it off. I never know when, like putting the pillow on a different spot on the bed. Usually I leave and go to a hotel. You're supposed to feel safe in your home but I can't feel safe in my home. This has been happening for, for, ummm three years. This time . . . my mother . . . I knew she had been doing volunteer work for a victim's group. She's on the East Coast so I went there. I told her, I think I'm being abused. She gave me books to read and . . . it was . . . it was like a light went off . . . suddenly there was a name for what I was going through. It all made sense. It wasn't my fault.

Before she entered this support group, Melanie had accepted the story of wife abuse as her own. She had read books and "suddenly there was a name" for her experiences: Hers was the story of wife abuse.

At other times, a woman might look back in retrospect and believe that she learned over time to change her story to that of wife abuse. Liz, for example, introduced herself to new members:

My name is Liz. I'm a regular. I've come a long way. You should have heard me when I started coming. I would look around the room and say, "you need to be here but I don't need to be here." I wasn't abused—that's what I thought. But I do need to be here. Because my husband has this sweet face—I always go for the ones with a sweet face—real clean-cut. We had everything but I was miserable. He called me every name in the book. The C word. What could be worse than the C word?

The explicit task of these support groups is to encourage their members to see their own stories as those of wife abuse. Just as magazine articles can give explicit advice for "what to look for" in order to categorize experiences as those of wife abuse, support-group facilitators give women sheets of information ("Why Women Stay," "Characteristics of Abusers," "The Wheel of Power and Control"). In these meetings women also might share the titles and contents of books they have read and they might watch films and then compare their own experiences to those of the characters in the films.

What is the most interesting is how interactions among women and support-group facilitators can lead women to embrace the story of wife abuse as their own. Margarete, for example, must have evaluated her experiences as potentially those of wife abuse because she came to a meeting publicly advertised as a support group for battered women. She starts her story, however, by voicing her hesitation that the wife abuse story is her own.

I don't know if I should be in a group like this. I thought my life was pretty normal. I just got sick of doing it all and not being respected. I never worked outside the home; my husband has a good job and I didn't have to work. I always did everything at home [she elaborates at some length]. He never appreciated it. Never sent me flowers or bought me a gift. Never took me out to dinner. I've been doing everything I could to make a wonderful home for us, cooking his dinner late because he worked late and it turns out he wasn't working late—he was with another woman!! I found out and confronted him and he said I wasn't going to break up our home. We argued and he got violent. That's the first time he ever touched me, but it will be the last. I filed for a divorce and I found out when he got served he broke down and cried. That really surprised me because I thought he'd be angry. He sent me flowers for Valentine's Day. She didn't get flowers, only me.

Notice how Margarete does not describe the one-way violence of wife abuse. Rather, she only alludes to violence ("he got violent") and she situates this violence within a mutual interaction ("I confronted him" and "We argued"). At this point, Margarete's story might be titled "Loyal and Unappreciated Wife Betrayed by Her Husband."

The conversation continues. Another group member, Megan, hears infidelity as Margarete's central theme and compares this to her own experiences. Then the support group leader ignores Megan's talk as well as Margarete's theme of infidelity and redirects the story toward violence by asking Margarete to be specific about "what he did to you."

Megan: I give you a lot of credit. My husband was always running around but I kept trying to get him back [she continues for two minutes detailing the unfaithfulness of her own partner].

Facilitator: So, Margarete, you say he got violent. Can you tell me exactly what he did to you?

Margarete: Well, as I said, I found out he was seeing someone else and we argued. He pushed me and I fell against the coffee table, and he put his hands around my neck and told me he wasn't going to let me break up his family. When I think about it, he had pushed me around at various times during our marriage. Usually when he thought I had spent too much money, but I never got hurt before.

Margarete's story has changed. The violence now seems severe ("he put his hands around my neck") and, critically, she adds that she "got hurt." Margarete also has changed her description of the history of violence in her marriage. Upon first telling, she said, "that's the first time he ever touched me," but now she recalls how "he had pushed me around at various times during our marriage."

Although Margarete has directed the conversation to violence, Megan attempts to redirect it back to her own interests in infidelity:

Megan: How did you find out he was seeing someone else?

Margarete: Uh, a friend saw him with her at a restaurant [she talks about where and when this happened]. I don't know how I could have been so blind. I guess a lot of people probably know about this and that is really embarrassing. I feel like such a

> fool. Now I see that there was always emotional abuse. He was always putting us down. We—the kids and I—never could do anything right in his eyes. I'm glad I came.

In explaining to Megan how she learned about her husband's infidelity, Margarete talks about her embarrassment and feeling "like a fool." She then adds emotional abuse to her story, emotional abuse that "always" has been there. In the end, Margarete reassesses her initial hesitation that this was an appropriate support group for her. Now she is "glad" she came to this group. Notice how Margarete's final story is a result of responding to questions and comments from the group facilitator and from another group member. In the process, Margarete has changed her story; now it is a story of wife abuse.

In summary, some women enter support groups for battered women already accepting the wife abuse story as their own; through their experiences in the group, other women learn over time to think of their lives in this way. But my data from these support groups do not allow me to estimate the extent to which these groups were successful as measured by the number of members eventually embracing the wife abuse story as their own. Support groups were characterized by member transience in that many women came only once or twice and never returned. Consider the stories of two such women who each attended only one meeting. I'll start with Jane.

Facilitator: Is this your first night?
Jane: Yes. I'm here because I was in a relationship with a man that has caused me a lot of pain. I paid a price that I was not willing to pay so I ended it. CPS [child protective services] took my kids away. It's not just what they did, it's how they did it. They picked them up at school and I wasn't told until after it happened. So I couldn't explain it to them or say goodbye. They were in foster care for a while, that was about six months ago. Now they're with their fathers. My daughter—I don't get to see her because my ex-husband lives in [another state]—is doing OK. Her father is OK. He's a good man. He's remarried and I don't know his wife. But I'm really worried about my son. He's in [another city]. His father is remarried and they lost custody of his children by his second wife because of abuse. Now they have a new baby and my son. My son's hyperactive and I think his stepmother resents him being there. My boyfriend wasn't abusive to them but now my son's in a home with a history of abuse.

Jane's story starts in an expectable way: She is at this meeting because of a relationship with a man who caused her "a lot of pain." But rather than talking about the pain of wife abuse, Jane rather talks about how her two children were taken from her and that one of them might not be safe. She also is clear that her boyfriend was *not* abusive to them. The interaction continues with the facilitator's common-sense assumption that Jane is no longer with her boyfriend.

Facilitator: So, you're not with this man anymore. Do you think you can get your children back?

Jane: Well, I have a restraining order, but I'm seeing him. I was living in a small town in [another area] with the two kids and taking care of my grandmother, too, in a little two-bedroom apartment. I was making $75 a week and the rent was $300. Johnny was calling and saying he was sorry, that he would change. He said he'd buy us some land and a trailer, he said he'd live with his brother. I took him up on it because I had to do something.... Once I got down here I started seeing him more since I thought he really wanted to change. But after a while things were just like they had been. The neighbors called the police several times. That's why CPS took the kids—they said it wasn't a healthy environment. I'm not willing to pay that price so I'm working on getting my life together.

Jane first corrects the facilitator's assumption that she no longer is with her boyfriend and then continues to offer reasons for this. But this story makes little sense because, while she replied that she was still with her boyfriend—a current condition—her argument is about why she was with him in the past—before the children were taken. The facilitator politely ignores this plot deficiency and pursues questions about the restraining order.

Facilitator: You know that if you're seeing him and you have a restraining order you are breaking the law? Think about the most important thing in your life. Is he more important than your children?

Jane: No. But I won't get my kids back unless I take care of my financial problems and I had to be here to do that. If he gets out of control, he'll be arrested.

Jane flatly denies she is putting her boyfriend above her children and rather frames her behavior as necessary in order to get her children back. Notice how Jane's story has gone on for some time but still does not contain abuse that is the central element in the story of wife abuse. The facilitator assumes Jane has experienced abuse:

Facilitator: Tell me about the abuse. Was it emotional, physical, sexual?

Jane: He got verbally and physically abusive when he was drunk— and that was a lot of the time. He has a temper. I might end up with bruises, he pushed me and slapped me. I never had a broken bone and I never needed medical attention. If the neighbors hadn't started to report it every time it got loud, we'd probably still be just the way we were. They probably called CPS, too. Because when he and I were going at it the kids would be screaming, STOP! So they probably thought the kids were being abused, but he was always good to them. And when he wasn't drinking he was the most loving man. I don't think he should be punished for the sickness of alcoholism. I loved him and thought it was my duty to try to help him.

Facilitator: But he was abusive to your children. It hurt them to see him hurt you. That's why CPS stepped in. Sometimes that's what it takes to make women realize that they are in an unhealthy relationship. I'm sorry you had to go through that. [Moving on to the next woman] Maggie, can you tell us what happened to you last week?

In answering a direct question about the violence she experienced, Jane tells a confusing story. She acknowledges abuse and injuries but simultaneously denies their severity; while she does not offer a specific scene containing violence, she does encourage her audience to understand these scenes were mutually created ("when he and I were going at it"). She concludes with a testimony about the inherent goodness of her boyfriend and returns to complaints about the neighbors who initiated contact with child protective services. Before moving on to the next woman, the facilitator's final comment challenges Jane's testimony that her boyfriend was the "most loving man" when he was sober and she makes Jane's story an example of what it takes to "get women to realize they are in an unhealthy relationship."

While audience members might evaluate Jane's story as one of wife abuse, it remains that Jane did little to develop her own story in that way. True, when asked directly, she did include violence in her story, but the major theme remained her effort to get her children back. Further, Jane does not construct herself as a battered woman who needs help. On the contrary, her character is a strong woman doing what she needs to do in order to achieve her goal. Still further, the villain in Jane's story is not the boyfriend who she characterizes as a "most loving" man when sober who does not abuse her children. The villains in Jane's story rather are the neighbors who called in CPS and CPS that took her children from her.

Women's stories of lived realities are complex and they do not always see violence as the central problem in their lives. I return to the evening when group interactions led to Margarete redefining her marriage as "always emotionally abusive." Recall that another group member, Megan, kept directing Margarete to talk about her husband's infidelity. Megan also was a new member that evening and her story follows. When the facilitator asked her to "tell us a little about yourself and why you're here," Megan replied:

> I'm Megan. I got my divorce. I have my boys. We're living in [another county] and things are really going good. I'm on probation because of him but I'm dealing with it. I beat up his girlfriend and slashed the tires on her car—and I'd do it again if I had to do it all over [laughing]. I admit to that—they got me on B and E [breaking and entering]; that's why I'm on probation. I still don't now why he left me for her. He had everything. I worked, he never did. He took off for months at a time on his bike and that was okay. The kids are doing good. They were always used to him being gone a lot anyway. He pays his child support.

Because the prompt of "tell us why you're here" happened in a support group for battered women, the answer should explain why a woman is in this particular type of group. Megan's story, however, does not contain any elements of violence toward her while it does include a sub-story of how she was violent toward her former husband's new girlfriend. Megan's characterization of her former partner also is not that of an abusive man. Other group members learn only that he was irresponsible in the past (he never worked and he left for months at a time), but is responsible in the present (he pays his child support). In brief, nothing in Megan's story characterizes her experiences as those of wife abuse and her characterization of herself as proudly violent toward his new girlfriend seems antithetical to understandings of the battered woman type of character. Given this, it is not surprising that another group member, Jessie, specifically asks Megan to enlarge her story to include violence:

Jessie: Was he physically abusive?
Megan: You name it, he did it; physically, emotionally, sexually. But I wouldn't have left. In fact, I tried to reconcile for months after he left. I guess I just couldn't handle the fact that I had always done everything for him, supported him, put up with everything he did and he left me for her . . . What does she have that I don't have? That's what I can't take. She went to court in a white knit low-cut dress that showed everything, slit all the way up one side. I'll be okay, it's just that it makes me so mad to think about him with her. Why do I still care?
Facilitator: He's still controlling you. He knows just what to do to make you angry. He doesn't want you to be free even although he is in a new relationship.

When directly asked to talk about the violence she experienced, Megan minimally answered the question but quickly returned to the central theme of her story—jealousy of her former partner's new girlfriend. Megan's character is a "jilted wife" rather than a "battered woman." Nonetheless, the facilitator understands Megan's story as one of wife abuse because she characterizes Megan's former husband as an abuser who is intent on controlling her.

In summary, some women readily tell their stories as those of wife abuse while others apparently learn over time to do so and still others resist understanding their lives in this way. The complexity, confusion, and indeterminacy of practical experience means that not all women will see the story of wife abuse as their own. This leads to a final set of questions: What has the public story of wife abuse accomplished? What are the problems when this narrative is used as a model to evaluate the meaning of personal experiences? What are the possibilities of changing the public story of wife abuse so that it can be more responsive to the complexities of women's lives?

STORIES AND SOCIAL CHANGE[26]

Narratives, the stories people tell, are pervasive and persuasive in social life. My focus has been on the story of wife abuse and my argument is that this publicly circulating story has been a component of social change. In comparison to arguments based on statistics or formal logic, stories have the power to encourage audiences to *feel* the desperation, pain, and devastating consequences of wife abuse. Stories personalize what otherwise might be merely abstractions and put unique human faces on what otherwise would be anonymous others. While the public story of wife abuse originally written by feminists conveys a whole series of values about gender equality, audiences do not need to consciously embrace these in order to evaluate wife abuse as a story of morally intolerable violence. Such an evaluation supports calls to take abuse seriously.

What I have focused on here is how widely circulating stories can be used by individuals; there are myriad empirical examples of how accepting the wife abuse story as their own encourages women to leave life-threatening relationships. Hence, the success of the public story of wife abuse can be measured in terms of the number of women's lives it has saved. While the importance of this, of course, cannot be discounted, I nonetheless want to explore some of the unintended consequences of the content of the story of wife abuse. This first requires considering relationships between public stories and personal experience.

My topic here has been the work narratives do in social life. In public, narratives can spark attention, encourage audiences to feel in particular ways, and hence, to support calls for social change. However, it is very difficult to author stories with widespread appeal for the simple reason that Americans are not united in our visions of how the world works or of how the world should work. Simply stated, achieving widespread appeal requires circumventing the countless ways in which

Americans make moral evaluations. While in daily life we evaluate violence on a case-by-case basis and are remarkably sensitive to details, publicly circulating stories are so clear that they are incontestable: Stories of wife abuse contain violence that is most assuredly and without a doubt abusive and illegitimate; the woman is none other than saintly and the man is none other than barbaric. This characteristic of popular public stories of all types to feature melodramatic plots and simple characters is precisely what makes them persuasive in public life. At the same time, this simplicity and clarity can make publicly circulating stories of less-than-obvious use to individuals who are trying to make sense of unique experiences. That is, while effective stories in the public realm achieve their clarity by denying complexity, effective narratives in personal life are those that make sense of this complexity. While the stock characters in public stories are one-dimensional characters, individuals do not experience themselves and others so simply. Indeed, while effective stories in public tend to feature extreme cases, extreme case images actually decrease the possibility that individuals will evaluate their own experiences as similar to those in the story.

There are indications that some women experiencing violence refuse to embrace the story of wife abuse as their own because they do not evaluate the harm they experience as extreme and/or they do not see themselves as the virtuous victim. Research also has found that service providers use the public story of wife abuse as a yardstick by which to evaluate stories told by their patients and clients, and many women are judged to not meet the standard of extreme harm and absolute moral purity set in the public story.

Regardless of the good the story of wife abuse has accomplished in public life, there are negative consequences when it is used to evaluate the experiences and characteristics of individual women. I am certainly not the first to note these problems. On the contrary, these are very troublesome to advocates who want to change the plot and characters of the wife abuse story in order to make them more responsive to the unique experiences and characteristics of individual women. Countless advocates for women have argued that narratives of wife abuse should condemn *all* forms of violence rather than focusing on obviously extreme violence. Such arguments, however, primarily are located in works written by and for a relatively small audience of feminists; they rarely appear in public because Americans in general remain concerned primarily with extreme violence. Offering stories in the public realm of less-than-extreme violence is risky because they reduce the possibility that audiences will evaluate wife abuse as morally intolerable behavior. Furthermore, many advocates argue that women must be offered sympathy and services even if they do not seem to be absolutely morally pure, but that argument also has not been accepted by a large audience because Americans typically categorize individuals as victims only when they are evaluated as good people lacking responsibility for creating the harm they experience. Hence, advocates have found that public support is lost if women seem other than absolutely pure victims:

> ... it has been extremely difficult for researchers, advocates, other practitioners, and some battered women themselves to talk about women's use of violence. These discussions quickly career off into polemics about women being as violent or more violent than men, women "participating in" or "provoking" their own victimization, and women not being "good" (or pure) victims, or even being victims at all.[27]

In brief, although advocates repeatedly have attempted to widen the story of wife abuse to include less-than-horrid violence and less-than-saintly victims, stories featuring graphic violence, virtuous victims, and vicious villains remain the most popular in the public realm.

There also are indications that individual women sometimes refuse to identify themselves as the victim in the story of wife abuse because they perceive victims to be powerless and passive and therefore not socially respected. Advocates also worry that the woman-as-victim identity emphasizes weaknesses rather than strengths. This has led to calls to reauthor the battered woman character in the wife abuse story from a victim to a survivor. While obviously well-intentioned and theoretically justified, such a change might be risky because it is the weakness of victims that supplies the mandate for offering them assistance. Stated otherwise, survivors are strong people who deserve respect for their strength but who do not require assistance because of this strength.

The remarkable social change in how people respond to the tragedy of wife abuse would not have been predicted in the 1970s given general beliefs that violence in marital relationships—at least among those in the middle class—was "normal" and "legitimate" and that women experiencing violence either caused it or liked it. Advocates and others authoring stories of wife abuse successfully challenged those notions so that now most Americans are willing to accept that some violence in marital relationships is morally intolerable abusive violence and that some women victims of this violence deserve sympathy and assistance. However, it remains that the wife abuse story as popularly understood does *not* challenge the systems of ideas surrounding the evaluations of violence and victims. Rather, the wife abuse story condemns violence that is most clearly abusive and illegitimate as assessed through the system of ideas surrounding the evaluation of violence, and it calls for sympathy and assistance for those women who are most certainly virtuous victims as assessed through systems of ideas for evaluating victim status. In other words, the public story of wife abuse does *not* challenge commonly accepted ideas about what is necessary for an incident of violence to be evaluated as "abusive/illegitimate" versus "normal/legitimate"; it does *not* challenge commonly accepted ideas about what is required for a person to be evaluated as a victim worthy of sympathy and attention.

The importance of social change since the 1970s certainly cannot be—and should not be—denied or diminished. Much has changed and this has been none other than lifesaving for countless women. But much more must be done to stop the continuing devastation of violence against women. Continued social change requires encouraging the public to take violence seriously *before* it yields irremediable injury and to stop demanding that women seem saintly in order to receive sympathy and services.

While my call to enlarge the plot and characters in the story of wife abuse leads to very practical questions of how this might be done, here I want to retain my focus on narratives and conclude with raising a perplexing question that would require considerable thought to answer. My argument is that the wife abuse story as now told ignores too much violence experienced by too many women. In very important ways, the story as now commonly understood is an "end of the line" story in that by the time women are easily recognizable—to themselves or to others—as living the story of wife abuse, there typically has been incredible damage already done and their relationships are simply irreparable. Expanding the story of wife abuse would encourage much earlier detection and intervention and that seems very good indeed. At the same time, the more the plot of wife abuse is expanded to include a broader range of violence, the more the female character loses her saintly qualities and the more the male character becomes less villainous, the more the wife abuse story would be indistinguishable from the stories of "mutual combat" and "marital troubles." And this would bring us right back to why the wife abuse story was authored in the first place: Both the mutual combat and the marital troubles stories hold women accountable for the violence they experience, and both hold promises that relationships can be saved. Most certainly, this has very practical consequences because women who are blamed for their experiences receive no sympathy or assistance; women's attempts to save their relationships are precisely what allows abuse to increase in severity over time, and this is exactly what leads to the physical and psychological devastation associated with wife abuse. So, expanding the story of wife abuse to include more violence and more women is fraught with complexity because of the systems of ideas surrounding the evaluation of violence and victims. Still, it is sad that we make individual women live the story of wife abuse and be the battered woman character before we find their stories worthy of our thoughts, feelings, and assistance.

NOTES

1. For a review, see D. R. Loseke, "The Study of Identity as Cultural, Institutional, Organizational, and Personal Narrative: Theoretical and Empirical Integrations," *The Sociological Quarterly* 48 (2007); and D. R. Loseke, and M. Kusenbach,

"The Social Construction of Emotions," in *Handbook of Constructionist Research*, ed. J. A. Holstein, and J. Gubrium (New York: Guilford Press, 2008).

2. K. Cuerelo, *Deciphering Violence: The Cognitive Structure of Right and Wrong* (New York: Routledge, 1998).

3. U.S. House of Representatives, *Research Into Violent Behavior: Domestic Violence* (Washington, D.C.: United States Government Printing Office, 1978), 147.

4. D. Martin, *Battered Wives* (San Francisco: Volcano Press, 1976), 1–5. Courtesy of Volcano Press, www.volcanopress.com.

5. Ibid., 5.

6. S. Schechter, *Women and Male Violence: The Visions and Struggles of the Battered Women's Movement* (Boston: South End Press, 1982), 12.

7. Ibid., 12–14.

8. I am indebted to Nancy Berns, who so graciously shared with me the data she collected on portrayals of violence against women in magazines targeted to a general audience of women.

9. "I Was a Battered Wife," *Good Housekeeping* (September 1987): 22, 24, 26, 28.

10. "I Was a Battered Wife," *Good Housekeeping* (May 1979): 36, 37, 40–42.

11. S. Burns, "On Being an Abused Wife . . . And Living in Fear," *Mademoiselle* (December 1979): 56.

12. "A Mother Burned Alive by her Husband," transcript, *The Oprah Winfrey Show* (New York: Harpo Productions), originally aired April 19, 2006.

13. D. Lewis, "When Love Turns Violent," *Glamour Magazine* (August 1990): 234.

14. Alexis Jetter, "How Battered Wives Can Learn to Leave," *McCall's* (September 1994): 98, 104, 106, 109.

15. J. Blumberg Victor,"He Beat Me: Battered Wife Tells Why She Took it for Seven Years," *Vogue* (January 1978): 177, 185, 186.

16. "A Suburban Mother's Nightmare Captured on Tape," transcript, *The Oprah Winfrey Show* (New York: Harpo Productions), originally aired May 8, 2007, 13–14.

17. C. Ostrom," The Secret Problem that Destroys Marriages," *Ladies' Home Journal* (October 1986): 87.

18. "A Mother Burned Alive," transcript, *The Oprah Winfrey Show* (New York: Harpo Productions), originally aired April 19, 2006, 10.

19. "A Suburban Mother's Nightmare Captured on Tape," transcript, *The Oprah Winfrey Show* (New York: Harpo Productions), originally aired May 8, 2007, 1.

20. "An Abusive Husband's Desperate Plea for Help," transcript, *The Oprah Winfrey Show* (New York: Harpo Productions), originally aired April 19, 2006, 1.

21. B. Mesch, "Why Women Stay With Men Who Beat Them," *Essence* (April 1983): 86; J. Ralston, "When Young Love Hurts," *Ladies' Home Journal* (June 1998): 71; R. J. Weems, "When Love Hurts," *Essence* (October 1988): 71; and J. Rosen, "When Someone You Love Hits You," *Mademoiselle* (October 2000): 85.

22. In the next two sections I draw heavily from previously published work: D. R. Loseke, "Lived Realities and Formula Stories of 'Battered Women,' " in *Institutional Selves: Troubled Identities in a Postmodern World*, ed. J. F. Gubrium, and J. A. Holstein (New York: Oxford University Press, 2001).

23. J. Marks, "My Husband Became Violent," *Ladies' Home Journal* (August 1983): 12.

24. L. Werner, "My Husband Hit Me," *Ladies' Home Journal* (November 1986): 14.

25. Data in this section were previously published in D. R. Loseke, "Lived Realities and Formula Stories of 'Battered Women,'" in *Institutional Selves: Troubled Identities in a Postmodern World*, ed. J. F. Gubrium, and J. A. Holstein (New York: Oxford University Press, 2001), which also contains the methodology for this research.

26. In this section I am drawing heavily from D. R. Loseke, "The Study of Identity as Cultural, Institutional, Organizational, and Personal Narrative: Theoretical and Empirical Integrations," *The Sociological Quarterly* 48 (2007).

27. A. Bible, S. Dasgupta, and S. Osthoff, "Guest Editor's Introduction," *Violence against Women* 8 (2002): 1,268.

FURTHER RESOURCES

C. Clark, *Misery and Company: Sympathy in Everyday Life* (Chicago: University of Chicago Press, 1997).

A. Goetting, *Getting Out: Life Stories of Women Who Left Abusive Men* (New York: Columbia University Press, 1999).

D. R. Loseke, *The Battered Woman and Shelters: The Social Construction of Wife Abuse* (New York: State University of New York Press, 1992).

D. Martin, *Battered Wives* (San Francisco: Volcano Press, 1976).

M. D. Pagelow, *Woman-Battering: Victims and their Experiences* (Beverly Hills, CA: Sage, 1981).

S. Schechter, *Women and Male Violence: The Visions and Struggles of the Battered Women's Movement* (Boston: South End Press, 1982).

Chapter 2

Film, Violence, and Gender[1]

Karen Boyle

It has become common practice when faced with apparently inexplicable acts of interpersonal violence—particularly those perpetrated by young, privileged, white men and boys—that media commentators turn to the question of possible media influence. Within this coverage, violent movies feature prominently with lurid headlines suggesting a causal relationship between repeat viewings and horrendous real-world crimes. What hides behind these headlines, however, is typically a more mundane story of male violence that finds support not only in horror movies but in other aspects of culture and society. Blaming the more explicit forms of film violence for real-world male violence distracts our attention from the male perpetrators themselves while also avoiding more complex questions about the ways in which male violence is normalized and celebrated across a wide range of representations and practices.

The "copycat" story creates a comfortable distance between "them" (the abusers) and "us" that is based more on cultural taste and media literacy than on a *choice*, a *decision* to act violently or not: *they* identify with film violence, but *we* with better tastes and values do not. For those who are concerned about real-world violence and its fictional referents on screen, such narrow understandings of media influence are therefore hugely problematic. However, such simplistic, sensationalist arguments *have* proved seductive for a range of thinkers concerned with male violence, including some feminist critics. For instance, in the context of a volume focusing on femicide (the killing of women because they are women), Chris Domingo comments:

> The public and media reaction to serial killings is quite disturbing. Not only is femicide ignored by mainstream news and discourse, it is joked about and used as grist in the R-rated movie mill. Serial murder is actually enjoyed—not only by the woman-haters who commit the murders, as evidenced by the usual presence of semen at crime scenes—but by a large percentage of the male population, as evidenced by attendance at "slasher" films and the popularity of photographs in which women are victims of violence.[2]

Domingo here raises troubling questions about the entertainment function of serial murder. However, her argument—echoed in recent protests against so-called "torture porn" films[3]—is based on an assumption that the pleasures of these movies are entirely straightforward (viewers identify with the killers and take pleasure in the murder of women) and their relationship to the sexual serial murder of women in reality self-evident (they reflect reality and promote violence against women). But is this a safe assumption? Are these the only pleasures on offer in slasher and other violent movies? Where does this leave women in the audience? What about male victims? Can enjoying violence on-screen really be equated with enjoying violence in real life? This chapter seeks to address these questions by discussing some of the popular American genres that have generated concern and critical interest for their portrayal of violence, gender, and sexuality.

THE VIOLENCE OF THE MALE GAZE

Violence has been central to feminist film theory and criticism since its inception. Early studies were primarily concerned with how images of women on-screen related—or, rather, didn't relate—to the lives of women off-screen and considered how anxieties about changing gender roles were played out in spectacles of violence.[4] However, like Domingo's much later criticisms, these early works focused on content at the expense of form. That is, there was little consideration of film *as film*—an audiovisual form of mass entertainment.

The publication of Laura Mulvey's hugely influential essay "Visual Pleasure and Narrative Cinema" in 1975 was an important intervention in this respect, focusing on the particular kinds of gendered pleasures cinema offers its viewers. Mulvey's most significant contribution was her argument that mainstream narrative cinema privileges a "male gaze" regardless of the sex of the actual spectator. She argued that there are two forms of pleasure offered by cinema—identification and objectification—and that both are fundamentally gendered. We—whether male or female—*identify* with the male character on the screen (the protagonist who drives the action forward) and *objectify* the female character(s) who embodies what Mulvey calls "to-be-looked-at-ness."

That is, the men *do* (and we identify with their action), while the women *appear* (and we enjoy looking at them).

Moreover, the conditions of viewing in the cinema privilege a *voyeuristic* spectatorship. We are "Peeping Toms," watching others—and taking pleasure in this—while we ourselves remain unseen. Feminists in other fields have identified voyeurism as a form of gendered violence: The "Peeping Tom" is nearly always male, watching a woman without her knowledge or consent. The power of his look is a reminder of women's object status, sexualization, lack of power, as well as (in a very real sense) a violation: part of what sociologist Liz Kelly influentially described as the *continuum* of men's violence against women.[5] In the cinema, the characters on-screen may not be "victims" in this sense, but *for the spectator* the two situations parallel one another offering a sense of mastery and control over the objects of the gaze. Film, therefore, offers an entertaining extension of men's social sense of entitlement.

This sense of entitlement is not, however, without its anxieties. Making use of Freudian psychoanalysis, Mulvey argues that the female figure poses something of a problem for the male unconscious: because she lacks a penis she symbolizes for the male the threat of castration. Although there is not the space to fully explain these arguments, what is significant for the purposes of this chapter is Mulvey's argument about how this threat is contained cinematically. According to Mulvey, cinema's fascination with the female figure provides a means of compensating for this as the woman becomes the *object* of the male gaze and of narrative fascination—looked at, investigated, probed, contained, and controlled. This works both at the level of the story (what happens to the female character) and at the level of the image (how she is shown, her body stylized, fragmented, and displayed for maximum male pleasure).

The crux of Mulvey's argument, then, is that Hollywood cinema privileges a male gaze that is characterized by power and control. In other words, the pleasures offered by mainstream cinema are underpinned by gendered violence. The legacy of Mulvey's work is to encourage us to consider the potential violence of film's form as well as its content. Mulvey's work has, of course, been revisited and revised by feminist critics over the thirty-plus years since its initial publication; in this chapter we will consider some of this work, particularly in relation to genres such as the slasher. However, it is also important to note that Mulvey's use of psychoanalysis led her to privilege *sexual* difference. While feminist critics following on from Mulvey have rightly noted how other differences—most notably race—also structure the gaze,[6] the majority of the work considered in this chapter has similarly privileged sexual difference in its consideration of mainstream (and primarily U.S.) genre cinema. For critics interested in violence, it is certainly notable that the gender norms that are supported or transgressed by violent behavior have racial, class, national, and sexual inflections. Unless otherwise stated, this chapter is primarily concerned with *dominant* (read: white, middle-class, and Anglo-American) cinematic constructions of gendered violence.

SLASHERS

In her influential account of horror-film spectatorship, Carol Clover writes: "The horror movie is somehow more than the sum of its monsters; it is itself monstrous."[7] Clover's concern here is with the self-reflexive aspects of horror or, more specifically, how *looking* is itself made horrific. She suggests that horror films repeatedly present a challenge to, if not a direct assault on, the viewer. Eyes are attacked on-screen in gruesome, lingering close-ups, while the act of viewing (particularly of videotapes) makes characters vulnerable to violation. So, counter to Domingo's arguments and to the theoretical approach taken by Mulvey, Clover suggests that there is a *masochistic* element to viewing these films: that they offer pleasure in being subjected to pain, horror, and fear. To investigate these claims we need to consider not only what these films *show* (what we actually see of the violence) but also how they position us in relation to what's going on (who we identify with and how).

There is no doubt that much of what we see in conventional horror films—and in the slasher film in particular—is the mutilation of women. As director Alfred Hitchcock put it, "I always believe in following the advice of the playwright Sardou. He said, 'Torture the women!' The trouble today is that we don't torture women enough."[8] Certainly, in the slasher films of the 1970s and 1980s, much screen time is taken up showing women in terror and pain. Sex equals death for both male and female teens in the slasher, but it is generally only *women's* deaths that are sexualized and lingered upon.

The more difficult question, however, is how we are positioned in relation to the violence on-screen: do we—as Domingo suggests—identify with the killer and delight in the violence, or is there more to it than that? The slasher film certainly offers us moments of identification with the killer. It's not accidental that these movies are also known as "stalkers": for much of the film we—along with the killer—stalk the teens who will become his victims. We see through his (and it is usually his) eyes and hear his breathing, heartbeat, and footsteps on the soundtrack. Our vision is compromised as his is—obscured by bushes, window blinds, and so on—and as we see through his eyes the killer himself remains unseen (as, too, do we in the audience).

Perhaps the classic example of this is the opening of *Halloween* (Carpenter, 1978) where we are positioned with the killer, go with him into the kitchen, up the stairs, and into the bedroom where we look through the Halloween mask he wears as he/we kill his postcoital teen sister. The killer himself is not revealed until after the murder when it is something of a shock for the spectator to discover that the killer is an emotionless six-year-old boy. And this is where it gets complicated. The revelation—that we've been identifying with a disturbed *child*—arguably undercuts any sense of mastery and control that we may have enjoyed up until this point. *Halloween* is by no means unique in this respect. The slasher-killer is *rarely* a figure with whom we would want to identify: juvenile, deformed or diseased, drooling, overweight, lacking in social skills and verbal dexterity, gender-confused, and/or ostracized from society. Further, the sequences from his point of view—while striking—are actually few and far between and there is rarely a stable point of identification in the first stages of the slasher film. Indeed, part of the way the slasher creates tension is by playing around with point of view to implicate other characters in the killings and/or to suggest a pervasive sense of threat. Early in *Friday the 13th* (Cunningham, 1980), for example, we adopt the perspective of the unseen killer lurking in the woods as she watches the camp counselors at the river (unusually, *Friday the 13th*'s first killer is a woman). When two of the counselors return to the river, we are again allied with an unseen voyeur who watches them making out. In this instance, the voyeur is their friend; allying his point of view with that of the killer makes him (briefly) a subject of suspicion before he becomes the real killer's next victim.

More significantly for Clover, by the end of the slasher we have completely switched allegiances as we are aligned with the point of view of the female survivor (who she calls the "Final Girl") whose flight, fight, and fright dominates the final section of the film. The Final Girl may be terrified, but she is also resourceful and determined, surviving when her friends do not. This leads Clover to argue that the pleasures offered by the slasher movie may not be sadistically simple. Indeed, she suggests that the Final Girl is the only coherent point of identification, providing the male spectator with the opportunity to live out *masochistic* fantasies (of powerlessness, feminization, and/or pain) in relative safety. So, the (male) spectator identifies with a *girl*, but one who is masculinized—in name (for example, Laurie, Stretch), appearance (distinctly less feminine than her female friends), and in her assumption of an active, investigating gaze. As such, she is "a congenial double for the adolescent male":

> feminine enough to act out in a gratifying way, a way unapproved for adult males, the terrors and masochistic pleasures of the underlying fantasy, but not so feminine as to disturb the structures of male competence and sexuality.[9]

This does not mean the slasher is necessarily progressive, but it does alert us to the fact that more may be going on than we might at first assume.

While Clover's model is useful in alerting us to other kinds of pleasure that might be provided by the slasher film, there are inevitably complications and contradictions when we try to apply her model to the slasher as it developed across the 1980s and beyond. First, we should note that the Final Girl is not consistently "final" (in a number of the early slashers, including *Halloween*, she must be saved by someone else), nor consistently a "girl" (in the 1980s horror franchises there are both male and female survivors). Further, her "survival" looks very different when we consider films in series: Alice (Adrienne King) may survive *Friday the 13th* but is quickly dispatched in the sequel; Laurie (Jamie Lee Curtis) survives *Halloween* but lives in terror through *Halloween II* (Rosenthal, 1981) and seventeen years on is an alcoholic living in the shadow of Michael's violence (in *H20*, Miner, 1998).

Most importantly, while the killer may be a marginal figure in individual films, the slasher *cycles* emphasize the killer. Freddy Kreuger, Jason Voorhees, and Michael Myers are the most enduring and memorable figures in the franchises in which they appear even if they are also somewhat interchangeable and lacking in conventional characterization. For instance, from John Carpenter's original to Rob Zombie's 2007 *Halloween* remake, Michael Myers—sometimes appearing in credits simply as "The Shape"—has been played by thirteen different actors. This may complicate any easy *identification* with the killers, but they have a life beyond the films (in merchandizing and other cultural reference points) that renders them "safe" and "fun" at the same time as reveling in their splatter-killings. Their ability to survive for sequel after sequel, not to mention the increasingly bizarre means of their resurrection, render the narrative obviously and deliberately implausible, and the films are typically both self-reflexive and self-deprecating in this regard. In the first *Halloween*, for example, Michael survives a stabbing and six bullet wounds to the chest to walk away at the film's end: in the sequels he will survive much more. Indeed, the special effects are a key part of the films' appeal with each movie pushing the boundaries that bit further in terms of bloody spectacle and incredible methods of killing. In this respect, Domingo's criticisms seem particularly wide of the mark: at least part of the fascination with the most popular slasher-killers (and killings) is that they are so patently *unreal*.

Yet, the fears these films tap into are very real, just as the "bogeymen" of children's rhymes can be traced back to real-life cases of sexual murder. While it is a mistake to simply read these films "straight" as a *reflection* of real-world anxieties and a *catalyst* for future violence, they *do* contribute to our understanding of gender and violence. However, this is not always in the detrimental way that critics like Domingo suggest. For instance, the sociopolitical context in which the slasher flourished through the 1980s was also a period in which "the family" became a contested political site, not least as a result of feminist research and activism around domestic and child sexual abuse. As the decade wore on, the response of more mainstream films—where they dealt with families in crisis at all—was often to demonize career women and victimize men, as most infamously in *Fatal Attraction* (Lyne, 1987). In contrast, slashers offered one of the few fictional spaces where families, fathers, and father figures were not uncritically celebrated. This is not to argue that these films are, therefore, promoting feminism—they are clearly more complicated than that—but to acknowledge that they engage with gender politics in a more complex way than the (understandable) knee-jerk reaction of some feminist critics might suggest.

THE HORRIFIC 1990S AND 2000S

At the conclusion of *Men, Women, and Chain Saws*—published in 1992—Clover claims that "the slasher film proper has died down."[10] However, the slasher has since had something of a revival. Films such as the *Scream* trilogy (Craven 1996, 1997, and 2000) and *I Know What You Did Last Summer* (Gillespie, 1997) and its sequel (Cannon, 1998), self-consciously use and transform aspects of the slasher. Yet some things have not changed: It is no accident that Jennifer Love Hewitt and Sarah Michelle Gellar reputedly referred to the film in which they costarred as "I Know What Your Breasts Did Last Summer!"[11] Similarly, *Scream* may be extremely knowing in its use of generic conventions, but the on-screen movie buffs do not comment on the differential fates of male and female characters. Rather, the film simply reproduces these conventions: the killings of female characters are significantly more protracted, they have time to register the danger they are in, and their fear and (attempted) flight takes up considerable screen time. The twelve-minute opening sequence in which Casey (Drew Barrymore) is tormented by a menacing movie buff clearly demonstrates this point. While her boyfriend is dispatched quickly and silently (he is gagged), Casey's dawning terror is the focus of the scene, and her death—when it comes—is long and bloody: she is repeatedly stabbed, dragged across the ground, and her body hung from a tree.

The ironic, knowing, and self-aware tone of *Scream* does, however, complicate a straightforward critique: an observation that applies equally to Quentin Tarantino's bloody reappropriations of generic situations and characters from the same period. Tarantino's early films as writer/director—most notably *Reservoir Dogs* (1991) and *Pulp Fiction* (1994)—were described by some critics as representing a "new brutalism" in early 1990s filmmaking, but Tarantino was (and is) always explicit that his generic reference points are far from "new" and the self-conscious intertextuality of his films finds a parallel in the postmodern slasher franchises. While the knowingness of these films can open up possibilities for subversive pleasures, it can also function to reinforce hegemonic power relations by replicating misogynist patterns of looking, speaking, or killing while using irony to hold any attempt to critique these representations at a distance. In her discussion of Tarantino's early work, bell hooks sums this up brilliantly, arguing that he

> represents the ultimate "white-cool": a hardcore cynical vision that would have everyone see racism, sexism, homophobia, but behave as though none of that shit really matters, or if it does it means nothing cause none of it's gonna change, cause the real deal is that domination is here to stay—going nowhere and everybody is in on the act. Mind you, domination is always and only patriarchal—a dick thing.
>
> [...] The fun thing about Tarantino's films is that he makes that shit look so ridiculous you think everybody's gonna get it and see how absurd it all is. Well, that's when we enter the danger zone. Folks be laughing at the absurdity and clinging to it nevertheless.[12]

In other words, for hooks, irony can go hand in hand with "clinging" to structures of domination. Indeed, some critics have argued that this applies even to a film like *Kill Bill* (2003, 2004), which excises its references to world cinema from their political, historical, and cultural contexts and implications, emptying them of anything other than aesthetic meaning in the process.[13] With this in mind, it is perhaps not surprising that the ironic take on the slasher provided by films like *Scream* was so quickly followed by a more straightforward return to slasher aesthetics and concerns, both in remakes—*The Texas Chainsaw Massacre* (Nispel, 2003), *Halloween* (Zombie, 2007)—and new franchises (*Saw, Hostel*). Clearly, the "ironic" take on the slasher could happily coexist with the genre itself.

While the original slashers were dubbed "gorenography" by some feminists as a way of emphasising their debt to the misogyny and sexual objectification of pornography, more recent films have been labelled "torture porn." Yet a closer look at these films suggests that to dismiss them as celebrations of sexual violence may be to oversimplify their appeal and significance. As male victims litter the screen and point of view becomes increasingly unstable, mastery (or its illusion) is rarely on offer for the male spectator. For instance, *Saw* (Wan, 2004) opens with two men trapped in a room with a "corpse" and tape-recorded instructions for escape that depend upon one man killing the other and mutilating himself. One of the men, Dr. Lawrence Gordon (Cary Elwes), has had previous contact with the likely mastermind of their predicament—a man known only as Jigsaw (Tobin Bell). However, the explanatory flashbacks anchored by Gordon's narration are intercut with the competing accounts of police officers with the result that we have no coherent point of view from which to watch the story unfold, and every male character falls under suspicion. Arguably, the games of spectatorship have here become the point, and the threat of violence has become both more pervasive and more diffuse than in the classic slasher film. While his victims—chosen for their amorality and apparent disregard for life—attack themselves and each other, Jigsaw himself plays dead for most of the film, keeping his hands clean and his eyes shut. Therefore, it is too simplistic to suggest that male viewers are offered the pleasure of identification with a misogynist killer. Indeed, the game playing—both at the level of narrative (the games the victims are forced to engage in) and form (the games the director plays with his viewers)—arguably precludes both identification and empathy.

It is also worth noting that it is the torture *of women* in these films that has attracted the most critical concern. This is understandable because it is still the mutilation of women that provides the most gruesome spectacles. For instance, in *Hostel* the torture of the three central male characters is dealt with relatively quickly and, predominately, in long shot. In contrast, a secondary female character is tortured with a blowtorch in a lingering close-up in what has become the film's most infamous scene. The woman's screams dominate the soundtrack even after her rescue, her dislocated eyeball hanging from its socket until it is cut by her rescuer, the camera lingering on the blood and pus oozing from her wound.

It also remains true that violence against women is often explicitly sexualized in a way that violence against men is not: a comparison of *Hostel* with its sequel neatly demonstrates this point. The first film focuses on three male friends who are backpacking in Europe, a trip that largely consists of leering at and trying to have sex with as many women as possible. For the spectator, fairly conventional soft-porn pleasures are on offer in the first third of the film as the camera follows the backpackers' lusting looks at semi-naked, young, and conventionally attractive white women. The women are, we later discover, working for a murder-for-profit business and are paid to seduce and capture young men. As such, the torture of the main characters can arguably be understood as a punishment of the male gaze (and, specifically, its pornographic aims), placing the spectator identifying with these characters in an uncomfortable position. However, unlike in the rape-revenge film that I will explore later, for the spectator these pains are temporary: the beheading of the first backpacker takes place off-screen, and the surviving member of the trio escapes and takes his own revenge on the torturers.

In contrast, the soft-porn pleasures of the sequel (which focuses on female backpackers) are almost exclusively linked to scenes of violence. The first backpacker to die is naked, trussed-up, and hung upside down over a shallow, candlelit pool where she is tortured by a naked woman. The torturer lies beneath her victim, licking her red-painted lips provocatively as she drags a curved blade across the backpacker's naked flesh (in lingering close-ups) before slicing at her body and bathing orgasmically in her blood. The murder of the second backpacker is presented as black comedy: dressed up in a showgirl outfit and tied to a chair, the young woman is taunted by her would-be killer as he "accidentally" embeds a circular saw in her face. The squelching and tearing of flesh on the soundtrack underscores the bloody, if more briefly glimpsed, spectacle. The third backpacker—this film's Final Girl—survives only by castrating her torturer, a move that sexualizes her as she desexualizes him. The horrific double standard is clearly alive and well.

Finally, it is worth noting that these films have an equally complicated relationship with reality. Director Eli Roth has claimed that *Hostel* was "very much a reflection of my disgust with the Iraq War and the Al-Qaeda beheadings.... It's not just about people who want to kill us, but about capitalism gone awry and American imperialism."[14] In their focus on unsympathetic Americans abroad, the *Hostel* films may raise questions about the morality of the victims, but they do so by reversing the traffic in (primarily) women and children from east to west, a context that has been much less discussed. It is also telling that Roth describes his films as a *reflection* of these real-world conditions (and not, for instance, a commentary or challenge). Indeed, I would suggest that Roth *replicates* for the viewer the lack of empathy, casual disregard for non-American victims, and fascination with the image that was (and is) essential to the original violence he references. As Shane Danielson notes, torture porn is "a set of sensations, calibrated for maximum efficiency and effect. One might say its very blankness is the most terrifying thing about it."[15] Like the porn to which it is often compared, the effectlessness and effectiveness of these films is a disturbing combination, suggesting something of the culture's broader subordination of male emotion and empathy to immediate physical gratification. It is this failure to engage the spectator's empathy (for instance, through identification with characters or situations)—rather than the scenes of violence themselves—that should be a key concern for feminist critics of these films.

KILLING AND THRILLING

The killer may be an often-shadowy figure in the slasher movie, but—since at least *The Silence of the Lambs* (Demme, 1991)—mainstream cinema has betrayed a fascination with the serial killer and his actions. I want to briefly consider the kind of pleasures these films might offer their spectators.

The thriller movie, far more than the slasher, is interested in the individual character of the serial killer and the distinctive aspects of his crimes. The process of detection focuses on the "signature" of the killer (the killer is an artist, a unique and talented individual); on patterns in killing (when, where, how, and who he kills); and on the bodies and lives of the victims. This gives a structure to the thriller narrative, pitting the investigator, with whom the spectator is most often aligned, against the killer in an intellectual battle conducted against the time pressures inherent in the serial nature of the killing and the running time of the film. As Richard Dyer writes in the cinema magazine *Sight and Sound*:

> Seriality emphasizes anticipation, suspense, what will happen next? It also emphasizes repetition, pattern, structure. We may enjoy the excitement of the threat posed by a serial killer—when will he strike next and whom? when will they get him?—but we can also enjoy discerning the pattern in his acts. This may be the same basic pattern in each act—the same selection of victim, the same method of killing—or it may be that a pattern emerges out of all the killing seen as a sequence. The commonest form of the first kind of pattern is explanation—each act becomes an expression of the same underlying pattern of motivation. A classic example of the second kind of pattern—that virtually only exists in fiction—would be a series of killings based upon some numerical or alphabetical sequence.[16]

Seriality, then, is a source of pleasure and reassurance for the spectator: the puzzle is solvable, the killer containable, the crimes explicable. While these serial killers are recognizably human in a way that serial slashers often are not, they are not "normal" men. Rather, as in fact-based accounts, they are typically "evil geniuses" and/or "madmen," fascinating and somewhat romanticized figures.[17] With the notable exception of Hannibal Lecter, it is unusual for serial killer characters to return outside the slasher. However, as so many serial-killer films use the same real-life cases as their inspiration (or are reported to do so), there is a sense in which they too are involved in a process of demonic resurrection: replaying real killings, contributing to the celebrity of the killer.

To illustrate some of these points, I want to consider *From Hell* (Hughes and Hughes, 2001), the latest in a long line of films focusing on the killings attributed to Jack the Ripper. Here, the real women murdered in Whitechapel in 1888 are given a fictional backstory that provides a link between them and a pattern to the brutal killings. What they share is (fictionalized) "knowledge" that the Duke of Clarence (Queen Victoria's grandson) had an affair with a prostitute who then gave birth to his child. The killer, Sir William Gull (Queen Victoria's physician), is trying to cover up this indiscretion by killing the women. The establishing of a pattern undoubtedly heightens the narrative tension—we know, and the women themselves know, that they are in specific danger—but the imposition of pattern also deflects the more disturbing randomness and misogyny of the original killings. In 1888, these women were killed because they were women, they were poor, and they were available, not—as *From Hell* would have it—because they were linked by exceptional circumstances.

Further, by establishing a pattern, the film's investigator, Inspector Abberline (Johnny Depp), is able to "solve" the crimes that eluded his historical namesake and "save" Mary Jane Kelly (Heather Graham), the woman he loves whose murder, in reality, was the final one attributed to the Ripper. Unlike the Final Girl, the investigator is rarely in mortal danger himself; rather, the dangers he faces are moral (he must not get too close to his subject) and emotional (putting his loved ones in jeopardy). *From Hell* has Abberline fall in love with Kelly precisely so that he has something to lose and someone he must protect. Although a stroke had left the real Gull with little strength and made him an extremely unlikely suspect, Gull's intelligence, professional standing, and status make him an attractive (and recurring) suspect in Ripper fictions, consolidating the broader cultural construction of the serial killer as exceptional individual. The conspiracy theory also provides an apparent explanation for the real-life failure to close the case that therefore restores the moral and intellectual authority of the hero (he *does* solve the case) while downplaying any understanding of the Ripper killings as *gendered* (Gull is protecting the throne, not murdering women as women). As such, although women are central to *From Hell*—and to the serial-killer phenomenon more generally—it is the men who drive the narrative and provide points of identification for the spectator.[18]

Female investigators are, unsurprisingly, differently positioned. While the female investigator has a more distinguished history on television than film,[19] a number of films do position women in this role, and merit brief comment here. Notably, the female investigator rarely works alone and is usually positioned in relation to a male mentor in a world dominated by men. The anxiety around women's assumption of active and violent roles means that the female investigator is frequently provided with multiple motivations for taking on these roles—avenging prior assault or avoiding future victimization; following in her father's footsteps; protecting her family or other children—motivations her male counterparts rarely require. As with representations of real-life violent women,[20] the investigator's assumption of the violent role is frequently allied to experiences of victimization and plays on her apparent vulnerability. For example, while Clarice Starling (Jodie Foster) has an active, investigating role in *Silence of the Lambs*, her gendered identification and empathy with the victims is in contrast to the male investigator's typical identification with the killer. Starling is thus able to "read" the bodies and lives of the victims in a way that eludes her male colleagues. Starling is the only woman other than the victims to inhabit the male-dominated world of serial murder and its investigation and her gendered isolation is consistently underscored by positioning her in male groups where her small stature and clothing make her "out of place." The incarcerated killer's probing also reveals her motivations for following this career path (motivations male characters rarely require) and underscores her vulnerability.

RAPE AND REVENGE

This movement between positions of action and vulnerability is even more obvious in the rape-revenge film that similarly challenges any easy assumption that watching violence on-screen is necessarily a sadistically pleasurable experience. However, like the slasher, the rape-revenge genre has garnered its share of controversy for allegedly presenting sexual violence as a pleasurable spectacle. For example, in an infamous article that begins with his experience of viewing *I Spit on Your Grave* (Zarchi, 1978), critic Roger Ebert condemns "women-in-danger" films for aligning their spectator with the point of view of the rapist:

> The audience seemed to be taking all this as a comedy, and there were shouts and loud laughs at the climaxes of violence. And then, beneath these noises, as a subtle counterpoint, I could hear my neighbor saying, "That's a good one.... Ooh—eee! She's got that coming! That'll teach her. That's right! Give it to her! She's learned her lesson...."[21]

These men's apparent appreciations of the rape scenes cannot be easily dismissed. However, it soon becomes clear that it is not simply men's responses that trouble Ebert: as the revenge section of the film progresses, he notes that women's voices begin to dominate. Now, he suggests, "the 'victim' is the poor, put-upon, traumatized male in the audience. And the demons are the women on-screen."[22]

Unlike in the slasher movie—where identification with the Final Girl provides a masochistic pleasure for the male spectator distanced from his own gender identity—in *I Spit on Your Grave* (and rape-revenge films more generally) the gender politics are rarely so ambiguous. Here, the Final Girl—or avenger—is quite definitely *female* and her attackers are quite definitely *male*. Brutalized *as a woman*—and, specifically, as a *white* woman (feminine vulnerability is always racialized)— in the first half of the film (through gang rape), *I Spit on Your Grave*'s heroine turns the tables on her attackers in the second half by using their misconceptions about female sexuality against them. In other words, the rape-revenge film makes the gendered nature of violence explicit and unavoidable.

Further, Ebert's outraged commentary disguises the fact that the rape scenes in *I Spit on Your Grave* are far from erotic. The frequent use of long shots, interspersed with an emphasis on the *rapists'* faces and reactions, frustrates the voyeuristic look at the female body to align us

with the point of view of the raped woman. There is absolutely no suggestion here that Jennifer (Camille Keaton) "enjoys" the rape: her violation and degradation is horrifying to watch (and listen to—her cries
dominate the soundtrack). This provides the justification for what follows. If sex is used as a weapon to victimize Jennifer, in her transformation to hero/avenger sex becomes *her* weapon: she lures two of the
rapists with the promise of sex before hanging one and castrating the
other. Like the other avenging women on-screen who follow her, Jennifer plays on men's willingness to believe in rape myths (she asked for
it, she enjoyed it) in order to seduce/kill her rapist(s), manipulating
both her appearance and demeanor in the process.

Herein lies one of the central contradictions of rape-revenge horror:
although presenting graphic scenes of sexual violence as "entertainment," it is also one of the few spaces where feminist analyses of
violence as a gendered and structural phenomenon are literalized.
However, while such self-conscious performances of rape myths arguably draw attention to their absurdity, by sexualizing revenge these
films arguably present *women's* sexuality as dangerous and, therefore,
justify male violence.[23] Nearly three decades on, a similar process is
arguably at work in *Hostel*: it is the men's willingness to believe in
women's sexual availability that renders them vulnerable and this
proves lethal for some of the men and all of the women. Further mirroring the slasher movie and its contemporary variants, in the revenge
section of the typical rape-revenge film there are also some fairly conventional soft-porn pleasures on offer for the male viewer in the representation of the sexualized, near-naked avenger. As the rapist is rarely
presented as a point of identification for the male spectator, he can take
pleasure in this display without having to confront the ways in which
his own gaze might mirror that of the rapist. Yet, as film studies academic Peter Lehman notes, "it is not just the women who are
watched—it is also the men in their horror and pain."[24] The pleasure
in other men's pain comes not only from *identifying* with the raped
woman in her revenge but also, Lehman argues, from a homosexual sa-
dism which resolves the heterosexual male spectator's anxiety about
his gaze at (and desire for) other men. In other words, the violence
provides an alibi for the male viewer to look at the bodies of other
men, which I will discuss in more detail in the next section.

Before I move on to this it is worth commenting briefly on *male*
rape-revenge. Although this is by no means an established subgenre,
the mid-1990s saw the release of a number of films which featured
male rape and vengeance: *Pulp Fiction* (Tarantino, 1994), *The Shawshank
Redemption* (Darabont, 1994), and *Sleepers* (Levinson, 1996).[25] However,
there are important differences between the female and male rape-
revenge traditions. First, as Joe Wlodarz argues, male rape-revenge
films—through their incessant scapegoating of gay men—go out of

their way to recuperate and reinstate patriarchy and heterosexual masculinity. For this to be effective, male rape-revenge films reverse two of the commonplace aspects of female rape-revenge films. Here, the rapist is a *deviation* from "normal" masculinity and not a continuation of it, and, secondly, there is nothing erotic about the raped man's revenge. The male victim can only move into the hero position if he moves out of a position of sexual objectification/victimization. This is also true of films that—like *Sleepers* or *The Prince of Tides* (Streisand, 1991)—focus on male survivors of child sexual abuse. For the survivor to become a credible (heterosexual) protagonist, he cannot—simultaneously—be seen as a victim, and so these films are evasive about the details of male victimization (specifically its sexual nature) while shoring up the authority of the narrator by increasing our reliance on his point of view. In other words, male victimization and sexual objectification sit uneasily with the narrative conventions of mainstream cinema as well as with cultural constructions of heterosexual masculinity more generally.[26]

THE MALE BODY

This tension between men's victimization, violence, and sexual objectification is by no means unique to male rape(-revenge). To begin to think through what might be at stake in these representations for the male spectator, we need to return to theories about the male gaze that were introduced earlier in this chapter. In an important development of Mulvey's work, Steve Neale argued that the male spectator's identification with the male character on-screen is not as straightforwardly pleasurable as Mulvey assumed. While Mulvey suggested that this is an identification based on a sense of power and control, Neale argued that this process can be profoundly contradictory for the male spectator, arousing anxieties about his own inadequacies in comparison to the idealized man on-screen.[27] This mismatch creates a distance between spectator and character and, as a result, the spectator shifts between an (uneasy) identification with the screen male and a more distanced contemplation. As such, the male character is not only the *subject* of the action (and identification) but also the *object* of the gaze.

However, while the female object is a sexualized and contained figure, there is a taboo around representing the white male body as the object of another man's—or woman's—look in a heterosexual and patriarchal society. (To be objectified is to be feminized, powerless.) Specifically, the taboo is around the *eroticism* of the look, and Neale's key contribution to the debate was to argue that the eroticism of the look at the male body is continually denied or disavowed in mainstream cinema, and one of the key ways in which this happens is through violence. So, instead of the male body as an erotic object, we are offered the male body as an object of violence (mutilated, hurt). And instead of the display of the body in and of itself, the male body is positioned within a highly ritualized (and generally violent) scene. The spectacle of male bodies is a spectacle of *action* and *movement*: the characters act (fight, attack, and defend) and their actions have clear narrative purpose (defeating or escaping an enemy or gaining information or status). These bodies are not, therefore, simply passive *objects* of the gaze, they drive the narrative forward.

This has implications for thinking about the portrayal of violence on-screen as it suggests that the tension between male victimization, violence, and sexual objectification touched on briefly at the end of the last section may be a more general feature of representing the male body in and through violence. By way of illustration I offer a brief analysis of the introduction of Arnold Schwarzenegger's character—the Terminator—in *Terminator 2: Judgment Day* (Cameron, 1991). Brought back from the future, the Terminator is "reborn" (naked) in the film's present and immediately heads for a biker bar where he acquires clothes and a vehicle from a patron. As the naked Terminator walks through the bar, male and female patrons alike look him up and down with both bemusement and admiration. But, it is *his* desire (for clothes and a vehicle) which drives this scene and the looks of the bar patrons are heavily mediated: we see him, seeing them, looking at him. For instance, we cut from an image of the Terminator's face as he looks at the patrons to a shot of the patrons through his (electronic) eyes: The Terminator's body is never the direct object of another character's look. The Terminator's body may be fragmented by later close-ups (of his muscular torso, legs, and arms) but it is a body-in-action, a body-in-motion, a body that is both the subject and object of violence. The display here is not superfluous, but drives the narrative forward.

So far, this sequence would seem to offer a fairly clear-cut example of the processes Neale describes but this reading is complicated when we factor in Schwarzenegger himself. After all, our gaze is not just at the (non-human) Terminator, it is also a look at a human, champion body. Yet, where once muscles and a tan signified manual labor and man's productive role, Schwarzenegger's built-body carries none of these connotations: his is a body built in the gym. Moreover, as the built-body is a body built to be posed and, so, to be looked at, it carries feminine connotations and so might be argued to symbolize the *instability* of masculinity. This tension is perhaps even more explicit in the "birthing" sequence in the third installment of the *Terminator* saga. More than a decade on, *Terminator 3: The Rise of the Machines* (Mostow, 2003) sees Schwarzenegger's Terminator seeking clothing and a vehicle not in a biker bar but in a strip club where a male stripper performs for a female audience. The Terminator's aggressive appropriation of the male stripper's outfit is, in some ways, consistent with arguments that erotic objectification is disavowed through violent action. But the presence of the stripper and the female audience also point to what writer Susan Faludi has described as the increasing *ornamentalization* of masculinity in contemporary culture: the muscles are for display, not for use; they are a product in themselves, not a by-product of manual labor; and they are *looked at*, clearly and explicitly.[28]

It is also significant to note that the body of the Terminator can be damaged as well as do damage and in this the Terminator is not alone among action heroes. The violence done to the heroic body is one of the means whereby the eroticism of the gaze at that body is disavowed, but there is something more at stake here. Whether man or machine, these bodies withstand abuse and heal themselves. So, for example, John Rambo (Sylvester Stallone) stitches his own wounded arm in *First Blood* (Kotcheff, 1982) and spectacularly cauterizes a shrapnel wound in his side using gunpowder in *Rambo III* (MacDonald, 1988). These scenes typically provoke discomfort from audiences: They are visceral scenes, the camera lingering on the wound, demonstrating both the vulnerability and exceptional strength of the hero.[29] While the heroes are not "victims" in any straightforward sense, the focus on the violence done *to* their bodies—of which their scars and torn and bloodied clothing serve as continual reminders—arguably legitimates the violence done *by* these bodies. The male characters are immersed in a world of violence and their own actions are legitimated and comprehensible within that context. Indeed—at the risk of stating the obvious—in the vast majority of action movies, violence is a predominately male preserve. Clearly there are action heroines and stars—Angelina Jolie's roles in the *Lara Croft: Tomb Raider* films (West, 2001; de Bont, 2003); *Mr. & Mrs. Smith* (Liman, 2005); and *Wanted* (Bekmambetov, 2008) being just some recent examples—but women remain in the minority both within the genre as a whole and within the narratives in which they function. (Although they have attracted a disproportionate amount of academic attention.) Action heroes may be isolated within the fictional world they inhabit—lone crusaders, vigilantes, and/or visionaries—but it is not the fact of their violence (or capacity for violence) that isolates them from other men. Violent women, however, are another matter, as we will now see.

WOMEN, VIOLENCE, AND SEXUALITY

I want to begin my discussion of women's violence with Oliver Stone's *Natural Born Killers* (1994) a film that, with its very different constructions of the male and female mass-murderer, usefully highlights some of the difficulties in representing women's violence. Reflecting on the motivations of his anti-heroes, Mickey (Woody Harrelson) and Mallory (Juliette Lewis), Stone suggests:

Mickey is a total predator. He understands the universe only from a predatory standpoint and he justifies what he does that way. Mallory is a different question because she comes from a whole different space, and we clarify their different motives.[30]

This "whole different space" is defined by victimization (Mallory's sexual abuse at the hands of her father) and sexual objectification (throughout the film, there are moments where she embodies Mulvey's idea of "to-be-looked-at-ness").

Of the child sexual abuse story, actor Juliette Lewis notes:

[...] I mentioned that [Stone] might wanna show that something happened to this girl in her background. *It's hard to see a girl be that cruel.* [italics added] I didn't want to disgust the audience; I want them to understand the character a little.[31]

Notably, Lewis suggests that it is specifically because Mallory is female that such a strategy is necessary, cruelty on the part of women inviting audience disgust and precluding identification. This oscillation between victim and perpetrator positions is, therefore, rather different than that undertaken by the action hero: like the raped avenger, she is victimized *on the basis of her sex* in a way male heroes very rarely are. Further, while Mickey too comes from an abusive home, his backstory functions quite differently, establishing a *continuity* between him and his abusive father. As Mickey comments: "I come from violence. It's in my blood. My dad had it, his dad had it. It's my fate." Mickey is positioned as the latest in a long line of violent men: in his own family, in the world of *NBK* (the prison inmates, abusive guards, and cops are all male), and in a broader sociocultural context (references to Charles Manson, Ted Bundy, John Wayne Gacy, and the Menendez brothers, among others, provide a recognizable context for Mickey's behavior and the public consumption of it). Clearly, it is not hard to imagine a *man* being that cruel.

The kind of cruelty perpetrated by Mallory Knox may be hard to imagine on one level, but there is no shortage of violent women on-screen across a range of generic contexts. For many feminists, these women offer rare glimpses of female agency on-screen and, as such, are a source of fascination and possibly even a cause for celebration. But, we might ask, what price visibility—particularly as female violence is so often linked to an active and desiring female sexuality? This link should not be entirely surprising: As perpetrators of violence or as desiring subjects, women transgress the *object* position that Mulvey argues they are typically assigned in mainstream narrative film. Women's sexuality and women's violence are arguably equally threatening to the status quo.

Indeed, in her classic article, Mulvey finds in film noir a perfect example of the sadistic aspects of the male gaze. Although the femme fatale is central to noir, Mulvey argues that she is not central *in herself* but for what she signifies for the male character—she is the mystery he must decipher, the character whose motives and sexuality he must investigate—and she is ultimately punished for her sexuality, controlled and contained by the film's end. Yet, other critics have pointed out that for this punishment to be meaningful, the femme fatale's sexual strength and threat must first be convincingly established. Precisely because such representations are relatively rare, we might argue that it is the femme fatale's attitude and strength that we remember rather than her inevitable demise.

Film noir emerged in a prefeminist period of gender-role flux in the aftermath of World War II. As such, the femme fatale has been read not only (following Mulvey) as a manifestation of men's *unconscious* fears of female sexuality, but also as a historically specific response to men's anxieties about shifting gender roles. In this respect, it is significant that the themes, characters, and visual style of noir experienced something of a resurgence from the 1970s against a backdrop of feminist activism and the almost simultaneous backlash against the movement. Like classic noir, the fatale figure of neo-noir has been both celebrated and condemned by feminist critics who have variously delighted in her assertiveness and rallied against the equation of women's sexual subjectivity with criminal violence. Neo-noir clearly owes something to the feminist movement but typically positions itself "post"-feminism in the sense that it depends upon *and* repudiates feminism. In planning her violent schemes, the more contemporary figure frequently uses feminist-inspired arguments around sexual pleasure, men's violence, and women's work. But these arguments are transformed so that feminism's threat to male privilege becomes a threat to individual men's lives and livelihood. Moreover, feminist demands for women's sexual autonomy here legitimate a sexualized display of women's bodies and sexual pleasure in the name of female sexual freedom. There are parallels here with bell hooks' arguments about the use of irony in Tarantino's early films: while these sexually aggressive women make male preconceptions of female sexuality look absurd, the sexualized presentation of these women for the pleasure of the films' spectators suggests that we are, indeed, clinging to the absurdity. The women may be powerful but that power is equated with their sexuality. Women = sex.

To illustrate some of these points, I want to briefly mention *Basic Instinct* (Verhoeven, 1991), a film that generated considerable controversy for its equation of lesbianism, bisexuality, and murderousness. The film begins with an unidentified naked blonde woman killing her sexual partner at the moment of his climax. As the film progresses, we are offered a series of explicit sex scenes and sexual displays in place of criminal investigation as the cop investigating the murder (Michael

Douglas) becomes sexually involved with both of the main suspects. The investigation of their guilt is thus inextricably tied to the investigation of their sexuality. Both women have had sexual relationships with men and women, their bisexuality evidence of a refusal of binaries and boundaries which makes them threatening to the hero and potential criminal suspects. The authenticity of their heterosexual acts is the key to the case both for the cop (for whom misreading the signs might mean death) and for the viewer (legitimating the "investigative" gaze at the female body).

Interestingly, *Village Voice* critic J. Hoberman describes Michael Douglas's men-in-peril films—*Fatal Attraction* (Lyne, 1988), *Falling Down* (Schumacher, 1992), and *Disclosure* (Levinson, 1994), as well as *Basic Instinct*—as role-reversing slasher movies.[32] The comparison is a striking one, underlining the extent to which challenges to white male privilege are explicitly envisaged as a form of violence against white men. Douglas himself frequently recasts interviewers' questions about his films' treatment of women and minorities in order to focus on "political correctness" as a censoring discourse, victimizing and restricting white men. In this context, women's violence—including women's resistance to misogyny—is overdetermined and endlessly scrutinized, while men's violence (against other men as well as against women) is normalized such that it is invisible *as such*. In other words, it isn't *men's* violence—it's just violence. To point to the gender dynamic—to insist that specific actions are perpetrated *by men* on-screen and that this might have something to tell us about constructions of men and masculinity in our culture and society—is to risk predictable accusations of demonizing *all* men.

This takes us to relatively familiar ground: women's violence requiring explanation in relation to their gender role and/or their deviance from it, while men's violence just *is*. In conclusion, I want to turn to screenwriter Hilary Henkin's account of trying to put an alternative version of the violent woman in a mainstream movie. From script to screen, the heroine of Henkin's *Fatal Beauty* (Holland, 1987), Rita Rizzoli, went through an interesting transformation. Rizzoli started out as a female version of Dirty Harry—obsessive, violent, and lacking in backstory—a concept apparently too frightening for the studio:

> "It seems that similar sorts of male characters within the genre are allowed to indulge their obsession, with almost no reason, and when they indulge their obsession they are applauded by the filmmaking establishment and the audience. But the notion of the female character who does things for the sake of doing them seems to be frighteningly out of control for the system and its perception of how the audience would react to that idea [...] the studio didn't think that an audience wanted to see such a violent woman. Hence they built in a backstory. The movie

went through many incarnations on the way to production. It was turned into a comedy, and from being a comedic tragicomedy, it became a broad comedy. Rita was given the quintessential abused female backstory—which gives her a motive, but it is a far less profound motive than she might have had."[33]

Henkin's account provides a clear example of how women's on-screen violence requires explanation and personal, gendered motivation, which is rarely an issue for their male counterparts. While I make no claims that Henkin's heroine in her original form is necessarily more "feminist," it is the job of feminist criticism to identify the ways in which gender determines what can and cannot be said and shown about violence. For feminists interested in film violence, this involves thinking about not only what is (and is not) shown on-screen, but also—as I have argued in this chapter—thinking through the implications of how we are positioned in relation to this violence. This helps us move beyond the understandable but very limited knee-jerk reaction to explicit violent scenes with which I opened this chapter to engage more fully with questions about how we *all* make meaning of film violence.

NOTES

1. This chapter is edited and updated (by the author) from K. Boyle, *Media and Violence: Gendering the Debates* (London: Sage, 2005): 123–160. Courtesy of Sage Publications.

2. C. Domingo. "What the White Man Won't Tell Us: Report from the Berkeley Clearinghouse on Femicide," in *Femicide: The Politics of Woman Killing,* edited by J. Radford and D. E. H. Russell (Buckingham: Open University Press, 1992): 196.

3. "Torture porn" is a term widely used by media commentators to refer to contemporary horror films obsessed with mental and physical torture of which the *Saw* and *Hostel* series are perhaps the most famous examples.

4. M. Rosen, *Popcorn Venus: Women, Movies and the American Dream* (New York: Coward, McCann & Geoghegen, 1973); and M. Haskell, *From Reverence to Rape: The Treatment of Women in the Movies* (Chicago: University of Chicago Press, 1974). Both focus primarily on images of white, heterosexual women in Hollywood.

5. L. Kelly, *Surviving Sexual Violence* (Cambridge: Polity, 1988).

6. J. Gaines, "White Privilege and Looking Relations," *Screen* 29 (4) (1988).

7. C. Clover, *Men, Women and Chain Saws: Gender in the Modern Horror Film* (London: BFI, 1992): 168.

8. Ibid., 42.

9. Ibid., 51.

10. Ibid., 235.

11. S. Vint, "Killing us Softly? A Feminist Search for the 'Real' Buffy," *Slayage: The On-line International Journal of Buffy Studies* 5 (2002), http://www.slayage.tv/.

12. b. hooks, "Cool Tool," *Artforum* (March 1995): 63–6, 108–9. 64.

13. L. Coulthard, "Killing Bill: Rethinking Feminism and Film Violence" in *Interrogating Postfeminism: Gender and the Politics of Popular Culture*, ed. Y. Tasker, and D. Negra (Durham & London: Duke University Press).

14. J. Patterson, "Putting the Gory in Allegory," *The Guardian* (June 23, 2008).

15. S. Danielson, "Blood Brother: Director Eli Roth, Inventor of 'Torture Porn,' " *The Independent*, June 24, 2008.

16. R. Dyer, "Kill and Kill Again," *Sight and Sound* 7, no. 9 (1997): 14–7, 16.

17. K. Boyle, *Media and Violence: Gendering the Debates* (London: Sage, 2005): 60–68; and D. Cameron, and E. Frazer, *The Lust to Kill: A Feminist Investigation of Sexual Murder* (Cambridge: Polity, 1987).

18. R. Dyer, "Kill and Kill Again," *Sight and Sound* 7, no. 9 (1997): 17.

19. Y. Tasker, *Working Girls: Gender and Sexuality in Popular Cinema* (London: Routledge, 1988).

20. K. Boyle, *Media and Violence: Gendering the Debates* (London: Sage, 2005): 94–122.

21. R. Ebert, "Why Audiences Aren't Safe Anymore." *American Film* 6, no. 5 (1981): 54–6.

22. Ibid., 56.

23. M. Emerman, "Only a Reflection? Sexual Violence on Screen," *Metro* 103 (1995): 72–5, 73.

24. P. Lehman, "Don't Blame This on a Girl: Female Rape-revenge Films," in *Screening the Male: Exploring Masculinities in Hollywood Cinema*, ed. S. Cohan and I. R. Hark (London: Routledge, 1993): 107.

25. J. Wlodarz, "Rape Fantasies: Hollywood and Homophobia," in *Masculinity: Bodies, Movies, Culture*, ed. P. Lehman (New York & London: Routledge, 2001).

26. K. Boyle, "Gendered Narratives of Child Sexual Abuse in Fiction Film," in *Local Violence, Global Media: Feminist Analyses of Gendered Representations*, ed. L. Cuklanz, and S. Moorti (New York: Peter Lang, 2008).

27. S. Neale, "Masculinity as Spectacle: Reflections on Men and Mainstream Cinema," *Screen* 24, 6 (1983): 2–17.

28. S. Faludi, *Stiffed: The Betrayal of Modern Man* (London: Vintage, 2000).

29. S. Jeffords, *Hard Bodies: Hollywood Masculinity in the Reagan Era* (New Brunswick, NJ: Rutgers University Press, 1994).

30. D. Williams, "Born to Kill," *Film Focus* 2 (1994): 12–8, 16.

31. B. Kaye, "The Femme Fatale," *Vox* 52 (1995): 28–9.

32. J. Hoberman, "Victim Victorious: Well-fed Yuppie Michael Douglas Leads the Charge for Resentful White Men," *Village Voice* 7 (March 1995): 31–3.

33. L. Francke, *Script Girls: Women Screenwriters in Hollywood* (London: BFI, 1994).

Chapter 3

Media Frames of Intimate Partner Homicide

Lori A. Post
Patricia K. Smith
Emily M. Meyer

FAYETTEVILLE, GA—Police offered no motive Tuesday to explain why Chris Benoit, a World Wrestling Entertainment star, strangled his wife and suffocated his 7-year-old son before hanging himself at their home in suburban Atlanta last weekend. Benoit, 40, left no suicide note. He did leave Bibles next to the bodies of wife Nancy, 43, and their son, Daniel ...[1]

The excerpt on a murder-suicide with which we begin this chapter about media coverage of intimate partner homicide (IPH) is from a lengthy article in *USA Today*. The article is packed with extraneous information about the perpetrator—we learn he was a "great family man," for instance—but presents minimal information about the victims. The story provides an excuse for the murders, following a side story line on Benoit's steroid use as part of his body-building regimes, while simultaneously reporting that authorities offered no motive for the killings. We learn about the "shock" felt by friends and neighbors who "never expected this to happen," much less for a seven-year-old boy to die. The story line is classic: family man loved by his neighbors goes berserk because of ingested pharmaceuticals. Toward the end of the extensive piece are five sentences about his abuse, and evidence that the wife had taken out a restraining order, filed for divorce, and charged him with cruel treatment. There is no investigation of Benoit's abusive history, however, let alone any suggestion that this history might be the context for his acts. "Brute kills wife" is about as newsworthy as "Fish swims."

For researchers and advocates who work with violence against women (VAW), this murder scenario is eerily familiar. Unfortunately, so is the media coverage. In fact, what is unique is that there is any mention of the perpetrator's abuse at all, even though it is sketchy and not linked to other details of the crimes. While taking steroids may indeed have fanned this man's fire, the fact that dozens of men commit similar acts each year without the influence of drugs suggest that this particular murder/suicide isn't anything special. This article provides multiple examples of what is wrong with media reporting on IPH to be dissected throughout this chapter.

Our particular interest in media coverage of domestic violence was accidental. We were conducting research on violence prevention. During my first trip into the field to collect data, a pregnant woman in the catchment site was murdered by her husband. This pregnant mother of one had done everything right. She had left her abusive husband, contacted the police, sought help from social services programs, filed police reports, and showed up in court. Shortly after she took these steps, she enrolled in a university. After the first day of classes, her husband ambushed her at a church. He shot her once in the abdomen. Ironically, neither the sanctuary of the church nor the personal-protection order she was clutching afforded her safety or stopped him from killing her and their unborn child. This information never made it to press. What did make news was the fact that her murderer ironed his clothing, attended church, read the Bible, was neat and tidy, a model citizen, and a good man. While this woman was just one of hundreds in my sample of battered women, the media portrayal of her murder was "outside the scope of the study." And yet, the callousness and irresponsible reporting was striking and hard to forget. As the years passed, I began observing patterns in the deficient reporting of IPH. It made logical sense to examine coverage of IPH more systematically.

The media report daily on homicides and other violent crimes. While all journalism has its share of reporting biases, the coverage of intimate partner violence (IPV) seems to be fairly consistent in this respect. Notably, there is a disconnect between the *reality* of IPV—ongoing, cumulative in effects, comprised of multiple strategies, and oriented toward power and control—and the IPV reporting approach journalists select. VAW advocates and scholars cite bias in how IPV murder victims are described, the circumstances of the crime, the information the journalist chooses to include or omit, how the information is collected, and who is interviewed. These biases are reflected in shared assumptions about why victims die and by the extent to which the violence involved is abstracted from the abusive context and presented as a discrete event. Readers are left to fill in the gaps since newspaper reports tend to be relatively brief. VAW researchers and advocates are concerned that this style of presentation perpetuates myths about IPV, blames victims for their own deaths, minimizes or conceals perpetrator responsibility, and conceals the significance of the violence and related forms of coercion and control by isolating incidents from their larger social contexts.

WHY SHOULD YOU CARE?

Media outlets play a major role in the "construction of social reality" in this country. News organizations pass on information, shape opinion, and provide context for events that occur in a person's world. As sociologist Gaye Tuchman points out, through the reporting of selected occurrences, news changes "happenings into publicly discussable events."[2]

The way that newspapers present the stories of IPH can influence not only peoples' opinions and thoughts about the individual events reported, but about IPV itself. Through the selection by editors and reporters of specific cases deemed "newsworthy," the subsequent prioritization of these cases and the selection and organization of such components of news stories as facts, sources, and headlines, journalists can shape the public's view of what IPH is and who is involved. *New York Sun* editor John B. Bogart famously said, "When a dog bites a man, that is not news, because it happens so often. But if a man bites a dog, that is news." This quotation is commonly invoked to describe the journalistic phenomenon wherein an extraordinary event is more likely to be reported than a common occurrence. The result is that news covering "Man Bites Dog" occurs more often than "Dog Bites Man," making it seem as though the former event is more common than it actually is. With respect to coverage of IPH, this sort of distortion in favor of "newsworthiness" has substantial ramifications. Selective reporting may determine whether or not we take IPV seriously, how we assess its motives, whom we hold accountable and how, and whether we consider victims of IPV "worthy" to receive our support—and by extension public protections—or "unworthy," possibly because they are culpable for their own demise. News stories can also determine whether readers should be concerned about IPV as a social issue that can affect them.

WHAT ARE WE TALKING ABOUT?

IPH is at the far end of the continuum of IPV. According to the FBI, in 2006 at least 1,290 individuals were killed by their current or former spouse or by a current boyfriend or girlfriend. We know this is an undercount because cases involving all relevant victim-suspect relationships are not discernable in the FBI database. For example, it does not include homicides by same-sex partners or by former boyfriends/girlfriends from whom the victim is separated. Because it is more likely that a homicide victim will be killed by an ex-husband or estranged boyfriend than by a current partner, the term "intimate" is somewhat misleading. There are also cases in which the perpetrator is not identified as the current or former intimate partner until years later, if ever. In other cases, the perpetrator may consider himself a victim's "intimate" even though they have had no significant prior relationship. Other issues directly related to counting both fatal and non-fatal cases cloud the picture, such as the lack of a standard definition for "intimate partner," as well as of what constitutes IPV.

Homicide is simply the killing of one human being by another and does not denote whether the killing is a criminal act (that is, murder or manslaughter) or its criminal intent or consequences (for example, killing in self-defense). Therefore, IPH connotes a person killing his or her current or former intimate partner (with the qualifications above) either with *malice aforethought* (murder), with criminal negligence, during the commission of a crime other than those included with felony murder (manslaughter), or in self-defense.

WHAT MAKES A CASE?

All cases of IPH are not created equal, at least not in the eyes of reporters and their editors. Crime reporting in general, and violent crime reporting in particular, has been a staple of the American newspaper since the "penny press" came into being with the *New York Sun* in 1833. The mass media provide surveillance and meaning for events in our world, with the journalist surveying the environment for a story worth reporting and the editor furnishing the reporting context.

IPH is, relatively speaking, a rare and thus novel event, regardless of where it occurs. By the very nature of it involving human death, it has cultural relevance. As violent human death, it has novelty and most likely some degree of spectacle and unpredictability. However, not all cases of homicide, including IPH, are singled out for reporting by journalists. In Michigan, for example, from 1999 to 2001, newspaper stories were found for only 75 percent of 187 identified IPHs.[3]

So, why are some cases selected for attention and not others? And, once selected for coverage, why are some cases reported in more detail than others?

Not surprisingly, race, sex, and social status as well as the relationships involved appear to determine which homicides are reported and which are not. In the Michigan study, as well as in a similar study that compared homicide coverage in the *Los Angeles Times* to homicides committed in Los Angeles County over a five-year period, there was a distinct preference for reporting homicides involving persons classified as "worthy victims"—people who were white, older or very young, women, of high socioeconomic status, and/or killed by a stranger. Overall, homicides perpetrated by strangers were the most likely to be reported. Next were acquaintance homicides. Homicides committed by intimates are least likely to be reported.

Among intimates, the same status characteristics appear to affect the reporting of homicides as affect reporting of homicides generally. The converse, of course, is that IPH involving victims who are male, black, and living in large cities are considered relatively unworthy and are consistently underreported. In Michigan, for instance, while 11 percent of the IPH victims whose killing was reported in Michigan newspapers were men, 26 percent of the victims in cases where no story was found were male. Twenty-two percent of IPH victims in the newspaper stories were black. But more than three times this number (68 percent) of cases that were not reported involved African American victims. Finally, only 9 percent of reported cases of IPH occurred in Detroit, whereas 55 percent of the deaths that were not reported occurred there.

How a problem is reported influences public perceptions of it. In reality, the killing of a stranger usually takes place during the commission of another crime, such as robbery, and so is termed a "secondary homicide." At least outside the South, homicides occur most frequently in big cities, and the victims are disproportionately male, acquaintances, or intimates, and are from racial minorities or other disadvantaged groups. As we can see, selective reporting of these deaths creates a very different profile, highlighting the types of victims who are actually at lowest risk—relatively affluent white women killed by strangers—and so, by implication, minimizing the danger posed to intimates, for instance, and men and women of color.

Moira Peelo, a British criminologist, points out that " . . . a part of what makes a murder into entertainment is the shock of ordinariness invaded by the brutal or the corrupt."[4] If you think about "entertainment" as synonymous with "newsworthy" you can begin to see why the news media in general focus on particular IPH stories and why murders of white, pregnant, attractive middle-class women such as Laci Peterson are touted as national news while that of Barbara Baker, a poor African American woman, is found only in one story in the *Detroit Free Press*.

Reporters and editors use the level of drama or perceived importance of an event to decide whether it meets the necessary "threshold" to be considered newsworthy. In our college English classes, we learned that a good narrative should address the who, what, when, where, why, and how of an event.

Preacher killed wife, stuffed body in freezer, police say Anthony Hopkins, *thirty-seven, was arrested Monday night at the Inspirational Tabernacle Church of God in Christ in Jackson, Alabama, just after he had delivered a sermon to a congregation that included his seven other children, officials said*[5]

This "Man Bites Dog" IPH story gained international attention and was followed by media outlets from the initial discovery of the homicide throughout the trial and conviction. This illustration far exceeds the minimum threshold for "newsworthy" because of the "what" (cultural context): a wife is brutally murdered because she discovers her husband raping their daughter, and the "who" (social context): the murderer is a preacher and the head of a large family. After killing his wife, he resumes normal daily activities for years with his wife's body in the basement freezer.

Death has always carried weight as a reportable event, as has violent crime. Therefore, homicide (violent death) automatically ranks high as a reportable event. But the contexts combine with the news values discussed earlier to shape the selective newsworthiness of IPH cases. To illustrate this interplay, consider the relative influence of geography ("where") in relation to the bias favoring more affluent, female victims. Since killings of any type are relatively rare in small towns, an IPH is likely to be considered worthy of major coverage by local newspapers regardless of the race, class, or sex of the victim. A relatively large proportion of the population probably knew the victim and perpetrator, adding to the event's newsworthiness.

Logically, one would think that any homicide occurring within the geographic boundaries of a newspaper's primary readership would be newsworthy, which is true for papers with smaller catchment areas. In fact, we saw this rural trend exaggerated in our exhaustive collection of Michigan IPH stories collected from every media outlet in the state over the course of several years. Frequently, small community-based newspapers would "borrow" homicides from the surrounding vicinities in an effort to attract an audience. However, for the press in large cities with many homicides, other factors likely carry more weight. In a major metropolitan area like Washington, D.C., with large numbers of homicides and where a much smaller percentage of the population might know the victim and/or perpetrator, the social aspects of the case (in terms of the social status of the players) become more important in determining newsworthiness. Here, as we've seen, certain characteristics of the victims (for example, white, female, young, celebrity) or of the event itself (for example, multiple victims) add social "weight" to an event and make a particular crime more worth a newspaper's time and space. For example, in the study of homicide reporting in the *Los Angeles Times*, Taylor and Sorenson found that homicides with specific social contexts of gang-related and child victims were given the most visibility.[6]

HOW IS A NEWS STORY CONSTRUCTED?

Story Structure

Pan and Kosicki remind us that a report of a newsworthy event is essentially a story "with a beginning, a climax, and an end" and as such it is usually seen as "a relatively independent unit, because it appears to contain complete information."[7] Newspaper stories have a distinct structure often based on the "inverted pyramid" we all learned about in middle-school English class. With this structure, the most important elements or those likely to have the most impact on the reader come first and, of course, those deemed least important come last. Thus, of the six structural elements—headline, lead, episodes, background, and closure—the headline and summary lead, which answers the questions who, what, when, where, and how are the most powerful.

> *Grant killed, then sought sex, says prosecutor He cut up wife's dead body, defendant admits to judge*
> *As Tara Grant's dead body lay in their bedroom, her husband sent a text message to the couple's teenage au pair: "You owe me a kiss." A naked Stephen Grant then left a note on the au pair's bedroom pillow as a reminder.*[8]

Dangerous Reporting

Admittedly, sensational reporting with compelling and gruesome headlines does capture the public's attention and thus sells papers or increases readership. Advertisers target newspapers with larger readerships; thus, there is a rationale for promoting compelling headlines. We don't actually fault journalists or their editors for standard reporting practices. Nor do we think that this reporting technique is at the root of IPV myths and/or misleading to the audience. The real culprit remains with media framing.

Framing

Framing essentially involves *selection* and *salience*. To frame is to select some aspects of a perceived reality and make them more salient in a communicating text in such a way as to promote a particular problem definition, causal interpretation, moral evaluation, and/or treatment recommendation for the item described.

Framing is a common tool used in news reporting and story construction. By selecting which elements of the story to include or exclude, highlight or downplay, the reporter has the power to control, to a certain extent, how the reader will interpret the event being reported. As Gamson points out, "Facts have no intrinsic meaning. They take on their meaning by being embedded in a frame or story line that organizes them and gives them coherence ... A frame is a central organizing idea for making sense of relevant events and suggesting what is at issue."[9] So, although reporters pride themselves on reporting "the facts" about an event, the facts that are selected or omitted by the reporter and how they are presented create the "picture" or "reality" of the event for the reader.

The following article demonstrates how framing molds our perceptions of intimate-partner violence. First, the story begins with an overview of a woman being killed and her mother being injured by several gunshot wounds. The author proceeds to provide a rationale for the killing and subsequent shooting as the result of an "argument." There is no other detail about the dead wife except that she participated in a verbal disagreement. Following, there is considerable detail about the beating of the murderer by relatives. The same newspaper article includes an overview of homicides in the community and a detailed accounting of a hate crime. The two homicides are not related; however, including a hate crime along with an IPH has the effect of framing IPH as part of a larger societal violence problem. Finally, the principal homicide is framed as the result of an argument.

Family dispute turns deadly Man kills wife, shoots her mother before
A man killed his wife and shot his mother-in-law Tuesday afternoon, then was disarmed and beaten nearly to death by two relatives, police said. The shooting happened about 4 p.m. in a two-story house on the 4200 block of Othello Drive, near the intersection of Othello Road, in the Ardenwood neighborhood. The husband and wife were arguing in the kitchen when he pulled out a handgun and shot her, Detective Bill Veteran said. The mother-in-law, who witnessed the shooting, then fled out of the house, but was shot several times from behind, the detective said. She then staggered to a neighbor's home for help, Veteran said.

"She went and called two relatives, not the police," the detective said. Within minutes, two male relatives arrived at the home and confronted the husband—who had dropped the handgun but was armed with a baseball bat—and severely beat him, Veteran said. They then held him until police arrived. At first, police thought the man also had suffered a gunshot wound, but it turned out to be injuries from the beating. After being stabilized at the scene, he was flown by helicopter to a local hospital, Veteran said. Meanwhile, the mother-in-law was taken by ambulance to a local hospital. She is expected to survive, but her condition was not known Tuesday night, the detective said. The two relatives who beat the gunman were taken to the Fremont Police Department on Tuesday evening for questioning, Veteran said, but they were not arrested. It was unclear if the men could face any criminal charges.

Several relatives gathered at the scene Tuesday, but were too distraught to talk. A few of them wept loudly and yelled at police officers who tried to calm them down. At one point, one woman yelled, "He's the killer and he's alive." Minutes later, the same woman scolded police officers because emergency personnel provided medical aid to the husband and took him to the hospital. Tuesday's shooting was Fremont's fifth homicide of the year, and the third since August.

On October 19, 38-year-old Alia Ansari, an Afghan Muslim mother of six, was shot in the face as she walked with her youngest daughter in the Glenmoor neighborhood.

Some of Ansari's relatives believe the killing may have been a hate crime, but authorities have not been able to confirm that. No one has been arrested in the case, but police have identified a 28-year-old man as a "person of interest."

Manuel David Urango of Fremont was detained near the scene within minutes of the shooting because his clothing and vehicle matched the description of the gunman. He ultimately was arrested on an unrelated parole violation.[10]

Episodic Versus Thematic Reporting

Probably the most common framing devices used in news stories are "episodic" and "thematic" news frames. Typically, journalists present events as isolated incidents (episodic framing) rather than embedding them within their larger social context (thematic framing). Episodic presentation focuses on the "what"; thematic presentation focuses on the "why" and "how." Thus, IPV homicides are seen as a singular event rather than as part of the larger patterns that make up violence against women or of social systems that support male privilege and patriarchy. In the case above, the killing of the wife begins with an argument on that day and ends with her death. There is no context of IPV. It seems as though this event began on the day of her killing. There is no discussion of violence outside of the killing; there is no logical explanation for why he killed her beyond the proximate argument. In fact, however, the killing of a partner is almost always the culmination of a long string of events.

As Iyengar points out, individual news stories do not necessarily use an episodic or thematic frame exclusively, but one clearly dominates. Episodic reporting is actually typical of the way that crime in general is reported.[11] In a landmark study conducted in 1976, Doris Graber found over the course of a year that, while crime was a frequent topic in the media she was studying, only 5 percent of the stories included any discussion of cause; solutions were presented in only 3 percent of the stories.[12]

For example, one group of researchers found that cases of elder abuse are usually reported episodically, thereby implicitly or explicitly placing the responsibility for cause and control on individuals rather than bringing forth the idea that broader social issues are also involved in the cause and that society has a role in the solution.[13] Researchers have also reached similar conclusions when looking at issues such as youth violence.

Journalists rarely provide a look at the larger context in which the crime, be it rape, murder, or arson, is imbedded. The reader is then obligated to place the incident within a larger social context that is based on his or her own knowledge, assumptions, and biases. This is why story construction and framing currently used in most IPV-related stories are puzzling to VAW researchers as they look at the topic from a feminist perspective of power and control, a task that requires a societal-level lens.

Episodic Reporting of IPH Events is the Norm

Koch makes the point that the "why" is often the most complex part of a story, yet is often glossed over or buried.[14] This is typical of newspaper reports of homicides committed by intimate partners, in which issues such as the history of escalating violence by the suspect against the victim are either not uncovered by the reporter or not included in newspaper articles. Providing a broader context for the story concerning the factors that support IPV in our society is likely even rarer.

What are the Characteristics Specific to Crime News Reporting?

"[T]he media reports on a selected portion of criminal incidents—and this selection process is neither random nor is it necessarily an accurate representation of crime in contemporary America. In fact, it appears that the media emphasize the unusual and ignore the routine."[15]

CURRENT FRAMING RESEARCH

Bullock and Cubert have the only known study of media framing of IPH. They identify four frames commonly used in IPH coverage.[16] These are:

1. The "police frame"—stories presented in a "just-the-facts" manner, as an isolated incident that was under control. Police and medical professionals were the information sources.

    A murder-suicide over the weekend came about when a 24-year-old man killed his 25-year-old girlfriend and then himself, Milwaukee police said. A landlord found the bodies of a 24-year-old man, whose identity was not immediately released, and Miranda Monique Young, 25, in their North Side apartment. Relatives of Young told the Milwaukee Journal Sentinel that she planned to leave her boyfriend. They had last been seen together Thursday night. Friends had been unable to reach them since then. Investigators did not immediately specify a motive in the case.[17]

2. "The people involved were somehow different" frame—the victims and perpetrators were presented as culturally, ethnically, or socially different from the majority population; as having criminal pasts; and/or as being involved in alcohol or drugs. This removed them from the common social milieu and implied that IPH only happened to "certain types of people."

    Numerous prosecution witnesses were prostitutes and crack addicts who identified Hubbard as a crack-smoking pimp and a mean, jealous drunk. Several said Hubbard abused Bush, and that he was angry she left him and had miscarried his baby last summer.[18]

3. The "blame the victim and/or excuse the perpetrator" frame. The researchers point out that this was often the frame used in cases of self-defense, but that it was used in other cases as well.

But Randall Abbott's mother, Irma Abbott, said her son was obsessed with his estranged wife and upset when he discovered she was back with her first husband. She blamed the victim for the troubled relationship, and said Julie Abbott pushed her son over the edge. "She was not willing to work things out," Irma Abbott said. "Randy kept trying everything to get her to come back. He really loved the girl. It just kept escalating to reach this point."[19]

4. The "perpetrators/abusers are not 'normal' and should be easily identifiable" frame. Bullock and Cubert found that many articles expressed the surprise and shock of neighbors and others that such a normal person could do such a thing, while at the same time the story characterized the perpetrators as "deviant," distancing them from the "normal" reader.

A man accused of killing his wife outside a police station was distraught that his wife had left him, neighbors said Tuesday. Newton (Bill) McMurtrey chased down his wife and slammed his pickup truck into her SUV as they approached the West Linn Police Department on Tuesday, police said. Officials said McMurtrey pulled out a rifle, shot his wife, and then turned the gun on himself. Their neighbors, Laura and Richard Calliham, were in utter disbelief over the incident Tuesday night. Richard Calliham said he never thought McMurtrey would take it this far. "I thought something might happen, but hoped it would't," Calliham said. "He suggested things sometimes . . . but he said he was just kidding. I tried to help him and talk to him and tell him that's not cool." West Linn police confirmed the couple was estranged, but not divorced. The Callihams said even before Lisa McMurtrey left her husband and moved to West Linn, there were no signs of domestic violence. They said he was a friendly man who was upset his wife had left him. The Callihams said McMurtrey simply never got over the separation. "I find it very tragic. There's nobody else in the house, no children left in the house. They had a dog; I don't know what happened to him," Laura Calliham said. "They're my neighbors. I'm just shocked."[20]

Bullock and Cubert concluded that these frames misrepresented the broader social problem of domestic violence, "providing commonsense solutions to complex problems."

Another study that focused on story content was conducted by researchers on behalf of the Wisconsin Coalition Against Domestic and Sexual Violence.[21,22] The researchers examined newspaper articles on IPH in their state over a four-year period. They identified three major fault lines in this work, ways that journalists either failed to incorporate or inappropriately incorporated thematic elements into their stories:

- IPHs were rarely labeled as such, and the articles did nothing to place them within the broader context of IPV
- Coverage provided an inaccurate view of IPV
- Coverage supported IPV myths

Meyers noted that stories covering domestic violence are typically framed to support the status quo by representing the interests of the ruling elite.[23] Newspaper coverage frequently blames the victim, attributing consequences to some unacceptable behavior or a failure to take steps necessary to end the abuse. This frame relieves society of any obligation for the incident by providing simple explanations for complex crimes. Maxwell et al. also found that articles on IPH were incident-specific, placed blame or solutions on individual victims and perpetrators, and failed to offer broader solutions for the problem.[24]

In her book *Framing the Victim: Domestic Violence Media and Social Problems*, Nancy Berns (see the chapter by Berns in this volume) focuses primarily on popular magazine and TV coverage of IPV rather than solely on newspapers.[25] But her findings are similar: The stories she studied focus exclusively on victims, either celebrating their courage for leaving a violent relationship or blaming them for letting the abuse continue. Some frames even incorporate accusations. Of course, there are also stories that foster support for victims in the form of new legal protections, greater enforcement, and broader funding for shelters and other local services. Still, Berns concludes that current framing techniques have done little to develop public understanding of the social context of violence and "may impede social change that could prevent violence." She warns that, as a result of incident-specific frames, abuser violence is lost and IPV is not perceived as a social problem that originates with the abuser. Among the consequences of this method of reporting are that the frames through which IPV are presented actually reinforce rather than challenge the social and cultural context that tolerates and fosters abuse.

Bullock and Cubert analyzed the State of Washington's newspaper coverage of IPV fatalities, including the accuracy of victim portrayals and overall attention to the broader social issue of IPV. They too found that coverage was distorted in ways that supported common stereotypes and misconceptions of IPV. Taylor and Sorenson concluded that coverage of IPH was episodic, factual, and unemotional in its tone. Homicides perpetrated by intimates were covered differently than other homicides; they were less likely to be "opinion-dominated" and emotional, and more likely to begin with a "hook." For example, newspaper coverage of stranger homicides (mall or university mass killings) go into great detail about the victims, including personalities, dreams, hopes, and past kind acts. By contrast, coverage of intimate partner homicides tends to adapt a more clinical tone, describing the victim by her age and profession, for instance, and providing an exacting description of the crime. Lastly, Wozniak (2007, unpublished dissertation) investigated gender issues in the reporting patterns of IPH. She confirmed the view that the media sensationalize news by highlighting the worthiness of the victim and its role in how stories are reported. These stories tend to focus on white, educated women or how the husband was involved in an extramarital affair. She also found that abuse-related homicides were almost never linked to the broader issue of domestic violence (or IPV). In fact, the broader context was mentioned in only 1 percent of her sampled articles.

COMMON PROBLEMATIC IPH REPORTING TRENDS

There is a clear process that a journalist follows when reporting violent crimes and homicides. However, one major characteristic sets IPH apart from general crime reporting—a current or preexisting tie between victim and perpetrator. In at least at one point in their relationship, this tie is based on love, intimacy, reliance, dependence, hope, and trust. The victim or intimate partner is killed by the very person she once cared for and may still care about. This has obvious implications for researchers and journalists investigating story frames and the major reporting issues associated with IPV homicides. The following excerpts provide examples of problematic reporting.

- *"He loved UFO documentaries."* In our review of IPH stories, we found that journalists had a tendency to include extraneous or irrelevant information about perpetrators, seemingly humanizing them in ways that made their violence seem out of character. Whereas IPH stories included very little information about the murder victim, frequently relegating her to "white, female, 31, dead.... " they provided excruciating detail about the perpetrator, including information on his religiosity. He was:

A religious man who frequently read the Bible and listened to gospel tapes apparently let his inner demons consume him

or

read the bible every day

or

He never missed church.

Perpetrators also exhibit good personal hygiene ... For example,

He kept a tidy house.

He always wore a suit.

Other virtues were also described, including qualities identified with parenting, community service, and good citizenship.

He was such a protective father.

He was such a good father.

He was actively involved in community events.

Perpetrators were also linked to their side-interests and hobbies, giving them an interesting breadth of character with which readers can empathize....

In a murder-suicide case involving Brenda and Gilbert Hernandez, it was mentioned that Gilbert worked for DaimlerChrysler,

"... bringing home more than $800 a week. He also owned a 1999 Plymouth Prowler. He had hot rods, he loved the Woodward Dream Cruise," said Karen Kolcan, who lived next door. "He collected old Tonka trucks. Everybody loved him."

It is not entirely clear why victims are described so clinically, while perpetrators given a nuanced persona. Is it is more newsworthy if the "normal" guy next door kills his wife? Are journalists empathizing with the perpetrator? Is there an implicit defense here: If he is such a good guy, with so many broad interests, has he been provoked? Is the clinical description a way to invite readers to distance themselves from the victim? Whatever the intent, the effect makes the victim appear distant and somehow not completely human. On the other hand, if the perpetrator was such a great and interesting guy, why did he kill her? Why would such a good guy go to such extremes?

- **"He was a victim, too!"** Journalists frequently focus on how much the perpetrator loved his partner, and that the homicide was a result of this intense love. Most readers would recognize that murder is not the natural outcome of love. However, many of these stories reinforce the notion that, with the man's love in the background, something the woman did left her partner no choice other than to kill her.

He could not live without her!

Mark was devastated when she asked for a divorce.

He could not stand to see Barbara with another man.

If Steven Tierney couldn't have Sally Paajanen, in his mind, no one else could either.

My brother was a victim too. Dwayne never would have hurt anybody.

- **"Marital spat escalates."** Intimate partner homicides are reported as random gender-neutral acts borne out of disagreements, as examples of "love gone wrong."

Those two were always fighting...

This reporting trend is problematic for two reasons. First, without setting the incident within the context of coercive control, the act appears irrational. Why would a homicide spontaneously erupt out of a simple argument or disagreement? There are disagreements and expressions of anger in all couples. So why murder now? The impression left is that the killer was driven crazy, an impression that sets a chilling climate for an abuse victim on trial for murder. The second problem is that framing the killing as an argument gone awry implies that both parties contributed equally to the violence, or that the conflict was symmetric. Describing a homicide as the outcome of a symmetrical argument suggests that the victim is somewhat culpable for his or her own death. When this frame combines with the empathic description of the perpetrator, the balance of blame shifts toward the victim.

Describing intimate partner homicides as symmetric also negates the reality that men are responsible for the vast majority of deaths caused by intimate partners. It also diminishes the importance of self-defense as a motive when women kill male aggressors.

> Ray, 28, is still being held in the Clinton County Jail without bond for the July 1 killing of her husband, Dinesh Balagangadhar, 29. The two had been married a year. Balagangadhar, an assistant professor of mechanical engineering, died of a single stab wound to the upper chest area, which penetrated his heart and lungs. DeWitt police chief Douglas Rogers said Ray has claimed the stabbing was accidental, saying she was preparing a meal and somehow Ray turned into him or he turned into her.[26]

What was not stated in the coverage of this death was that Mrs. Balagangadhar was being dragged by her hair through the kitchen before she managed to grab a knife sitting on the kitchen counter. Nor was it noted that the wife had previously sought treatment at the local battered woman's shelter and that there were discarded papers in her husband's study with the words, "I will not hit my wife again, I will not hit my wife again, I will not hit my wife again" written over and over.

Newspaper articles sometimes bend over backward to create the illusion that an intimate partner homicide occurred on a level playing field. For example,

> He and his wife were arguing during a walk near Mill Creek in Lima Township when he started choking her. Then, he held her under the water.

It is hard to tell from this account whether the husband simply "lost it," perhaps because his argumentative wife is a "shrew"; whether the man became violent out of the blue after a peaceable, loving marriage; or whether he was provoked in some way. In any case, the man's propensity to go from disagreement to murderous rage is treated matter-of-factly rather than as the culmination of an abusive history. This is, the article suggests, the way men, or at least some men, simply are. The transition from walking and arguing to choking and drowning is treated as a natural progression, given her propensity to argue the status of a provocation. Nor are the power differences implied by the description—they *both* argue, but only he uses lethal physical force—reflected in the narrative.

Collateral Killing

In contrast to media portrayals of intimate partner homicides, collateral killings provide the most dramatic evidence of gender asymmetry in IPH. There are undoubtedly many cases in which women initiate violence against men or participate in mutual violence. But it most

certainly cannot be argued that small children incite their own killings. Collateral killing can be defined as those persons, other than the
focal victim, killed as a result of intimate partner violence. Specifically, the children, parents, siblings, new partners, of the primary
focal victim are murdered. Sometimes, the primary intimate partner
victim is not killed.

> *BAYOU LA BATRE, AL—A man angered after a dispute with his wife confessed
> to tossing his four young children off a bridge, authorities said Wednesday as they
> searched murky waters for the bodies.*[27]
> *Lam Luong, 37, who is charged with four counts of capital murder, told author-
> ities Tuesday night that he drove to the Dauphin Island bridge and dropped the
> children from a span that reaches 80 feet in places, said Detective Scott Rivera.*
> *Luong came to coastal Alabama from Vietnam in 1984 and worked in the com-
> mercial fishing industry as a shrimper, Police Chief John Joyner and a relative said.
> He had argued with his wife, Ngoc Phan, before taking the children, he said.*

This story positions the violence as symmetrical. A "dispute" connotes that both partners are equal in the relationship and that both
have the freedom to express their discontent with the other without
fear of retaliation or that both are freely able to discuss a problem.
Rather, this story is an example of a battered woman who was punished by her abusive partner. He also murdered their four children.
Yet, the homicides were reported to have resulted from a dispute.

An exhaustive review of all Michigan newspaper coverage of "collateral killings" between 1990 and 2007 identified 290 articles that
described 600 homicides with 413 persons killed besides or in addition
to the focal victim. Most of the collateral killings involved children.
Males were responsible for 100 percent of the collateral killings. During
this same time period in Michigan, there were rare cases of women
who killed their children as reported in the statewide child death
review. However, not a single one of these killings was the result of or
even related to a conflict with an intimate partner. Unlike intimate
partner homicides, most females who perpetrated filicide were mentally ill. If there is little gender symmetry in partner killing, there is
none where children are killed as well. Despite this, even when children are collateral victims, news stories persist in focusing on the fatal
violence as a response to a "dispute."

- *"He gave her every possible chance."* In this frame, the media contribute
  to victim-blaming by questioning why the victimized woman went back
  to or stayed with an abusive partner even after knowing her physical
  safety or life was at risk, refused to return when he gave her a chance
  to do so, or led the killer on by not providing unambiguous signs of
  rejection.

When Randall Abbott killed his ex-wife, Julie Abbott, Randall's mother blamed her for their troubled relationship, claiming, "She wasn't willing to work things out. Randy kept trying everything to get her to come back. He really loved the girl."

Defense attorney Tom Casselman had this to say about the situation. "Steven Tierney adored Sally Paajanen. He proposed to her more than once and offered her everything he had." He later said, "How difficult would it have been for her to tell him she was dating someone else and to please not call her anymore?" Casselman asked. "Instead, Steven Tierney felt like there was still hope for him and Sally." "Imagine how he felt when he saw her embracing and kissing Craig Fleck (who he also killed) that day," Casselman added. "His co-workers knew how he felt about Sally. He was the laughingstock at work."

The newspaper coverage of the murders of Sally Paajanen and Craig Fleck legitimized the actions of Steven Tierney. The story cites contradictory views: the mother who blames her for not returning and the attorney who cites her failure to make a clean break. By highlighting these views, the story joins these conflicting threads into a single theme: the victim was at fault, bringing death not only to herself but her new boyfriend. In reality, of course, the unifying thread was the cumulative fear Sally felt, given the history of abuse, to both return to Steve or to openly reject him.

- *"Rural Community in Shock."* Perhaps the most perplexing set of observations provided by journalists in describing IPH involves the "shock and disbelief" statements they make or attribute to witnesses. These statements invariably emphasize that the murder "does not make sense," that it is inconsistent with the killer's profile as a "nice guy," and that bad things like this simply don't happen in safe places (small towns, rural areas, and the suburbs). This profile is confirmed only so long as we ignore the context of coercive control and focus solely on the incident of the homicide itself. The community's shock is understandable. However, if instead, intimate partner homicides are reported within the context of violence, coercion, power, and control, then the murder makes perfect sense as the logical, if tragic, outcome of an ongoing pattern of illegitimate, though rational and instrumental, behavior. Moreover, once power and control enter the picture, violence may actually play a much smaller role in explaining the killing, and sometimes none at all. To illustrate:

Jacqueline was in the process of filing for divorce. Ray Ponke was not physically abusive but a controlling man. "When she'd escape to her mother's, he would call and say, 'You'd better get your butt home. I've got a fire going in the fireplace and I'm going to burn everything you own,' " states Dr. Alan Bredin, her longtime employer and confidant. After a November 1993 attempted assault, Jackie filed for divorce. By Christmas time she was in fear for her life and was desperately trying to protect herself. After bringing their daughter to the house for a Christmas Day visit, Ray Ponke wrecked the house by smashing holes into every room, wrecking appliances, ripping cupboards apart, and clubbing furniture into pieces. On January

8, Ray Ponke went into the dentist office in which Jacqueline worked and beat her to death in front of two people.[28]

For once, the homicide is clearly linked to the history of abuse.

CAN REPORTING OF IPV BE IMPROVED?

As Iyengar reminds us, the typical news story is not presented within a strictly episodic or thematic frame, but rather as a blend, with one or the other predominating. The problem with IPH news stories is not simply that they are typically episodic, but that the important thematic elements are buried toward the bottom or least important part of the story or not included at all. Episodic framing is an integral part of reporting the "news" which is, after all, prompted by specific events. But what needs to be developed are the infrastructure, tools, and relationships necessary to make it easy and desirable for reporters to include thematic elements more centrally in their stories.

As a first step, we need to acknowledge how newspapers report IPH events and how that reporting supports the public's general view that IPV is a "private crime" wherein individuals carry the full responsibility for causation and prevention. If the only things that newspapers or news outlets in general bring to the attention of the public are select cases of IPH, then IPV will remain below the radar and not become a public issue and fail to elicit a public outcry.

Can advocates and journalists successfully work together to change the essence of newspaper reporting on IPH? The short answer is yes. The possibilities are demonstrated by an experiment conducted by the Rhode Island Coalition Against Domestic Violence (RICADV). Its aim was to "encourage reporters . . . to stress community responsibility, collective action, and prevention."[29] Working closely with journalists, as well as talking with survivors, the coalition developed a handbook of best practices for reporting IPV that acknowledged the constraints under which journalists work. This in turn became the template that coalitions in Arizona, Washington, and elsewhere have used to develop their own guidebooks for journalists.

"Participatory communication" between journalists and battered women's advocates led to major changes in the way IPH stories were presented. These included a significant increase in applying the label of "domestic violence" to events and to an overall increase in the use of "domestic violence language" by non-advocate sources. There was also a concurrent reduction in the frequency with which people close to the victim (family, friends, and coworkers) and casual bystanders were used as primary quotable sources and a concomitant increase in the use of police/criminal justice agencies and especially advocates as sources. Researchers noted that the agency not only saw the need to change journalists' behavior, but also realized it needed to change its own practices to respond to reporter needs. By calling police and reporters proactively after a domestic violence murder, reporters could reach the organization quickly and easily and get reliable information. Staff was made available to reporters to research suspects' criminal justice histories, and journalists followed up to see if the staff had editing suggestions. In sum, recommendations and strategies were developed to improve the reporting of IPV, in addition to building *relationships* and *infrastructure* necessary to assure that those recommendations were put into practice.

Is it a simple matter to change the journalistic traditions and conventions of reporting IPH? Probably not. But, as these examples illustrate, it is possible. Ryan, Anastario, and DaCunha summarized the findings from their experiment in communication as follows:

Only collective actors and in fact multiple collective actors, synchronizing their resources, can accrue sufficient experience, develop strategy, and consolidate skills and contacts to build an infrastructure sufficient to sustain a successful foray into the market-driven media arena. Thus, in the U.S. context, attempts to change public awareness via mass media require long-term interventions with ongoing collective actors.[30]

CONCLUSIONS

"[T]he nature of homicide reporting is critical because the news media can influence public beliefs and perceptions, help establish specific agendas, and influence public policy. Differences in the amount and nature of news coverage are likely to have a corresponding influence on the perceived importance of and potential solutions for an issue."[31]

First and foremost, the presentation of IPV in general must change. Homicides should be treated not as a separate entity from IPV, but as a tragic expression of the larger phenomenon. After reviewing the extant research on how journalists report crime and how those reports influence audiences, McManus and Dorfman offered three recommendations for journalists: (1) to report more thematically, helping audiences to see patterns; (2) when reporting episodes, to increase the level of context so readers will have more resources to fit the new knowledge into the old; and (3) to enrich stories with more frames describing causes and solutions.[32] One way to summarize these recommendations is to expect the reporting of IPV and IPH to be informed by research and to incorporate the relationship context into each story. Advocates often say that domestic violence cannot be understood apart from "context, motive, meaning, and consequence." Highlighting these elements, linking the meaning of specific episodes of IPH to the themes of violence and control in relationships, linking these themes to the larger problem of domestic violence in our society, and setting these connections in the context of the systemic forces that currently support IPV and IPH in interpersonal relationships would go a long way to meeting the responsibility of an informed press in a democratic society.

NOTES

1. *USA Today*, "Few Answers in Wrestler's Death," June 26, 2007, sec A.

2. G. Tuchman, *Making News: A Study in the Construction of Reality* (New York: The Free Press, 1978).

3. B. J. Biroscak, and P. K. Smith, *Intimate Partner Homicide in Michigan, 1999–2003* (Lansing: Michigan Department of Community Health, 2005).

4. M. Peelo, "Framing Homicide Narrative in Newspapers: Mediated Witnesses and the Construction of Virtual Victimhood," *Crime, Media, Culture* 2 (2006): 164.

5. CNN, "Preacher Killed Wife, Stuffed Body in Freezer, Police Say," July 31, 2008.

6. C. A. Taylor, and S. B. Sorenson, "The Nature of Newspaper Coverage of Homicide," *Injury Prevention*, 8 (2002): 121.

7. Z. Pan, and G. M. Kosicki,"Framing Analysis: An Approach to News Discourse," *Political Communication* 10 (1993): 60.

8. *Detroit Free Press*, "Grant killed, then sought sex, says prosecutor: He cut up wife's dead body, defendant admits to judge," December 8, 2007.

9. W. A. Gamson, "News as Framing," *American Behavioral Scientist* 33 (1989): 157.

10. *Oakland Tribune*, "Family dispute turns deadly. Man kills wife, shoots her mother before," November 22, 2006.

11. S. Iyengar, *Is Anyone Responsible? How Television Frames Political Issues* (Chicago: The University of Chicago Press, 1991).

12. D. A. Graber, *Crime News and the Public* (New York: Praeger, 1980).

13. T. J. Mastin, J. Choi, G. E. Barboza, and L. Post, "Newspapers' Framing of Elder Abuse: It's Not a Family Affair," *Journalism & Mass Communication Quarterly* 84 (2007): 777.

14. T. Koch, *The News as Myth: Fact and Context in Journalism* (Westport, CT: Greenwood Press, 1990).

15. S. Chermak and N. M. Chapman, "Predicting Crime Story Salience: A Replication," *Journal of Criminal Justice* 35 (2007): 351.

16. C. F. Bullock, and J. Cubert, "Coverage of Domestic Violence Fatalities by Newspapers in Washington State," *Journal of Interpersonal Violence* 17 (2002): 475.

17. *Milwaukee News*, "Man killed girlfriend, himself," October 26, 2008.

18. *Jackson City Patriot*, "Murder trial may go to jury today: Key witness testified accused slit victim's throat," May 13, 2004.

19. *Grand Rapids Press*, "Slaying suspect obsessed with wife, mom says," April 3, 2004.

20. *Portland News*, "Neighbors react to killing at police station," April 30, 2008.

21. Washington State Coalition Against Domestic Violence. 2002, revised 2006. "Covering domestic violence: A guide for journalists and other media professionals," http://www.wscadv.org.

22. Wisconsin Coalition Against Domestic Violence. 2004. "2002 Wisconsin domestic violence homicide report," http://www.wcadv.org/?go=download&id=216.

23. M. Meyers, "News of Battering," *Journal of Communication* 44 (1994): 47.

24. K. A. Maxwell, J. Huxford, C. Borum, and R. Hornik, "Covering Domestic Violence: How the O. J. Simpson Case Shaped Reporting of Domestic Violence in the News Media," *Journalism & Mass Communication Quarterly* 77 (2000): 258.

25. N. Berns, *Framing the Victim: Domestic Violence Media and Social Problems* (Hawthorne, NY: Aldine de Gruyter, 2004).

26. *The State News*, "Postponed hearing will help investigation," August 1, 2001.

27. Associated Press, "Cops: Angry dad hurls 4 kids off Alabama bridge," January 8, 2008.

28. *Detroit Free Press*, "Police turned backs to rubble," February 17, 1994.

29. C. Ryan, M. Anastario, and A. DaCunha, "Changing Coverage of Domestic Violence Murders: A Longitudinal Experiment in Participatory Communication," *Journal of Interpersonal Violence* 21 (2006): 214.

30. Ibid, 225.

31. C. A. Taylor, and S. B. Sorenson, "The Nature of Newspaper Coverage of Homicide," *Injury Prevention* 8 (2002): 126.

32. J. McManus, and L. Dorfman, "Youth Violence Stories Focus on Events, Not Causes," *Newspaper Research Journal* 23 (2002): 6.

Chapter 4

Domestic Violence in American Magazines

Kathryn Phillips Thill
Karen E. Dill

We don't think of listening to a song or other forms of entertainment as a learning experience. Nevertheless, lyrics from the hit song "Face Down" by Red Jumpsuit Apparatus tell a story about domestic abuse that will provide many listeners with new information and resonate with the experiences of others. The song tells the story of covering up, denial, trust, and power.

Of course, what we "learn" from the media may not be accurate. In a classic study, Ira Glasser probed what people thought about crime, police, and legal procedures.[1] Results showed something fascinating. What people believe has less to do with what actually happens in police stations or courtrooms than with what they see on TV, on shows like *Law & Order* for instance. The popular view is that television reflects reality; in fact television also helps to *construct* reality as we know it.

In reading magazine accounts about domestic violence (DV), women learn about what can and does happen to other women and how victims respond to DV. Through this process, magazines normalize the stories of women. In other words, they teach people to think about abused women in certain ways (and not in other ways) and to expect them to exhibit certain behaviors if they are truly victims. As with TV images, this normalization process can have negative as well as positive consequences. On the positive side, readers may get important information, such as that abusers often apologize after an assault and that victims often mistakenly conclude perpetrators won't hit them again. But a distorted picture can perpetuate public stereotypes that affect a myriad of outcomes, including empathy for victims and public policy and funding for victim support. Distortions can also confuse abused women about how to understand or respond to what is happening to them. They may conclude their situation falls outside the spectrum of abuse, feel more isolated than before, and even make decisions, such as to stay with an abusive partner, that increases their risk.

The reactions of viewers who watched *The Burning Bed* when it aired in 1984 should dispel any doubt that what we see on TV and read in magazines affects us. After the show, battered wife centers from Boston to Los Angeles were inundated with calls for help—many from men seeking counseling. Still, at least two people seemed to get a nontherapeutic message from the show. In Quincy, Massachusetts, a husband angered by the movie beat his wife senseless. "He told her he wanted to get her before she got him," said the director of a shelter that took her in. And in Chicago, a battered wife watched the show—then shot her husband.[2]

This chapter looks at magazine coverage of DV over the last three decades. We consider the extent to which DV was covered, which types of magazines covered it most frequently, and the composition of the audiences for these magazines. In analyzing whether DV coverage in American magazines changed over the years, we pay special attention to watershed events in the history of the public understanding of DV and what affect these events had on magazine coverage of DV issues.

Those who study mass media ask a variety of questions and employ a range of methods. Some study the content of a specific media source like a magazine; others focus on the effects of exposure to these media. This chapter discusses both the content of magazine articles on DV and their probable effects. We begin with the issue communications scholars call "uses and gratifications," or, in everyday terms, understanding why people read the magazines they do. Uses and gratifications theory suggests that magazine readers are active and motivated; they buy magazines to fulfill needs. The active role of the initial motive remains important even though the magazine doesn't fulfill all their needs in this area and their magazine buying behavior may morph into being more habitual over time.

There are three basic motives for buying magazines: diversion (escapism), surveillance (information gathering), and developing personal identity (to reinforce or adopt beliefs and values). Diversion includes reading to be happy, to relax, to gain a sense of companionship, and to help pass the time. Surveillance motives include reading to learn about common issues, to learn information needed for work, to keep abreast of events, and to understand what's going on in the world.[3] Finally, in reading magazines one can learn what beliefs and attitudes others value, what we personally value, and what we can share with others, and one can enjoy the sense that one's values are appreciated by others and important.

Related to what motivates readers of a magazine is how well magazines address their readers' motives. Magazines that appeal solely to diversion readers may strictly limit the scope and informational content of what they publish to conform with the overall image of the magazine as well as what the paying advertisers want to see on the pages. In such magazines, stories that might increase public awareness about DV or serve current or future victims, about DV law enforcement, shelters, and education focused on reducing violence or changing attitudes for instance, are least common. When diversion magazines cover issues like domestic violence, they tend to feature uplifting stories of empowered women who have successfully escaped their abusive relationship. These articles are "entertainment-driven" or "infotainment" because the stories are designed to provide diversion rather than accurate knowledge about the potentially depressing realities confronted by the millions of women who continue to be in abusive relationships.

At the same time, a number of the most popular women's magazines, such as *Redbook* or *Good Housekeeping*, appeal to all three motives. As media scholar Nancy Berns points out, "Women's magazines offer an interesting perspective on women's issues, often introducing social problems and issues in more detail than other mass media.[4] They also try to capture the changing roles and responsibilities of women." Many women turn to these publications for information on topics that are not widely discussed. Young women in particular may use them to guide lifestyle choices, hence to create a sense of individuality, as well as to make their subcultural identity more precise. There is some evidence than independent reading may be a more vital source of education on sex, for instance, than parents, peers, or schools. Like sex, domestic violence has been taboo.

Magazines have led the way in covering domestic violence cases involving major media figures, as well as in shaping the importance of these events and how they would be covered. For example coverage of the 1994 O. J. Simpson trial raised public awareness that batterers can be deadly. As the *Jet* article "O. J. Simpson's case brings new focus on abuse of women" explains: "Battered women's shelters were flooded with women following the murder (of Nicole Simpson, allegedly by ex-husband O. J.), apparently because many women realized that their situation was far more dangerous than they realized."[5] A January 1994 *Newsweek* article, "Bobbitt fever: why Americans can't seem to get enough" addressed a related obsession: this domestic violence story was a variation from the norm: The perpetrator and victim roles were hard to distinguish. Lorena Bobbitt claimed she was raped, and as we all know, her husband was infamously injured. The sensationalist focus on a male victim of domestic violence fueled a media-inspired "battle of the sexes."

When Nancy Berns studied magazine coverage of domestic violence between 1970 and 1997, she uncovered a tendency to frame the issue as the woman's problem and to place responsibility for solving it squarely on her shoulders.[6] (See her chapter in this volume.) A prototypical example was a series published in *Good Housekeeping* magazine in the 1970s titled "My Problem and How I Solved It." Apart from its victim-blaming connotations, we wonder how such a title would be interpreted in light of Lorena Bobbitt's actions.

The early years of domestic violence coverage painted the issue with a broad brush. This was appropriate because it was still unclear how many people were affected, whether it was primarily a women's issue, a criminal justice problem, or a dynamic in dysfunctional families primarily. These early articles laid out the terrain so to speak. However, as domestic violence emerged as a "known issue," the focus of coverage shifted to specialized subareas and more particular, individual accounts. Like Berns, sociologist Donileen Loseke found that the substance of domestic violence coverage became more personalized over time, as it was no longer necessary to justify the importance of the issue or define it.[7] Unlike Berns, however, Loseke found a tendency to define women as victims of a sexist society as well as of their husband's violence.

Both Berns and Loseke conclude that magazine portrayals do little to aid readers who are currently suffering domestic violence. Coverage highlights extreme cases of violence and dramatic escapes from abuse. One effect of this emphasis is to actually increase tolerance of typical but much less extreme instances of abuse, and to elicit public policies that target extreme rather than more typical cases. Women who don't fit the stereotype of extreme violence are referred to as "assaulted women" rather than as "abused wives" and there is almost no coverage of the core issues for victims, the emotional impact, the financial dilemmas created by abuse, the involvement of children, or the dangerous repercussions of trying to leave.

Loseke focused on the social construction of the term "wife abuse" in magazine articles published between 1974 and 1986. Like Berns, she documented the emphasis on "it happened to me" stories ending with simplistic advice to victims about how to solve their problem. Victims were urged to "Change your personality," "Increase your self-esteem," to "Take control of your life," and to "Refuse to be a victim." The message was that "You have the power to end abuse."

OUR STUDY: THIRTY YEARS OF DOMESTIC VIOLENCE COVERAGE IN AMERICAN MAGAZINES

"... awareness of the problem is the first step toward prevention. Once named, violence against women, in its various forms, is no longer socially and culturally invisible ... *naming is power.*"[8]

Though DV is a problem with a long-standing history in Western Europe and America, it entered contemporary public consciousness in the mid-1970s, when it was referred to by terms such as "wife beating," "wife battering," and "wife abuse." A landmark in this awareness was the publication in 1974 of *Scream Quietly or the Neighbours Will Hear* by Erin Pizzey, the founder of the first official battered woman's shelter in England. The cover pictured women with bruised and battered bodies, the result of spousal abuse. The earliest shelters in the United States were also started around this time. Though abuse had been widely tolerated for centuries, a public debate now ensued about how best to help victims and respond to perpetrators. The term "wife beating" first appeared in the *Readers' Guide to Periodical Literature* in 1974.

The importance of 1974 in the history of DV makes it a natural starting point for our research. Our intention was to cover content from each of the decades that followed up to the present. Because important events in the history of DV also occurred in 1984 and 1994, we decided to sample magazine articles that appeared in print in 1974, 1984, 1994, and 2004. Table 4.1 summarizes these landmark events. These events raised public understanding and awareness about domestic violence issues and include the opening of the first women's shelters and landmark legislation relevant to DV.

Especially appropriate to this paper are key media events relevant to domestic violence. In 1984, *The Burning Bed* was released, considered by many to be one of the major events in raising awareness about domestic abuse. This film told the story of the abuse of Francine Hughes, a Michigan housewife who was judged to have been temporarily insane when she killed her ex-husband Mickey by lighting afire the bed where he had passed out drunk after an abusive rampage. The year 1994 held the murders that sparked the infamous trial of O. J. Simpson, accused of killing his ex-wife Nicole Brown Simpson and her friend Ron Goldman. Although Simpson was acquitted of murder, the 1995 trial was a watershed in public awareness that abusers may kill their victims and prompted record numbers of women to seek help at shelters.[9] The resulting media frenzy may have expedited passage of the federal Violence Against Women Act (VAWA) that same year, the first large-scale federal effort to fund community-based services for victims and support the criminal justice response. As an article in *Essence* pointed out at the time, "Following the Simpson horror ... legislators throughout the nation have been scurrying to author laws and create support services to protect women from domestic violence."[10] Lorena Bobbitt was also acquitted in 1994 for cutting off her husband John Wayne Bobbitt's penis in reaction to years of abuse, including a forced abortion.

In 2004, Scott Peterson was convicted of murdering his wife Laci and their unborn son. While Peterson's crime clearly involved violence against a wife and so was relevant to an understanding of domestic

Table 4.1.
Landmark Events in the Modern History of Domestic Violence: 1974, 1984, and 1994

1974	Erin Pizzey publishes *Scream Quietly or the Neighbors Will Hear*, the first contemporary book to expose wife battering as a topic. Pizzey also opens a shelter for abused women in England—the first of its kind.
	First battered women's shelter in America, Woman House, opens
1984	The movie *The Burning Bed* tells the story of abuse victim Francine Hughes. A jury acquits Hughes of killing her husband on grounds of temporary insanity. Actress Farrah Faucett is nominated for an Emmy for her portrayal of Hughes.
	Congress passes the *Family Violence Prevention and Services Act*, allocating funds for victims of domestic violence.
1994	OJ Simpson is tried for murder of his ex-wife Nicole Brown Simpson. The trial brings into awareness the idea that domestic violence can result in murder. Record numbers of battered women go to women's shelters that year, apparently realizing the dangerousness of the situation.
	President Clinton signs the *Violence Against Women Act*, a multi-pronged public policy approach including educational, law enforcement, and legal reform.
	Celebrated trial of abuse victim Lorena Bobbitt, which garnered media attention because she cut off her husband's penis, ended with a successful defense of abuse-induced post-traumatic stress disorder.
	Event of interest to domestic violence:
2004	Trial of Scott Peterson for the murder of his pregnant wife Laci and their unborn son Connor. That same year, president Bush signed into law the Unborn Victims of Violent Crime, which was also called Laci and Connor's Law.

violence, we give it less importance than the other events because it involved a single dramatic instance rather than an ongoing pattern of abuse. The Laci Peterson murder did, however, draw attention given to partner violence during pregnancy, a particularly vulnerable time for victims of DV.

Following the methods used by other researchers, we used the *Reader's Guide to Periodical Literature* to identify all magazine articles relevant to domestic violence published in the target years.

This list of terms is interesting because it documents how the vocabulary used to describe DV changed over thirty years, as new titles and issues emerged. "Family violence" was first used as a heading in 1984, replacing the earlier term "wife abuse." In later years, however,

Table 4.2.
Domestic Violence Terms as Covered in the *Reader's Guide to Periodical Literature* in 1974, 1984, 1994, and 2004 and the Number of Articles Appearing in Those Years

Term	Year(s) Term Appears in RGPL (number of articles)
Abused Women	2004 (4)
Domestic Violence/Domestic Abuse	1994 (8), 2004 (9)
Husband Abuse	1994 (1), 2004 (2)
Marital Rape	1994 (13)
Family Violence	1984 (7)
O'Malley, Suzanne, 1951	1994 (3)
Press and Domestic Violence	1994 (2)
Spouse Murder	2004 (17)
Women's Shelters	1994 (1), 2004 (1)
Violence Against Women Act	1994 (1)
Wife Abuse	1984 (12), 1994 (4), 2004 (1)
Wife Beating	1974 (2)*

*Frequency of Articles by Year Published in the U.S.**

Year Published	Number of Articles
1974	1
1984	18
1994	67
2004	33

*Some headings had articles listed that were not published in magazines in the United States. Articles published in Canadian or English editions were not included in this study.

"family violence" was restricted to child abuse and "domestic violence" and "wife abuse" were used to refer to partner violence. While the term "murder" generated some articles related to domestic violence, "spouse murder" proved to be the more relevant heading.

Table 4.2 lists the relevant headings found in the *Readers' Guide*, the year they appeared, and the number of articles published underneath each heading. One can get a fairly clear picture of which topics were "hot" in domestic violence solely by looking at the headings in Table 4.2. The heading "wife beating" disappeared after 1974, for example, as increasing public education about abuse made its use politically incorrect. Nor, however, was "domestic violence" used in 1974 or 1984, as this issue was still emerging and lacked an adequate nomenclature. Thirteen articles were listed under "marital rape" in 1994, almost certainly because of the publicity received by the Bobbitt trial. But use of the new term declined soon after and was no longer used in 2004. "Spouse murder" made its debut in 2004 with seventeen articles, a result, in part, of the well-publicized murders of Laci Peterson, Lori Hacking, and other victims. Thus, simply from the headings and the number of articles in each, we can track how sensational events influence the portrayal of domestic violence in the mass media.

HOW MANY ARTICLES ABOUT DOMESTIC VIOLENCE ARE BEING PUBLISHED?

The number of domestic violence articles published varied markedly with each decade, rising from the single article identified in 1974, to eighteen articles in 1984, peaking in 1994 with sixty-seven articles, and then falling off to thirty-three articles in 2004, a drop of more than 50 percent. To gauge the relative importance of these numbers, we compared domestic violence coverage to coverage of abortion and breast cancer, two current issues affecting women, one controversial, one not. Domestic violence paled in importance compared to these concerns. In 1974, compared to the single article on partner abuse, forty-three articles on abortion and twenty-one articles on breast cancer were published. In 1984, coverage of all three issues increased and the proportional coverage of domestic violence rose to 60 percent of breast cancer coverage (eighteen versus thirty articles) and to 20 percent of abortion coverage (eighteen versus ninety-two articles). Coverage of all three issues grew again over the next decade, a reflection of women's increasing importance as consumers. Domestic violence articles peaked at sixty-seven in 1994, a gain of almost 400 percent over the decade. But coverage was still relatively low, about 65 percent compared to breast cancer (n = 101) or abortion (n = 103). By 2004, the gap between domestic violence and breast cancer had basically returned to the 1984 ratio (thirty-three versus sixty-three), while interest in abortion continued to rise (thirty-three versus 119), almost certainly because of increasing opposition to legalized abortion during this period.

WHAT TYPES OF MAGAZINES PUBLISHED DOMESTIC VIOLENCE ARTICLES?

Table 4.3 lists the names of the magazines publishing DV articles in the years surveyed, the classification of the magazines surveyed (news, entertainment, etc.), the number of articles appearing in each magazine, and the sales rank for magazines ranked in the top 100 sellers for 2004 by the Magazine Publisher's Association.

People magazine published far and away the most DV articles during this period (twenty-one), followed by *Newsweek* (twelve), *Jet* (eleven),

Table 4.3.
Characteristics of American Magazines Publishing Domestic Violence Articles-1974, 1984, 1994 and 2004 and their 2004 Circulation Rank

Magazines Publishing the Most[1] Domestic Violence Articles, in Rank Order

Magazine Name	# of Articles	US Circulation Rank-2004[2]
People	21	12
Newsweek	12	18
Jet	11	—
Time	6	11
Ms.	6	—
Redbook	4	27
Essence	4	79
New York Magazine	4	—
Parents	3	30

Breakdown of Magazine by Category in Rank Order

Magazine Category	Magazine Titles	Number of Articles
Entertainment	People	21
News	Newsweek, Time	18
Black Interest	Jet, Essence	15
Women's Interest	Ms., Redbook, Good Housekeeping	13
Parenting	Parents	3
Lifestyle	New York Magazine	3

[1]This table lists all magazines publishing more than two articles in the years covered by this study.
[2]2004 statistics for those magazines ranked in the top 100, according to the Magazine Publishers Association. Statistics available at www.magazine.org.

Time, and *Ms. Magazine* (six each). *Time,* ranking eleventh in sales of all U.S. magazines in 2004, and *People,* ranking twelfth, were the top selling titles in our sample. In terms of magazine category, entertainment magazines had the most relevant articles (twenty-one), followed by news (eighteen), black interest (fifteen), and women's interest (thirteen). The number of articles published in *People, Newsweek,* and *Time* largely accounts for entertainment and news being the top two categories. These distributions make it clear that DV is characterized in American magazines as an entertainment issue first and as a news issue second, almost certainly a reflection of coverage of celebrities and/or their trials.

Since *People* magazine gave the most coverage to domestic violence in the years we studied, we looked more closely at its mission and readership. *People* has a readership of 34 million weekly; one in eight Americans reads *People*. They advertise that they are the "world's most popular magazine." Eighty percent of the readers of both the print version of *People* and the online version People.com are women. The target audience is between eighteen and forty-nine years of age.

A 1974 spin-off of *Time* magazine, *People* explicitly states its focus is "on people and not issues." It aims for an approximately fifty-fifty split of celebrity and human-interest stories. This implies that *People* provides entertainment, meeting the diversion motive. But even diversion magazines move and inform people. As *People's* own advertising slogan points out, "Nothing grabs people like people." In addition, celebrity articles can speak to the audiences' desire to find models of identity.

Although entertainment articles certainly have a legitimate role in diverting people from their everyday problems, the fact that domestic violence is presented to its audiences primarily as a form of entertainment is worrisome. Thus, domestic violence is most frequently covered in a format that explicitly promises *not* to cover serious issues. Coverage in most other magazines also reflects the emphasis on infotainment or straight news stories that cover the details of public events such as trials.

The newsworthiness of domestic violence is second in importance to its use for entertainment. Third in importance is its portrayal as an issue relevant to women generally and to black women specifically. Although black interest magazines (three) made up a small percentage (6.8 percent) of our total (forty-four) magazines, the percentage of articles published in these outlets was more than twice what would be expected (13.4 percent) simply by their proportional representation.

The most obvious explanation for the disproportionate coverage of domestic violence in black interest magazines is the O. J. Simpson trial. However, while Nicole Brown Simpson's 911 call received a good deal of publicity, it was deliberately played down in the criminal trial, as was the domestic violence issue overall. The prosecutor, Marcia Clark, never called her domestic violence expert and neither, then, did O. J.'s defense team. Moreover, the discussion of race during the trial focused on whether a racial motive underlay O. J.'s prosecution, not on the risk of domestic violence. Interestingly, of the sixteen articles published in black interest magazines during the decades studied, only five discussed the O. J. Simpson trial. James Brown, another African American celebrity faced with charges of domestic violence, was the subject of two of the sixteen articles. The focus on domestic violence remains disproportionate even when these celebrity trials are omitted. Another explanation is a belief that domestic violence is more common among African Americans or among the economically disadvantaged. This belief may have led publishers to feel that domestic violence had special relevance to their readers, though a similar obligatory sense does not appear to have been shared by other publishers.

Loseke highlights a contrasting view, reporting the consensus among experts in the field and journalists who write for the magazines she studied that DV is *not* limited to specific racial or economic groups. She found that magazine articles made this point by giving examples of DV involving white, educated, high-income perpetrators.

Another finding, perhaps less surprising, is the dearth of coverage domestic violence received in men's magazines. There was one article published in a magazine of male interest, a witty, light, and trifling article discussing the relationship of John and Lorena Bobbitt, with an appropriately amusing title: "Separation Anxiety" (*Men's Health*, 1994).[11] This finding is consistent with the widely held notion that DV is a woman's and not a man's problem.

Also missing were domestic violence articles in magazines directed toward teens, male or female. This remained true even in recent years, when the issue of "dating violence" received widespread publicity. We also take this as a major missed opportunity to provide education with an eye toward early prevention.

WHY DO WOMEN STAY? THE CYCLE OF COERCIVE CONTROL

In *Coercive Control: How Men Entrap Women in Personal Life*, sociologist Evan Stark argues that control issues were part of the understanding of domestic violence when the issue came into the spotlight in the 1970s, but disappeared later, when abuse was increasingly identified solely with physical violence.[12] The changing focus of magazine articles about domestic violence supports Stark's point. The article "Wife-Beating" that appeared in *Ladies' Home Journal* in 1974 focuses on the broad socioeconomic context for abuse.[13] In explaining "Why do these women take it?" author Karen Durbin cites financial concerns, calling women "economic prisoners," and explains that one woman is "afraid that if she [leaves], she and the children will be forced into the humiliation of welfare." She also describes the "psychological bind of marriage," stating that, "A woman in this situation may see the end of her marriage as the disintegration of all meaning in her life, and she may tolerate an extraordinary degree of abuse from her husband before the balance tips and she leaves." Durbin gives the example, "When her husband began to abuse her, she didn't like it, and she was afraid, but the physical pain was a lot less frightening than leaving the marriage." The article captures a dilemma with which many readers could identify, trapped both by their partner's coercive and controlling tactics and by their fear of being isolated and unable to support themselves if they leave. More recent articles lack this level of insight and appear to highlight physical abuse almost exclusively.

Durbin's article also includes a nuanced understanding of abusers. In response to the question, "Why does a man start to batter his wife

in the first place?" she echoes a common theme in both domestic violence research and in the best popular pieces on abuse, that "There is
no neat thumbnail sketch of the violent husband. . . ." She identifies the
abusers' weaknesses as important, naming helplessness, fear, inad-
equacy, insecurity, and "a faltering sense of masculinity" as possible
motives for abuse and as commonplace feelings that may become man-
ifest as anger and violence. Importantly, this is tied to a gendered analysis. "The culture holds out violence as a channel of expression for
men. If a man is upset, he isn't supposed to cry. It's more manly to put
his fist through the wall. Only sometimes the wall is his wife." Since
domestic violence was only redefined as a problem for criminal justice
rather than individual counseling in the 1980s, it is not surprising that
Durbin emphasizes psychological and cultural dimensions of abuse.
Still, one effect of her description could be to feel sorry for perpetrators
of abuse rather than to hold them accountable.

Fluff articles are not completely devoid of similar substance. An article titled "The Other Nicole" in *People* magazine told the story of a victim of domestic violence who was shot and killed, like Nicole Brown
Simpson.[14] It quoted a psychologist's insightful description of domestic
violence perpetrators as "not so much in love as in obsession. But they
want to bring this woman into control so they can feel better about
themselves." The expert also reiterated the common observation that
"domestic violence can happen to anyone." While this insight was
commonplace, it spoke to a widespread public prejudice that only certain types of women were likely to be abused.

"IT HAPPENED TO ME" OR "FLUFF AND NONSENSE"

Aside from articles about specific news events, many articles focused
on telling "it happened to me" stories about everyday people. One
such story clearly blames the victim, echoing the long-discredited belief
that abused women are masochistic. One wife, for example, is quoted
as saying "I know I was completely dominated by Frank from the first
moment I met him and I suppose I wanted to be dominated."[15]

A classic belief described by Stark is that abuse results from "bad
luck" in men and that the antidote is "Mr. Right," the prince who res-
cues Cinderella from her life of tragedy and hardship. An infotainment
article that promotes this myth appeared in *Redbook* in 1994. "Beauty
and the Brave" describes the hardships faced by actress Halle Berry,
who "was abandoned by her father and abused by many of the men in
her life."[16] Enter the prince. "It took the strong, abiding love of baseball player David Justice to make her trust again."

The Cinderella premise is that David Justice (whom Berry subsequently divorced) saved the actress from a lifetime of abuse and
restored her trust in men. Men are thus divided into abusers and

saviors. A reader might well wonder how she is to tell which is which? Instead of helping women anticipate abuse by learning the signs of coercion and control, the article leaves the distinct impression that finding Justice was just a result of Berry's luck—the folklore premise that fate rather than reason determines our experiences in life. Another implication in this piece is that Justice has "saved" Berry, in part by his strength (as a superstar athlete) to protect her from abusive men. Since this same premise often leads abused women to seek protection from "strong men" who end up becoming abusive themselves when the seemingly helpless female shows a wit of independence, the messages conveyed by this fluff piece are worse than infotainment and can actually increase the risk of readers by teaching them to trust "good" men rather than their own prowess or strength. Thus, despite their insistence otherwise, diversion magazines *do* cover issues, though not always in a socially responsible manner. The story on Berry—an African American Oscar winner—uses her sexiness and personal tragedies to manipulate the hopes and dreams of readers, all without even a dose of reality.

Happily, there are examples of magazines getting it right. One good example of accurate and helpful coverage came from an article in *The Progressive* called "Blame it on Battered Women."[17] This article raised substantive issues such as why the focus is on a "battered women" syndrome instead of a battering men syndrome. Also, the article analyzed how the celebrity of O. J. Simpson overshadowed the opportunity to reach broader audiences with information about domestic violence during his trial.

The Progressive is a left-leaning, issues-focused magazine with a relatively small and largely white and middle-class readership. A more important exception to the fluff rule appeared in *O, The Oprah Magazine*, a top-ten seller with an audience that is 89 percent women.[18] *O* has other unique attributes including being trusted by readers and attracting a wide range of reader ages (readership is roughly equal among four age ranges starting from eighteen and ending at fifty-five and older). One *O* goal is "to help women see every experience and challenge as an opportunity to grow and discover their best self."[19] Here, as in the early article from *Ladies' Home Journal*, the emphasis is less on physical assault than on broader aspects of coercion and control. Quoting Rita Smith, the executive director of the *National Coalition Against Domestic Violence*, the article "She's Come Undone," relates:

> When a partner is criticizing everything you do, who you see, how you spend the money, and telling you how lucky you are that you've got him because you're fat, ugly, and stupid, you start to question your own reality. The more isolated you are, the less you hear from other people and the more his reality becomes yours. Most of the women I've met prefer

the physical violence because it's the thing people can see and believe ...
We all intuitively agree that it's not good to be subjected to name-calling,
degradation, and belittling, but it's almost impossible to take any kind of
legal action. If the bottom line is controlling a partner, a man with financial resources and verbal skills can control a woman quite successfully
without ever having to hit.[20]

This is one of the very few instances when a critical important truth
about battering reached a mass audience.

MAJOR NEWS STORIES DOMINATE DOMESTIC VIOLENCE COVERAGE IN MAGAZINES

Perhaps the most sobering finding from our research is the extent to
which coverage of domestic violence in American magazines over the
last thirty years was dominated by a limited number of high-profile
media events. The watershed events summarized in Table 4.1 exhaust
the lion's share of topics covered. With the marked exceptions of the
articles singled out above, the articles reviewed are "it happened to
me" stories, either about celebrities or everyday citizens.

The remainder of the chapter focuses on how these high-profile events
were covered, beginning with the landmark film *The Burning Bed* and pro-
gressing through the O. J. Simpson and Lorena Bobbitt trials to the trial of
Scott Peterson. We again examine the degree to which the pieces were substantive and informative versus infotainment. Since we purposefully chose
the dates we did because of their importance in the history of domestic violence awareness, the focus on key events is not surprising. Given the burgeoning of a huge research literature on domestic violence during this
period, we wondered whether magazine coverage would be limited to
news stories and infotainment articles, or whether the importance of
watershed events would also spawn independent and informative articles
about domestic violence generally. In fact, it did not.

The Burning Bed

Articles that discussed the 1984 film *The Burning Bed* were generally
of two types: those that retold the story of Francine Hughes and those
who interviewed actress Farrah Fawcett about her experience in the
role. The articles about Francine Hughes fit the pattern of the "it happened to me" stories and generally ended with the mandate that
women should "refuse to be a victim." Here, DV is a woman's problem, and she needs to solve it. Interestingly, the interviews with Farrah
took the same general form, often asking her opinions about domestic
violence. Responses were sometimes on target and sometimes not. Consider, for example, these commentaries from Farrah that express a
tendency to blame women and victims.[21]

Why do husbands beat their wives? I think it's largely due to the confusion of roles today. My parents had a traditional loving relationship
where he was big and strong and the breadwinner and she took care of
the home. Today men come home from a stressful day at work to find
wives who demand equal say because they work too. Men traditionally
have dominated and their masculinity is threatened.

Farrah did point out correctly the cycle of hope and self-blame
abuse victims suffer, saying: "The women assumed it was their fault
and they had this incredible hope that they could change the man
back. They'd say 'I should be prettier' or 'I didn't have dinner ready
and that irritated him.' " Again, though, the emphasis is on understanding why perpetrators are abusive rather than on depicting their
acts as willful and criminal. Farrah was also apparently offended by
the emphasis on Hughes as a more-or-less passive victim of her circumstances. She told the reporter, "I kept saying to *The Burning Bed*
director, 'I want to hit back, I would never let a man treat me that
way. Why does Francine stay?' " Sadly, this last quote proved untrue
when Farrah herself was abused.

Coverage of Francine Hughes also echoed the "it happened to me"
theme, albeit in dramatic ways that fit the "infotainment" model. *Murder
Was Her Last Resort* gave details of abusive episodes between Francine
and her ex-husband Mickey: "I was afraid he would break my nose or
knock out my teeth," she was quoted as saying. "While he pounded on
me I slumped down farther and farther, sinking into the corner."[22] The
story emphasizes a number of issues raised by Rita Smith in the *O* article,
including the pattern of control and financial and educational manipulation that accompanied his coercive tactics. The reader learns that
Mickey "... was calling me every filthy name, saying I was *gonna* quit
college, and if I didn't say it, he would break every bone in my body." In
the film *The Burning Bed*, Mickey uses other coercive tactics such as dis-
abling the car so that Francine cannot drive and slapping her in front of
guests for going into town without him, but the coverage never reaches
beyond individual narrative. Readers may recognize themselves in Francine Hughes' abuse. But the article does nothing to enhance their understanding of her predicament.

The Murder of Nicole Brown Simpson and the Trial of O. J. Simpson

Because of the public obsession with the Simpson trial, 1994 was a
bounty year for domestic violence coverage, as we've seen. Of the
sixty-seven articles listed for 1994, twenty-four discussed O. J. or the
murder of Nicole Brown Simpson and her friend Ron Goldman to
some extent. Interestingly, the articles revealed a new self-conscious-
ness about their own role. Most (sixteen) of the articles commented on

the effect the O. J. case had on the media, often stating their responsibility for finally bringing attention to the issue of domestic violence:

In 1992, in fact, the U.S. surgeon general ranked abuse by husbands and boyfriends as the leading cause of injuries to women aged fifteen to forty-four. Despite these warnings, it took O. J. Simpson's arrest for his ex-wife's murder and the accompanying revelations that he beat her during their marriage to make Americans pay attention to the staggering statistics—and the women behind them.[23]

Probably because knowledge of domestic violence had been more widely disseminated in 1994 than a decade earlier, coverage of the Simpson trial often included a number of general points about domestic violence, extending from the effects of a sports-focused culture on young males ("Football players are taught to hurt people ... if they don't see the guy across the line as a human being, how can they see a woman as a human being?") to the effects of the trial on women's shelters.[24] *Working Woman* noted, for instance, that, "The media widely publicized how the murder of Nicole Brown Simpson brought battered women to the doors of shelters everywhere ... despite all the publicity, donations have yet to rise."[25]

Although it was rarely mentioned in magazines, there were a number of news stories of batterers at the time who "juiced" their partners or ex-partners by threatening or attacking them during the trial. In the main, magazine articles kept to the "it happened to me" story line, with reports from women who shared their personal stories about how they got out, often realizing the danger of their situation only after learning of the murder and the history of abuse that had plagued Nicole Brown Simpson's relationship with O.J. Typical is this report from *Time*:

> Last Tuesday, however, Dana finally came to believe her life was in danger. Her change of mind came as she nursed her latest wounds, mesmerized by the reports about Nicole Simpson's tempestuous marriage to ex-football star O. J."I grew up idolizing him," she says.
>
> "I didn't want to believe it was O. J. It was just like with my husband." Then, she says, "the reality hit me. Her story is the same as mine—except she's dead."[26]

As *The Progressive* had, so now its conservative rival *The New Republic* critically observed domestic violence coverage, criticizing more popular magazines for giving so much attention to the trial: "An irritating by-product of the O. J. Simpson tragedy is the blizzard of balderdash about wife battering that has been loosed in the main-stream media."[27] Meanwhile, a leading Canadian news magazine asked, "I mean, who is O. J. Simpson? What makes him rate all this attention? Why is this a national event?"[28] However unwarranted fascination with this case may have been, the tragedy undoubtedly brought this issue to the forefront of attention, even only for a brief period, raising awareness and hopefully saving lives.

"You have to have tremendous compassion for Nicole Brown Simpson, for it took her death for people to realize that even the most wonderful public persona can still be a wife-beater," says Richard Gelles, who heads the Family Violence Research Program at the University of Rhode Island. "But the real tragedy, and I hope we don't lose sight of this, is the 1,400 women every year who are killed by their husbands or partners. It is a tragedy for them, their families, and their children."[29]

The Bobbitt Trial

The Bobbitt trial also marked 1994 as a peak year for domestic violence coverage. Lorena Bobbitt's assault on her husband received such media attention because of its sensationalistic nature, reversing the usual story of husbands assaulting wives. Moreover, there was enormous ambiguity about whether to treat the event humorously or to take it seriously. Fourteen of the sixty-seven articles from 1994 were devoted to news-driven coverage or commentary on the Bobbitt trial. "Some observers argue that the media focus on such trials—including this very story—can have redeeming social value. 'The Bobbitt case has sparked a great deal of discussion,' said Rita Smith"[30] (the Executive Director of the National Coalition Against Domestic Violence). More than ten of the articles provided up-to-date coverage of the trial or commented on aspects of the trial, such as Lorena's testimony or the final verdict of insanity. "For John, who watched the last day of the trial on TV, the verdict had to be an enormous letdown. But for the rest of us, there is considerable joy in the prospect that the word 'penis' can now once again be reserved for special occasions."[31]

Due to the unusual symbolic nature of this event, the issue of feminism was automatically intertwined with this story, giving birth to a media-evoked "battle of the sexes." One *MacLean's* article, entitled "The Male Myth," was devoted entirely to the anger males felt toward females, especially feminists, as a result of this event: "The fable of John and Lorena has brought out extremes of pathos and farce in the gender war."[32] Interestingly, the only article concerning domestic violence published in a men's interest magazine was an article aptly titled "Separation Anxiety," in which the battle of the sexes over the incident was reported thusly:

> ... at breakfast tables everywhere, amazement seems to have been followed by laughter, at least from one side of the table. A woman friend tells me of the exceptionally high spirits among the females in her office that morning; with jokes on the excellent quality of cutlery these days and the kinds of commercials that might be shot to prove it, above all,

thinking back on it, about what each of them would like to have done to this or that ex if the only the occasion had arisen.[33]

Originally, the media focused attention on the unusual act of violence Lorena perpetrated, though eventually people began to wonder what would drive her to commit such a deed. Lorena's answer—or, at least, the explanation offered by her psychiatric expert at trial, Susan Feister—was that she had been driven to temporary insanity after years of physical and emotional abuse, most recently by the alleged rape that occurred just hours before she sought retribution.

The events leading up to the Bobbitt trial led some magazines to take marital rape more seriously. Although marital rape laws had been passed in most states by this time (or the marital exemption had been removed), marital rapes were rarely reported, as few women realized that they were protected from a husband's sexual assaults. As an article in *Ladies' Home Journal* observed, "Martial rape is, for many, a complicated issue. For most people, 'marital rape' is an oxymoron."[34] Regardless of whether sympathy for Lorena Bobbitt or fear that other women would retaliate as she had, by the time the trial began, all fifty states had passed legislation prohibiting marital rape, though it remains a lesser offense than stranger rape in thirty-three states.

Speaking to North Carolina's Senate Judiciary Committee, which was balking at giving the bill its approval, Representative Bertha Hold said, "I want to remind you, in light of recent occurrences, that unless you give women legal recourse, they may take matters into their own hands."[35]

The Peterson Trial

Fourteen of the thirty-three articles published in 2004 pertaining to the issue of domestic violence concerned the trial of Scott Peterson for the murder of his pregnant wife, Laci Peterson, and the star witness in the trial, his former mistress, Amber Frey. All but one of the Peterson articles focused completely on the trial, hardly mentioning the disappearance and murder of Laci and her unborn son. Typical was this description from *People:*

> He walks into court each morning wearing his familiar nonchalant grin, as seemingly carefree as a man strolling to the first tee for a round of golf. But whether Scott Peterson is simply confident in the outcome of his murder trial—or perhaps just disconnected from the possible death sentence that hangs over him—is unclear.[36]

Since none of the participants in the trial had celebrity status, these articles were largely driven by news events rather than infotainment. The focus on Amber Frey, though, made it appear that infidelity was the major issue in the case rather than domestic violence.

Scott Peterson may have told Amber Frey he wanted her to play a big role in his future, but certainly not like this.

> Taking the stand last week in Redwood City, California, as the prosecution's star witness in Peterson's murder trial, Frey cut a more respectable figure than she had as the tabloid siren who had an affair with him in the weeks before his wife, Laci, disappeared.[37]

One popular article went a bit further, linking the obsession with the trial's outcome to the widespread belief he should be punished.

> As a clerk solemnly pronounced Peterson guilty of murdering his wife and the couple's unborn son, strangers huddled around radios on the courthouse plaza exploded into cheers and tearfully embraced each other as though Boston had won the World Series all over again. "There was this huge release," says Winnegar. "I think people were worried how awful it would be if it was like O. J. and they weren't able to put him away.[38]

Indeed, so strong was this sentiment that attention to Laci or the named but unborn child was largely lost behind a running moral commentary on the trial from media figures and ordinary citizens.

Though there was no evidence of an abusive history in the Peterson relationship, the story provided a shocking example of domestic violence. Nevertheless, we found only one reported article concerning the Petersons that addressed this issue, and it did so in the context of violence against pregnant women. Mentioned earlier, the 2004 *Ms. Magazine* article titled "A Buried Statistic" discussed how Laci Peterson and Lori Hacking (a later, similar case of a pregnant wife murdered by her husband) were not unusual.[39] Mirroring several theories about domestic violence and coercive control, this article discussed why there is such a danger of abuse to pregnant women by stating that some men feel a loss of control and experience jealousy when their wives or girlfriends become pregnant.

The article also provided staggering statistics about violence during pregnancy and noted that most of these victims remain anonymous. "The number one cause of death for pregnant women in America is murder.... Between 1994 and 1998, pregnant women in Maryland were twice as likely to be murdered as nonpregnant women of the exact same age ..."

Ms. Magazine is a feminist magazine, so it is not surprising it took the Peterson trial as an occasion to educate its readership about a relatively unknown facet of domestic violence. But why didn't the problem merit more discussion, particularly, with two similar cases reported in the media almost back to back (Laci disappeared in December and Lori seven months later in July)? As we've seen, the murder of Nicole Brown Simpson produced a spike in both the coverage of domestic violence and in the utilization of shelters as well as a spate of articles about women who heard about Nicole's story and realized they had to get help. Similarly, the Bobbitt incident renewed attention to marital rape and stimulated discussion in state legislatures as well as in popular magazines. One explanation is that unlike these cases, the Peterson case was not defined as a domestic violence issue but as a murder mystery involving a missing victim.

This trend supports what was found in past research, that article content continues to focus less on the real issues of domestic violence than on providing a news feed with just enough juice to keep audiences interested. By 2004, the multiple facets of domestic violence—coercive control, intimidation, and feelings of inferiority—discussed in 1984 and particularly in 1994 had largely disappeared from popular magazines. And none of the articles in 2004 were anywhere nearly as comprehensive as the *Ladies' Home Journal*'s 1974 article "Wife-Beating." Perhaps societal awareness of domestic violence made it possible to use it as fluff. Another possibility is that an issue that was initially appealing as infotainment had lost its shock value and with this also its cache as news.

CONCLUSIONS

The single popular article on domestic violence published in the *Ladies' Home Journal* in 1974 was an informative and substantive piece. Interest grew over the next decade at least in part due to the publication and then release of *The Burning Bed*. But the vast majority of the eighteen articles published in 1984 treated domestic violence as infotainment rather than as an opportunity to educate readers about the dangers and dimensions of abuse or its growing redefinition as a crime rather than as a problem for counseling. Infotainment pieces consisting largely of stories about abuse against or by celebrities and "it could happen to me" narratives were even more in evidence by 1994, when interest in violence against women was peaked by the trials of O. J. Simpson and Lorena Bobbitt. Indeed, so marked were the obsessions with these watershed events that coverage of domestic violence by mass media itself became worthy of critical commentary in issue magazines like *MacClean's* and highbrow intellectual magazines like *The Progressive* and *The New Republic*. Interest in domestic violence remained far less than coverage of other issues affecting women primarily, such as abortion and breast cancer.

Still, media coverage of events leading up to these famous trials almost certainly contributed to expanded protections for women. On the one hand, coverage of the Simpson trial appears to have caused a spike in the use of shelters by abuse victims. On the other hand, as news articles on the trials drew on the growing body of empirical research on domestic violence and commentators focused attention on "the battle of the sexes" and marital rape elements of the Bobbitt case, political pressure mounted to enact the VAWA (passed by the U.S. Congress in 1994) and for states that had not yet done so to eliminate the marital exemption from rape charges or to redefine sexual assault by a husband as rape.

Media interest in domestic violence appears to have diminished after 1994. While the number of articles published in 2004 was much higher than the number published in 1984, it was 50 percent less than the number published in 1994. Significantly, *Ms. Magazine* took the trial of Scott Peterson as an occasion to highlight the importance of domestic violence during pregnancy. And *O, The Oprah Magazine* ran a broadly focused piece on abuse that was on a par with the 1974 article in the *Ladies' Home Journal* in its scope and sophistication. Importantly, however, magazines exploited the Peterson case as an instance of jealousy and marital intrigue rather than as an opportunity to educate audiences about domestic violence.

The early piece in the *Ladies' Home Journal* (like articles in *O* and *Ms.*) addressed coercive and controlling elements of partner abuse other than bone-breaking physical violence, a theme powerfully portrayed in the popular 1991 film *Sleeping with the Enemy* (with Julia Roberts playing a wife who is stalked and controlled as well as assaulted by her husband). But the more general trend in the decades studied was to narrow the depiction of domestic violence rather than to broaden it.

How can we explain these trends and what do they tell us about magazine coverage of domestic violence, a vital issue that may affect as many as one woman in five in the United States? The news is mostly disheartening, though not entirely.

It is possible that interest in domestic violence waned because it became a less serious problem after 1994, particularly with the passage of the VAWA and the widespread adoption of mandatory arrest policies by local police departments throughout the United States. In other words, it was no longer important enough to feature. Supporting this view are claims by federal agencies and some researchers that partner homicides and assaults have declined significantly over the last few decades, though these changes appear to have benefited some groups (males and African Americans, for instance) more than others. Even if legislation did not have the effects claimed, it is possible that, as the police and service responses to domestic violence were normalized, the sense of urgency that surrounded the issue and was heightened by the publicity surrounding the Simpson trial simply waned.

A less optimistic interpretation is that attention to domestic violence peaked and waned in response to the events that obsessed the media, the impact of which we have traced, and that coverage declined as the issue lost its value as entertainment. Apart from the cynical view this supports, that attention to an issue is only warranted by sensational and horrific events, the focus on tragic instances of fatal or near fatal violence masks the more typical reality faced by abused women, wherein violence and other forms of abuse are terrifying, manipulative, controlling, and psychologically devastating but not necessarily life-threatening. Someone should not have to die for an issue with so much consequence for women to be newsworthy.

Clearly articles that address substantive dimensions of domestic violence and provide a realistic picture of women's alternatives are more useful to the mass audience of female readers of popular magazines than the fluff typified by celebrity sagas and "it happened to me" stories. But those who control media content insist they publish what their readers want, not what they "need," and that their survival in a competitive media market depends on this strategy. An analogy would be to say that readers would prefer morbid accounts of victims who died or survived horrible automobile accidents to realistic information about how to drive safely. Even if we grant that readers prefer to read about real-life nightmares and heroic stories of escape than about facts and resources, it is hard to believe they are still satisfied with the belief that "Mr. Right" will save them from "Mr. Wrong," or that how one negotiates for safety in relationships is largely a matter of personal willfulness or "luck," the core messages in the "it happened to me" stories.

The idea that magazine editors are not concerned with what is best for their readers is hardly new. Researchers studying women's magazines have shown the extent to which damaging women's self-esteem through ads and articles that highlight physical or personality deficits contribute to the "beauty myth," the idea that personal problems, and particularly problems involving love, work, and marriage, can be solved by buying the products on whose ads magazines depend. Horrific accounts of domestic violence, particularly when they involve celebrities, increase women's general sense of discomfort (if it can happen to anyone, it can happen to *you*) with their lives and create an inchoate fear that might be salved through buying. Meanwhile, stories of individual escape from abuse perpetuate the notion that social problems like abuse can be addressed by individualized makeovers. From this vantage, stories highlighting available services, resources, or effective means to cope with the psychological consequences of abuse are not merely boring. They also threaten the bottom line. Thus, even if a story would greatly benefit readers, if it could be predicted to also lower revenues from advertising, the magazines will side with the big money and literally "sell out" their readers. If "it happened to me" stories offer little beyond entertainment for most magazine readers, they may inform those who are unaware of the potential dangers of abuse in relationships.

The ideal formula—one which could meet the entertainment needs of marketers and readers as well as inform—would seem to be a combination of personal stories with education about the typical dynamics in abusive relationships and available resources. There is no way to know how often articles submitted with this ideal combination lose their substance to the demand for advertising space.

We are not implying that individual editors conspire to keep from their readers the truth about domestic violence and other current issues affecting women. We are merely suggesting that they hone to issue selection and presentation that follow themes whose ultimate test is in marketing, not in the quality of public discourse or information.

In other areas of women's lives, particularly with respect to issues related to health such as weight loss, diet, and exercise, the most popular women's magazines have found ways to provide practical information within the infotainment formula. Although it is unclear why this has yet to happen on a large scale with domestic violence, one answer might be to treat what one observer terms "terror on the home front" as a matter of personal health.

AUTHOR'S NOTE

The authors wish to thank research librarians Burl McCuiston and Virginia Moreland for their invaluable help locating the articles reviewed here. Great thanks also to Mariko Tada (Bachelor of Journalism, University of Missouri-Columbia) for expert advise on magazine journalism.

NOTES

1. I. Glasser, "Television and the Construction of Reality," *Applied Social Psychology Annual* (1988): 44.

2. N. Karlen, "Copycat Assault," *Newsweek* (October 22, 1984).

3. G. Payne, et al., "Uses and Gratifications Motives as Indicators of Magazine Readership," *Journalism Quarterly* 65, no. 4 (1988): 909.

4. N. Berns, *Framing the Victim: Domestic Violence, Media and Social Problems* (Hawthorne, NY: Aldine de Gruyter, 2004): 194.

5. T. Moore, "O. J. Simpson's Case Brings New Focus on Abuse of Women." *Jet* 86, no. 11 (1994): 14.

6. N. Berns, *Framing the Victim*, 194.

7. D. Loseke and J. Best, " 'Violence' Is 'Violence' ... Or Is It: The Social Construction of 'Wife Abuse' and Public Policy," in *Images of Issues: Typifying Contemporary Social Problem* (Hawthorne, NY: Aldine de Gruyter, 1989): 191.

8. M. Crawford and R. Unger, *Women and Gender: A Feminist* (New York: McGraw-Hill, 2004): 440.

9. J. Hyde, *Half the Human Experience* (New York: Houghton Mifflin, 2006): 593.

10. S. Taylor, "Owning Your Life." *Essence* 25, no. 5 (1994): 65.

11. H. Stein, "Separation Anxiety." *Men's Health (10544836)* 8, no. 8 (1993): 28.

12. E. Stark, *Coercive Control: How Men Entrap Women in Personal Life* (New York: Oxford University Press, 2007), 452.

13. K. Durbin, "Wife-Beating," *Ladies' Home Journal* (1974): 64–65.

14. B. Hewitt and M. Eftimiades, "The Other Nicole," *People* 42, no. 2 (1994): 36.

15. K. Sandiford and A. Burgess. "Shattered Night," *Good Housekeeping* (1984): 72.

16. V. Coppola, "Beauty and the Brave," *Redbook* 183, no. 3 (1994): 46.

17. S. Douglas, "Blame It on Battered Women," *The Progressive* 58, no. 8 (1994): 15.

18. C. Carr, "You Can Read Her Like A ... Magazine." *Broadcasting & Cable*, January 24 (2005): 57.

19. *O, The Oprah Magazine*, "The O Media Kit," http://www.OMediakit.com/r5/home.asp.

20. A. L. Ball, "She's Come Undone," *O, The Oprah Magazine* 5, no. 9 (2004): 300.

21. "Farrah Talks About Her Role of a Lifetime," *People Weekly* (1984): 109.

22. F. McNulty, "Murder Was Her Last Resort," *Redbook*, no. 198 (November 1984).

23. L. Randolph, "Battered Women," *Ebony* 49, no. 11 (1994): 112.

24. R. Lipsyte, "O. J. Syndrome," *American Health* (1994): 50.

25. F. Hermelin, "Women's Shelters: Demand Up, Donations Down," *Working Woman* 19, no. 11 (1994): 9.

26. J. Smolowe and A. Blackman, "When Violence Hits Home" (Cover Story), *Time* 144, no. 1 (1994): 18.

27. K. Dunn, "Truth Abuse," *New Republic* 211, no. 5 (1994): 16.

28. F. Bruning, "Wife Beating—A Nation's Obsession," *Maclean's* 107, no. 30 (1994): 11.

29. T. Namuth, "When Did He Stop Beating His Wife?" (Cover Story), *Newsweek* 123, no. 26 (1994): 21.

30. M. Nemeth and W. Lowther, "Hot Off the Presses," *Maclean's* 107, no. 4 (1994): 66.

31. J. Seligmann and F. Chideya, "Bobbitts: Temporary Insanity," *Newsweek* 123, no. 5 (1994): 54.

32. B. Johnson, "The Male Myth" (Cover Story), *Maclean's* 107, no. 5 (1994): 38.

33. H. Stein, "Separation Anxiety," *Men's Health* 8, no. 8 (1993): 28.

34. A. Gross, "A Question of Rape," *Ladies' Home Journal* 110, no. 11 (1993): 170.

35. Ibid.

36. B. Hewitt, L. Stambler, R. Arias, V. Bane, J. Dodd, C. Clark, and F. Swertlow, "Can He Escape His Lies?" (Cover Story), *People* 62, no. 15 (2004): 66.

37. K. Breslau, R. Ricitiello, and B. Jackson, "She Glitters, but Is She Really Gold?" *Newsweek* 144, no. 8 (2004): 31.

38. Op. cit. K. Breslau, R. Ricitiello, and B. Jackson, "Why We Watched," *Newsweek* 144, no. 21 (2004): 44.

39. K. Browne, "A Buried Statistic," *Ms. Magazine* 14, no. 3 (2004): 18.

Chapter 5

Domestic Violence and Victim Empowerment Folklore in Popular Culture

Nancy Berns

Once upon a time there was a battered woman who lived with her abuser.... Do you know the rest of the story?

I should have known there would be violence in the children's play at my daughter's school because it was based on "Snow White." Naively, though, I had thought because it was for children, it would be gentle. I was wrong. High school students in a children's theater program had adapted the classic story for all the elementary schools in town. I looked around as the play unfolded. The children were engrossed, even scared at times. I also watched the reactions of the adults in the room. Was I the only one disturbed by the frequent use of words like "kill her," "she must die," and "I will put an end to her"? The knife was fake, and the character only raised the knife above Snow White's head, stopping short of actually killing her. The dramatic effect came from the threat, the possibility that he would kill her. At some schools in this district, a student wielding a fake knife could be suspended under a zero-tolerance policy. I was struck by the irony. So long as it was considered entertainment, the fake knife was not only acceptable in the play, but its use also appeared to meet with adult approval.

Fairy tales are full of violent acts, creepy characters, winsome heroes, and happily-ever-after endings. They are frequently accepted as folklore, part of a normal childhood. Academic studies have occasionally assessed how fairy tales perpetuate gender stereotypes. But they have rarely targeted the lessons they convey about violence. In any case, literary criticism seldom reaches a nonacademic audience. Even if it did, I suspect many people brush off fairy tale violence as just that, as pretend. Fun. Harmless. In the end, the hero (or, less frequently, the heroine), triumphs over evil, sometimes using violence to do so. We celebrate the happy ending but do not question the means used to get there, the narrative of a triumph achieved through violence.

This chapter is not about fairly tales per se but rather tales of domestic violence. Yet I suggest that our stereotypical media images and the dominant public understanding of domestic violence have a lot in common with fairy tales. The characters are introduced: a victim and a villain. The plot is propelled forward, often with acts of violence. The plots I examine have a twist on the usual formula: the victim has to become the heroine and rescue herself. To do this, she must become "empowered." Then she lives happily ever after. The story celebrates the end of the abuse, but the abuser is a minor character or may not even make an appearance. The violence also seems incidental, a mere means to propel the story toward its positive conclusion. This is an outline of the most common domestic violence narrative found in our mass media. It is a story about what I term "victim empowerment"—a key motif in American domestic violence folklore. I use the term folklore to refer generally to cultural stories that are shaped over time and passed along through various avenues, including media and everyday conversations. Domestic violence folklore reflects people's "common knowledge" about domestic violence: part "true story," part myth, part hope, part politics.

This chapter draws from my research on domestic violence in popular media and everyday discourse. For this research I systematically examined articles about domestic violence found in women's, men's, political, news, and other types of magazines. This chapter includes examples from these articles to illustrate my points, as well as examples from other media. I focused on media because research suggests that most people rely on media as a main source of information about social problems like domestic violence. For many issues, people use the media as their only resource for considering social problems. This is not surprising if you just look around. Think of the easy access we have to television, radio, newspapers, movies, the Internet, books, and magazines. From these resources, individuals construct their own conceptions of what is normal and acceptable. Since media images contribute heavily to public understanding, it is important to consider the stories they tell about domestic violence. (For more information on the importance of narratives, see Donileen Loseke's chapter in this volume.)

I will use the term "frame" as both a noun and a verb to discuss these stories. The term has been adopted from the work of sociologist Erving Goffman to describe how people identify, interpret, understand, and label their experiences. Frames provide a way for people to make sense of their experiences. We might think of this type of framing as similar to the framing a photographer does when deciding how to compose a shot. The photographer tells a particular story about a scenic landscape by focusing on, say, a single blooming flower. A lot of information will be left outside that frame. Another photographer (or the same one on another shot) may instead take pictures of herd of deer, or a mountain range on the horizon, or the sky. Each composition involves making a decision to focus on some things while leaving out other things. One of the main findings of my research is that the stories we tell about domestic violence focus on, or frame, victims of domestic violence while leaving out offenders and structural, cultural, and institutional factors that contribute to violence. One of the most popular versions of this story is the "victim empowerment perspective," or "victim empowerment frame." After describing this perspective, I will explain why it emerged as the most popular perspective and why that is a problem.

VICTIM EMPOWERMENT FOLKLORE

One of the most important themes in American domestic violence folklore is victim empowerment. The victim empowerment story is sympathetic to victims and yet holds them responsible for solving their problem. Victim empowerment is the most common perspective on domestic violence in mass entertainment television, movies, and magazines as well as a frequent frame found on the Internet and overheard in everyday conversations.[1] This perspective portrays domestic violence as a private problem and, more specifically, the victim's problem and charges her alone with solving it. (I use gendered language in describing the victim and abuser because the majority of victims of domestic violence are women and their abusers more typically men. Furthermore, most stories in the media about domestic violence reflect this pattern. Significantly, men are also victims. I do not mean to downplay that occurrence.)

If you read enough of them, you find a pattern in media accounts of domestic violence that is as familiar as a fairy tale. For the purposes of this chapter, I divide the victim empowerment narrative structure into four parts. First, the characters and situation are introduced. Most stories about domestic violence begin with the abuse victim's situation, including how the couple got together and the early signs of abuse. This orients us to the story from the vantage of the victim's experience. Particularly in women's magazine articles, TV talk shows, and movies, we may also learn something about the victim's life before the abuse starts and how she got involved in the abusive situation. Even in this foreshadowing, we get a hint that the victim has some responsibility for getting involved in an abusive situation. Next, the problem is presented. In domestic violence stories, the problem is abuse. We are told how and when the abuse started and given some horrific examples of it. The third, and most consequential segment, involves the rise of the heroine and the resolution of the problem. This is the crux of the victim empowerment narrative: when we learn how the victim gained the courage to end the abuse, usually by going to counseling and/or by simply leaving. The fairy tale ends with the heroine and others she rescued, such as her children, living happily ever after. The message is unambiguous: like the heroine, other victims can enjoy the same happy ending if they only assume responsibility for being abused, take back their power, and change their lives.

The following sections concentrate on the third part of the victim empowerment narrative, the transformation of the abused woman into a heroine. Though this frame is in many ways sympathetic to the victim, it also holds her responsible for solving the problem. Though others may advise or counsel her, she has to rescue herself. After describing this story in more detail, I will explain why this particular frame dominates media accounts of domestic violence.

Rescue Yourself: Victim Empowerment

In the victim empowerment story, the battered woman is encouraged, and at times berated, to finally wake up. The awakening of the victim, so the story goes, consists of the realization that something needs to change and that this will only happen if she takes control of the situation. She needs to take back the power. By not leaving the relationship, she is allowing herself to be abused. The examples here are from *Essence* and *Redbook*.

> Making a decision to leave your home and a life of abuse will be difficult. Your husband may even try to stop you, but you must take action now! Abused wives must come out of the closet and put an end to this terrible practice.[2]
>
> "Don't be a victim," Dr. Briggs said. I knew he was talking to me. "If you don't like your life, fix it. Don't feel sorry for yourself. It will destroy you. If you want to be happy, accept responsibility for your own lives.[3]

One battered woman told readers in *McCall's*, "I'll never shake my fear of him, but if I've learned anything from all of this, it's that women cannot allow themselves to be silenced by abusive men."[4]

Typically, something dramatic happens to awaken the victim. An article in *Glamour* describes such a breaking point:

> A woman involved in a violent courtship can break that cycle and change her life, if something happens to make her want to. She may be so badly beaten that she fears she will die. Or she may simply wake up one morning and decide that she's had enough.[5]

Personal testimonials are presented that illustrate how a particularly violent act makes women finally ready to leave or get help, as in this story from *Glamour*.

> ... the marriage had ended for me forever the moment I felt the blade of the knife against my throat. I'd wanted to leave Steve before, but that night I knew I had to leave him. I realized then that it was beyond my power to save him, but that I must save myself.[6]

The testimonials show current victims they have the power to stop the abuse, if only they would use it. Moreover, these stories are filled with self-recrimination and guilt about waiting so long. The not-so-subtle subtext here is that women who wait or fail to act decisively can be blamed for not doing more to stop the abuse. So the reader is urged not only to think, "If she did it, I can too," but also "if I don't act now, I am foolish." Here is one of those cautionary quotes from *Essence*:

> "The signs that he would one day attack me were everywhere, but I ignored them," she says. "I didn't love myself enough to end it. I accepted his 'I'm sorry's,' his tears, his candy, and I went back into the lion's den every time."[7]

A victim's anger is turned inward rather than at the abusive partner or situation, as illustrated in the following quotes from *McCall's* and *Teen*.

> "A lot of my anger now is directed toward myself," she told me recently. "I'm mad at *me*, I didn't have to stick around and be abused all those years!"[8]
> I'm not bitter. I don't blame Jake for everything that happened in our relationship. I hold myself responsible for my own actions and choices. Forgiving myself has been the hardest part.[9]

Victims are portrayed as being confused as to why they let the abuse continue. This is true even of professionals who are acquainted with domestic violence, as is illustrated in this *Essence* article:

> Even now I'm baffled that I allowed the abuse to continue for so long— and all while I prosecuted other abusers. I now listen to the advice I have so often given to other women: No one can steal my dignity and self-worth unless I give them up.[10]

Formerly battered women tell their painful stories to inspire others to act and not be as "foolish" as the author in these articles from *Good Housekeeping* and *Ladies' Home Journal*.

> That's why I decided to write about my experience ... in the hope that other women who may be secretly suffering as I did will be helped by

knowing that they are not alone. There is something that can be done about ending marital violence.[11]

These memories are painful to recollect, but perhaps other women out there reading this will sigh in relief to find they are not the only ones who made foolish choices, then even more foolishly stood by them. More important, perhaps they will be moved to get help and get out.[12]

Most women's magazine articles, many domestic violence movies, and frequent talk show episodes about the topic claim to empower and inspire current victims of abuse to solve their problem by taking charge of their life. Of course, this is a common theme in self-help literature generally, whatever the problem. And, in fact, the women in the stories do achieve "success" by solving their problem, becoming what the historian Linda Gordon calls "heroes of their own lives." As in the following *Good Housekeeping* fragment, most stories show how much better the victim is doing since she left.

I want victims of emotional abuse to know that a new start *is* possible. I didn't realize just how miserable I was until I got out of my abusive situation. Shortly after the divorce, Robert moved away. My friends tell me that I rarely smiled in the later years of my marriage, but now I smile all the time. I've also begun dating. But I no longer tolerate certain behaviors.[13]

Healing—and preventing a subsequent abusive relationship—often includes figuring out why women let the abuse happen, often with the help of a professional.

Seeing a therapist is also crucial to making a new life for myself. It's not enough to just escape Dave. I need to understand who I was when I was with him and why I put up with the abuse if I really want to make sure I never get in that kind of relationship again. I just keep telling myself, 'Today I'm strong enough for today, and tomorrow I'll be strong enough for tomorrow.' I've been through so much already, and it's time to start living life for me.[14]

"Life after abuse" articles began appearing in women's magazines in the 1990s, presumably to allay the fears of women in currently abusive relationships that such a life was not possible. Although these stories also recount the abuse women suffered and how they got out, their inspirational core comes from what the former victim is doing now, and usually includes helping other abused women. "Life after abuse" articles complete the picture of the battered woman as the hero of her own life. The empowerment perspective frames the victim as heroic—but only if she solves her problem.

Victim Empowerment Becomes Folk Wisdom

Victim self-empowerment is not only the most common theme in women's magazine articles about domestic violence, but also pervades the coverage of domestic violence by other media and everyday talk. Made-for-TV movies about domestic violence such as those presented on the Lifetime cable station feature individual women who have escaped abuse. Even such otherwise compelling Hollywood films such as *Sleeping with the Enemy* (Ruben, 1991) and *Enough* (Apted, 2002) clearly identify abuse as the victim's problem and dramatize how she solved it.

Television talk shows are another popular format in which victim empowerment stories become folk wisdom. Whether these shows feature the pop psychology of hosts like Dr. Phil or Oprah or outside "experts," the same message is given to guests and to the viewing audience. Victims need to wake up, reclaim their power, and acknowledge how they are allowing themselves to be abused. Notes of empathy may creep in. But the message is often presented as an admonition as well as counsel, as if the victim's failure to act is a character flaw. Sometimes the victim's role in the abuse is portrayed as subtle. In other cases, victims are blamed for actually provoking the abuse. Phil McGraw, or Dr. Phil, is a television talk-show host and author of several best-selling books. During an episode he did jointly with Oprah, Dr. Phil asked women who were being emotionally abused by their partners what they were doing that told the men they could do this. The men were "getting away" with the abuse only because victims were signaling that it was acceptable. Oprah also told the women to stand up for themselves and regain their power. In the following excerpt, Dr. Phil begins by addressing the abuser and then quickly turns to the victim's role in the abuse:

Dr. Phil: "Any man who goes home and closes a door and abuses his wife and children is a coward and a bully. Do you get that?
Jimmy: "I get it."
Dr. Phil: "You get that. If you do that, you're nothing but a coward and a bully and you choose where to do it where it's safe, because you don't do it down at some biker bar, do you? You don't do it at [your] job where they can fire you. You don't do it with somebody like me. You want to abuse me? That's not going to happen, is it? Because I don't teach you to do that. And you've [looking to the victim] taught him to do that and you need to teach him otherwise. And it isn't about being 6'4" and 230. It's about having a spirit that says 'I'm not going to take this from you.' And more importantly, Jimmy, you've got to say 'I'm not going to take this from me.' Because when you look in the mirror after that, how do you feel?"
Jimmy: "I feel bad."[15]

While Dr. Phil does send a clear message that the man is a bully, the ultimate responsibility lies with the victim who has taught him that he can get away with abusing her. When the victim seems confused about how she contributed to the abuse, Oprah joins in with a forceful voice on victim responsibility.

Unidentified Woman: Honestly, I don't know what I've done to create this. I mean, I know that . . .

Dr. Phil: You have to figure out what am I doing to set this up that way, because you can send a message. You can send a message, treat me with dignity and respect or not.

Unidentified Woman: I don't know. I really don't know how I've set it all up.

Oprah: Doggone it, this ticks me off. You know why? It ticks me off because you're not taking responsibly for your own life and your own situation.[16]

Note how Oprah's anger is now focused on the victim, a pose with which her abusive partner can identify. This dynamic intensifies when Dr. Phil invites the abuser to blame the victim for his actions.

Dr. Phil: Tell us, Jimmy, why do you do this at home instead of at work?

Jimmy: Because she stays there and takes it.

Dr. Phil: Duh!

Here, the victim empowerment story is illustrated by negative example. The victimized woman demonstrates the truth of self-empowerment by failing to embrace it, showing that she is flawed. One wonders what messages viewers get. Are they encouraged to take back their power in relationships? Or do they feel that their instinctive sense of fear and powerlessness in the face of abuse is a weakness of which they should be shamed? Are they more or less likely to come forward for help?

The rest of this chapter examines why this perspective emerged so prominently and why it is a problem.

WHO IS BEHIND THE CURTAIN?: EDITORIAL GUIDELINES

In the *Wizard of Oz*, when Dorothy is frustrated with the wizard, her dog Toto pulls back the curtain, exposing an ordinary man controlling a giant mechanical head. The wizard instructs Dorothy and her friends to "Pay no attention to that man behind the curtain!"

If media stories of domestic violence appear as first-person victim narratives, there is always someone else behind the curtain to whom we should pay attention. The writers, editors, and others who produce media stories frame social problems to please advertisers as well as to sell magazines or attract viewers. To explain why the victim empowerment narrative is constructed in the ways that it is, I draw on my interviews with editors and an in-depth analysis of writers' advice guides.

Four main guidelines shape almost all articles for women's magazines: service, empowerment, personal stories, and uplifting endings. Editors said they are there to provide resources, tools, inspiration, and hope for their readers. They claim to serve women by "empowering" them. Editors keep it personal: focusing on one woman's story rather than more comprehensive, social complexities of any issue. Keeping the articles primarily about one woman helps achieve their goal of empowering women and maintaining uplifting endings. These guidelines capture the essence of the victim empowerment model and why social problems are turned into inspiration.

Service and Empowerment

The belief that they are providing a service is one key to why articles about abuse in women's magazines emphasize empowerment. An editor for *Essence* contrasted service-oriented articles with those that were merely sensational and titillating, insisting they would always "include some kind of resource or resources that would help people figure out how to get help or prevent abuse." At *Ladies' Home Journal*, an editor described their mission: "We inform, inspire, and educate women. That is really our goal."

As in fairy tales, at some point in a magazine article we find out who is responsible for solving the problem. In most articles about abuse in women's magazines, the victim is the one held responsible. The editorial buzzword for this perspective is empowerment. A *Good Housekeeping* editor said that empowerment was "absolutely core to our mission." When I probed what she meant, she defined empowerment as giving women the "tools, resources, understanding, knowledge to make the best decisions for their lives. This is true whether they are buying a washing machine or seeing their daughter in an abusive dating relationship." In other words, empowerment is the main service they provide. And empowerment includes a strong dose of self-help. According to an editor from *Ladies' Home Journal*, "I think that with this issue [domestic violence] the most important thing to say [is] that if you are a victim, don't take it anymore. Get out. Get out of the situation."

Keeping It Personal and Positive

In addition to service and empowerment, editors of women's magazines emphasize personal narratives and upbeat endings. Editors describe their favorite storytelling technique as "one-on-one," which allows the reader to have a personal relationship with the victim. *Good Housekeeping*'s most popular category of articles is the dramatic narrative in which a woman describes a problem she has overcome en route to providing education or inspiration for others who face similar problems. The emphasis is on the individual's personal strategy, not larger dimensions of change. When I asked the *Good Housekeeping* editor why they did not cover social and cultural aspects of domestic violence, she said, "That's not our role. We are a women's magazine."

Individualism and personal drama underlie popular culture, which the media draw on and support. So it is not surprising to find this emphasis in a majority of the domestic violence articles in women's magazines. An editor from *McCall's* explained that people want simple solutions.

> The subtext of many of these stories is that the individual can solve her problem. These magazines are not looking at problems of these kinds in a societal or cultural context. They're just not. I would imagine that editors think it would be too overwhelming for readers to think that there are all these cultural forces kind of arrayed against them. They don't want to hear that we live in a culture of violence. They like to know that by doing steps one through five they can get out of a lousy situation.

My analysis of magazine articles and reports from editors suggests that the number of comprehensive articles on the social and cultural contexts of domestic violence declined in the 1990s. In the 1970s, the problem of domestic violence was "new." The battered women movement introduced the problem to the public, and editors considered it news to write about the broad scope of the problem and the complex, intertwining issues. Within a few years, however, they assumed that readers were familiar with domestic violence and encouraged writers to target a single, narrow aspect of the problem.

In addition to providing service, empowering victims, and keeping it personal, editors of these magazines think that their readers want to be inspired, entertained, and uplifted by reading their magazine. Particularly with an issue like domestic violence, anything less than a positive ending feels like a "downer." *Good Housekeeping*'s editor explained that a positive resolution is important to good storytelling and to the empowerment message. "If you leave people unresolved and adrift, it is not going to give the reader the sense that she can also take charge in her life." A *McCall's* editor was even more explicit. She told me, "A positive ending is really important in women's magazines because editors feel that readers need to be given some hope that their situations can be changed. Women readers need to be given some hope that they can solve their problems in some way on their own. Readers don't like downers." *Essence*'s editor said that a positive resolution is so important because "if you are reading it and you are in an abusive situation, we want you to feel like you can get out. We want people to feel like it is possible to get out of an abusive situation."

In order to have happy endings, stories almost always feature women who have successfully ended their abuse—either through counseling or leaving the relationship through an act of will. Like most fairy tales, magazine articles using a victim empowerment frame give a skewed perspective of what most domestic violence victims experience. As readers of this chapter are probably aware, the reality for most abuse victims involves far more than a "stay" or "leave" option. In fact, the vast majority of abuse victims do separate from their abusive partners, often many times. Typically, however, they are drawn back into the relationship. Sometimes this is because of their own emotional ambivalence, concerns about their children, fear of being alone, or hope that their partner will change. Often, however, little changes when they separate because the abusive partner continues to stalk or harass them and may even step up his violence, an important reason that separation (or even talk of separation) is widely viewed as the most dangerous time for abused women. Studies show that victims' attempts to leave a relationship often result in escalating violence because the abuser becomes more desperate to maintain control. From this vantage, staying or leaving are not the end points they appear to be in personal stories of heroism, but tactical maneuvers within an ongoing process of disengagement, each step of which must be carefully calculated in terms of the relative risks it poses to the woman and/or her children. In taking such critical decisions out of their real-world social and cultural context, indeed by abstracting them even from the particular risks they pose in a given relationship, the empowerment narrative actually misinforms readers, including those who are currently being abused, and trivializes the important concerns that frame real-world decision-making.

SETTING THE STAGE FOR VICTIM EMPOWERMENT

Folklore both reflects and shapes popular culture. Several cultural trends have emerged in the past few decades influencing the emphasis on victim empowerment.

The Rise of Domestic Violence as a Victim's Social Problem

Social conditions that could be described as social problems are never in short supply. How and why public understandings of some social problems emerge is the work of social problem scholars. Though domestic violence has been around since Cain and Abel, it did not emerge as a "public" social problem until the 1970s. It is helpful to study the beginning of this movement to better understand why victims have become the central characters in most talk about domestic violence.

In the 1970s, a small group of activists wanted to raise awareness about domestic violence and therefore started what we now call the battered women's movement. The activists framed the problem in a way that emphasized the needs of battered women to end abuse, not the need to hold abusers accountable. Though the activists in this movement wanted to draw attention to the cultural and structural factors that contributed to domestic violence, the political context of the time made it difficult to focus on more than getting help for the victims. Battered women's movement activists wanted to exonerate victims from blame, identify abusers, locate abuse within the social and cultural context, and specify community responses and help for the victim.

The battered women's movement has three major assumptions. First, victims should not be blamed for the abuse they receive. Second, domestic violence is primarily a problem of men abusing women. Third, domestic violence is one component of a patriarchal system that includes other forms of discrimination against women. Local communities and the government were not comfortable with the argument that wife-beating was a result of a cultural and structural system of gender discrimination. In order to secure funding and support, many feminists had to censor their own political positions. Eventually, shelter founders from the feminist movement lost much of their control of many shelters, which drew more support from churches, community groups, and social services. Clinical language, psychotherapeutic intervention, and professional social workers took over many of the shelters.

Due to this political context and to the movement's initial focus on the needs of victims, the recognition of domestic violence as a social problem emerged as an issue about the victims. The battered women's movement also played a crucial role in shaping public and media understanding of domestic violence as a social problem about victims. I am not arguing that this is wrong or that it should have or even could have been done differently. Victims continue to need the resources provided by shelters and other programs. However, it is also important to recognize what happens when we fail to talk about abusers and the cultural and structural contexts of abuse. The battered women's movement is not the only event shaping the victim empowerment perspective. Other social movements and trends in popular culture have powerfully shaped our focus on victims.

Popular Culture: Framing Social Problems as Entertainment

Popular culture, including talk shows, movies, and television shows, has introduced formats and rhetoric that frame the victim. In the 1960s and 1970s, a new "pop psychology" emerged that popularized guidelines for how to help yourself heal after traumatic events. The self-help movement has also exploded into the world of television talk shows. Oprah's "change-your-life TV" and Dr. Phil's show lead the way in showing people how to "regain their power" and change their own lives. This pop psychology helped frame the victim as a cultural object to fix and opened up new narratives for victimization, healing, and the central role of therapeutic stories. Today most talk shows, movies, and news coverage about crime and other social problems include the victim as a central character and use emotions to drive the story. This reflects a larger shift in journalism to what the critic David Altheide calls infotainment. The past three decades have seen the rise of social problems as entertainment in the form of tabloid news and reality crime programs. Producers see victims, conflict, and emotion as keys to getting people to watch their shows.

The drive to make news entertaining and more profitable has resulted in news *as* entertainment. When television and other media adopted this format, they shifted the emphasis from gathering and presenting information to personifying news in ways that elicited intense emotional responses. "Capturing a sob, seeing tears flow down cheeks, looking into the eyes of the interviewee during tight camera shots merged as critical features of the message and, in some cases, the most important part of the report."[17]

Where once a clear distinction existed between drama and news, producers increasingly harvest social problems as a primary source of drama and sensationalism. Nowhere is this more evident than in the television talk show. Kathe Lowney compares talk shows to early religious revivals because of their interplay of personalized social problems, drama, confession, and salvation. Talk shows represent social problems by featuring victims and victimizers who are encouraged to enact their conflicts in full view of the audience. "Talk show staffs see social actors in conflict as creating 'good television,' for their disputes often involve dramatic tension, confrontation, and emotion."[18] Laura Grindstaff worked at two talk shows while conducting her ethnographic research. She explains that these shows are produced with one goal in mind: the money shot, which she defines as "concrete, physical evidence of real, raw emotion."[19] Producers work hard to lead guests to emotional outbursts, often achieved through the exploitation of sensitive, intimate, and volatile topics.

Media producers are more concerned with having a dramatic impact on their audiences in order to entertain them rather than to inform them. This is a stark contrast from past journalistic values that saw interviews as research and believed the story should be guided by the experts' information rather than preconceived notions of the story. The emphasis on interviewing or hosting guests has shifted from gathering information to satisfying entertainment goals that stress impact, shock, drama, twists, and morality plays.

A similar shift from gathering and disseminating information to producing entertainment can be seen in the advice given about writing for popular magazines. Today's writers' guidebooks place much less emphasis on in-depth research and using experts for information than on using experts to legitimate a preconceived story.

These changes not only affect how we are entertained, but also how we think about the causes of and solutions to social problems. This, in turn, affects not only how victims understand their predicament, but the kind of programs or solutions nonabused persons are likely to support as well as how they treat abused persons in their social network. As we have seen, the reduction of complex social issues like domestic violence into emotion-laden and simplistic morality tales of individual heroism is a conscious strategy by media producers designed to maximize revenues through infotainment. By comparison, the truth of domestic violence victimization is depressing.

A FAIRY-TALE ENDING: WHY VICTIM EMPOWERMENT IS A PROBLEM

Stripping the Politics from Victim Empowerment Exposes the Victim

"Victim empowerment" is the term I use to refer to the frame that saturates mass media, such as women's magazines and talk shows. However, the idea of empowerment did not originate with these media, and many scholars argue that an adequate theory of empowerment must go beyond the personal story. The concept of empowerment does not have to be primarily about the individual.

Empowerment has been a core principle of social work practice for decades. Here, as in the feminist literature, empowerment is a necessary response to the powerlessness that results when structural and institutional inequality deprives groups of power and control over basic resources. Empowerment describes the process by which individuals and groups come to understand the sources of their powerlessness and mobilize to achieve social justice. The social work literature describes three levels of empowerment: personal, interpersonal, and political. Each level of empowerment sets the stage for the next. Personal empowerment involves recognizing and identifying the power one already has. At the interpersonal level, people increase their skills at influencing others. Political empowerment involves social action and a process of transferring power between groups.

The political level of empowerment includes an understanding that different groups in our society possess different levels of power and control over social resources. Although empowerment is a means to help individuals overcome the effects of powerlessness in this model, its overall goal of achieving social justice and reducing social inequality is critical to the success of empowerment at an individual level. It is this critical piece that is absent from the notion of empowerment adapted by popular media. This is not merely an intellectual omission. By obscuring the institutional inequalities that make certain groups more vulnerable to victimization than other groups, as well as the fact that members of groups so disadvantaged are also less able to mobilize the resources needed to regain control over their lives, the media also misrepresent the realistic options open to abuse victims, increasing their risk.

The mass media also discuss power. However, they present power as a personal choice, something abuse victims can put on or take off at will. On talk shows and in women's magazines, victims are told to "take back the power" to "take charge of their life." But this idea of empowerment depoliticizes power, stripping it of its structural, cultural, historical, and gendered contexts. In this currently fashionable version, empowerment refers only to "individual self-assertion, upward mobility, or the psychological experience of 'feeling powerful.' "[20] Nowhere to be found are the ways in which gender socialization, patriarchy, the structure of family and society, and cultural tolerance of violence shape a victim's experience or constrain her options. Articles in liberal political magazines such as *The Progressive* and *The Nation* do address the political level of empowerment. But these media have niche markets and smaller circulations. For example, *Good Housekeeping* and *Ladies' Home Journal* each have over four *million* paid subscribers, which dwarfs the number of paid subscriptions at *The Nation* (at 150,000) and *The Progressive* (at 60,000).[21] And even women's magazines have a small audience compared to Oprah.

The movements organized in the 1960s and 1970s to support victims of rape or domestic violence or other forms of social oppression made it easier for people to identify themselves as victims. And advocates, such as those involved in the battered women's movement, wanted to use the label of victim empowerment to exonerate victims from blame, identify those responsible for the violence, locate the abuse within the social and cultural context, and specify community responses that could help victims. Again, the popular media take the same concept, victimization in this case, and employ it in their own style of storytelling. While advocates are framing a social problem in a way that they think will help them achieve the desired responses to the problem, the media are framing the problem in a way that will please their audience, be compatible with entertainment, and help ratings.

The principles and guidelines that shape mass-media stories emphasize the purely personal, dramatic, and uplifting. To the battered women's movement, the aim of describing victimization was to elicit public sympathy and institutional support for victims and to highlight the culpability of those who inflict it. But in the media story, the perpetrator's only role is to create the dilemma from which the woman must rescue herself in an inspirational act of heroism. Apart from this, he is missing.

The Moral of the Story: Why Doesn't She Leave?

People may be shocked by the explicit blame put on victims of domestic violence with questions such as "What did she do to provoke him?" or statements like "She deserved it." Although ostensibly more sympathetic to victims, "it happened to me" articles also imply they are ultimately responsible for their abuse. They do this both by implying that those who fail to follow the example of heroism recounted in the story are somehow inadequate and by telling victims to find solutions within themselves. The messages are: "Change your personality." "Increase your self-esteem." "Take control of your life." "Refuse to be a victim." "You have the power to end the abuse." The victim's experience is set within a narrow personal context from which not only the role of the abuser but also of society is largely absent, severely restricting our view of the domestic violence landscape. By implying that any woman could just leave if she really wanted to, the victim empowerment fairy tale reinforces the question "Why doesn't she just leave?" Not asked, and so never answered, is "Why does he abuse her?" or "How does our society foster the abuse?"

The victim empowerment folklore is not the only story told about domestic violence in the media. But it is far and away the most influential. In the past three decades, there has been an explosion of attention and social science research on the topic of domestic violence. This research ranges from the psychological studies of victims and abusers to sociological and feminist research that has advanced our understanding of how domestic violence relates to structural and cultural factors, such as society's tolerance for violence, structural power arrangements, and gender socialization. Even though academic theories have advanced our understanding of domestic violence to include structural and cultural factors, public understanding of domestic violence focuses primarily on the individual or psychological level.

It is important to analyze how the media frame victims because people use the media to understand social problems. The media are the gatekeepers for advocates who are trying to get their claims to the public. Media portrayals of social problems affect common understandings of the problem, which spill over into individual responses by police officers, judges, jurors, lawyers, clergy, friends, family, and counselors. These individual understandings are also used in making laws, developing policy, and creating prevention programs.

Given the role of the media in shaping public opinion, it is hardly surprising that public opinion about domestic violence lags far behind research. The victim empowerment frame normalizes the idea that the victim should be held responsible for solving her problem. It ignores the social and cultural barriers that victims face, including the need for shelter, law enforcement protection, employment, childcare, and family support. With the current media primarily framing the victim of domestic violence, the source of harm is generally ignored, resulting in very little public debate on why abusers abuse.

More people today than in the past recognize the suffering battered women endure, the complicated dynamics that typify abusive relationships, and why it may be hard for a victim to leave an abusive relationship. These changes are undoubtedly related to sympathetic accounts of abuse in the media. At the same time, even those who say domestic violence is wrong believe it is justified in some circumstances and "private" in others, and many hold the victim personally responsible for solving, and in some cases, for causing the problem. The media's sole focus on victims has also affected how the public views the best policy response. When asked about how we should respond to domestic violence, the majority of the public favor counseling services over alternative policies, such as stiffer penalties for batterers or any changes in structural and cultural factors that foster violence.[22] Thus, even as the media have helped make the tragedy of domestic violence and the dilemmas faced by battered women more visible, they have also helped obscure the source of the problem—the abusive partner, cultural and political contexts, and the most effective antidotes.

Deleted Scenes and Alternative Endings

The special features on DVDs often include deleted scenes or alternative endings. Viewers can imagine how the story would be different with these deleted portions added. In commentaries, the writer or director may explain why they chose particular scenes or images to tell their story. We realize that with other decisions in the scripts and edits, we would have watched a different movie. The situation involving domestic violence coverage by the media is similar, with alternative scenes, key characters, and different and more realistic endings lying on the cutting room floor. The challenge is to recover and reinsert this lost material, even if the resulting story line is more complicated, even if it is more depressing, than the happily-ever-after resolution.

Violence is already an everyday part of the entertainment and news we consume. The public seems less shocked that people are abusive or violent toward their loved ones than that the victims of this violence "take it" or fail to leave. Ironically, the fact that there are now more resources available for victims than there were previously adds to pressure for them to "just leave" and to the propensity for people to blame them if they do not.

What kind of new story do we need to change the questions people ask to "Why do people abuse others?" or "Why can they get away with that?" and to shift the focus of their disapproval from victims to abusers? The "added" scenes might highlight the ways violence and other forms of abuse play out in women's everyday lives rather than only in the most extreme instances. We need a heightened awareness of common abusive strategies. Stories should disclose the way abusers think and operate and show how well they manipulate situations, deny the harm, and minimize the problems. We need in-depth looks at how people first started using abuse, why they use violence and control strategies, and how they continue to get away with it.

We need to hear the abuser's story as well as the victim's. Commentary could explain how abusers choose when and toward whom the abuse will happen and why, showing that for many abusive men, violence and control are rational and instrumental choices designed to elicit very specific benefits, some of them tangible, like money or sex, and some symbolic, like a sense that they are more "manly" if they can control "their" woman. These scenes would challenge the belief that the victim "made me do it." These scenes need not be depressing. Portraying abuse as a behavior men learn to achieve specific ends offers hope because it suggests they can unlearn those strategies, master alternative ways to resolve conflicts, and learn to deal with their need to feel powerful or to discharge frustration—something women need as well—in nonabusive ways. These stories will not appeal to everyone. But they offer real hope that violence can be significantly reduced in everyday life.

Finally, we need more scenes that put domestic violence in its social context, that portray how the larger culture teaches us to tolerate and even to positively sanction the use of violence, particularly against women. If there is to be a fairy tale, let it include heroes who stand up against the culture of violence, resist its messages, confront those who use it to harm innocent others, and exhibit alternative means to transcend a sense of powerlessness. Can we create an environment in which the abuser's circle of friends, his employer, family, church, media, law enforcement, and colleagues send a consistent message that abuse will not be tolerated? This need not mean abandoning stories of personal empowerment. But it does mean that personal empowerment will be linked to the politics of empowerment, the transformation of the attitudes, and institutional responses to the use of violence.

CONCLUSIONS

Mass media continue to portray domestic violence as the victim's personal problem, which can be solved through empowering her. The "unfolding drama" has a beginning and an end—complete with dramatic images and descriptions of bruises, injuries, trauma, personal histories and characteristics, and acts of violence, including self-defense. The victim empowerment frame explains what a victim can and should do to solve the problem. Public responses to the problem are portrayed through psychological language and solutions. The "social problem" of domestic violence is replaced with syndromes, profiles, risk factors, and portrayals of women with low self-esteem, dependence, and related individual characteristics or pathologies. Counseling and advising (even telling) the victim to leave the relationship are the most common solutions in the media. The tragedy of abuse is ended by heroic acts of separation or escape. Marketing fears play a role in the marginalization of perspectives that emphasize the social and cultural context of domestic violence. Personal dramatic stories sell more newspapers, magazines, and movies than stories about the more complex social and political dynamics of a problem. The victim's dramatic story of rising from tragedy to happiness and success evokes sympathy, identification, and inspiration.

The victim empowerment perspective depoliticizes our understanding of power and hinders our understanding of how people learn to be abusive and why they continue to get away with this behavior. I have outlined the dimensions of the alternative story that media need to put at the center of how they represent abuse.

Lest I be accused of proposing one fairy tale to replace another, let me end with a note of caution. It will not be easy to enlarge the narrative of domestic violence to include the stories of abusers and the roots of violence, to portray the everyday reality of living with abuse, to capture its complex social, political, and economic dynamics, or to highlight that prevention requires that the community as a whole (rather than just the victim) assumes responsibility for ending it.

Replacing the current folklore with an alternative story will elicit controversy, flak, and perhaps open hostility. This is to be expected. Advocates in the battered women's movement have learned to live with political opposition. It is undoubtedly easier for the media to convey the "fairy-tale happy ending" to victim stories than the unsettling message that our culture needs to change. Keeping stories individual and personal allows us to distance ourselves from their more unpleasant implications by insisting, "that's not me." Focusing on the political and social dimensions of a problem affects everyone.

It is important to continue providing support for victims and raising awareness of their experiences. But little is gained by doing this without also discussing the bigger picture. The personal happily-ever-after story may be simple to convey, even inspiring; but it so distorts the actual causes, dynamics, and supports for abuse that its ultimate effects are to conceal what is most important—the responsibility of abusive men for their actions—and refocus expectations for change solely on the victim. In the end, then, empowering victims is inseparable from disempowering abusers and reshaping the social and cultural contexts that support the abuse. This story, albeit somewhat more complex than the fairy tale of personal empowerment, has yet to be told.

NOTES

1. This chapter builds on my earlier research on media images of domestic violence. For more detailed information on this research, see N. Berns, *Framing the Victim: Domestic Violence, Media, and Social Problems* (New York: Aldine de Gruyter, 2004).

2. L. Frier Webb. "Battered Wife's Dilemma," *Essence* 14 (November 1987).

3. A. Kays. "The Four Words that Saved My Life," *Redbook* 78 (April 1997).

4. E. Golding and Ronny Frishman, "My Ex-Husband Harassed Me From Prison," *McCall's* 69 (February 1996).

5. N. Baker, "Why Women Stay with Men Who Beat Them," *Glamour* 367 (August 1983).

6. D. Lewis, "When Love Turns Violent," *Glamour* 259 (August 1990).

7. E. A. Bowman, "Wheel Power," *Essence* 146 (September 1998).

8. M. Rock, "How Could This Happen To My Friend?" *McCall's* 58 (April 1983).

9. "Boyfriend Abuse: Troubled Love," *Teen* 53 (May 1995).

10. S. J. Harrison, "Her Toughest Case," *Essence* 94 (August 1999).

11. "Our Home Was a Battlefield," *Good Housekeeping* 86 (1972).

12. P. Davis, "Dangerous Liaison," *Ladies' Home Journal* 70 (April 1998).

13. L. Burgdorff and J. Block. "Invisible Bruises," *Good Housekeeping*, 89. (May, 1996).

14. A. R. Vander Pluym, "My Boyfriend Abused Me," *Teen* 75 (April 1999).

15. *The Oprah Winfrey Show* (September 10, 2002) All-Time Best Dr. Phil Moments, 16.

16. *The Oprah Winfrey Show*, 17. op cit.

17. D. Altheide, *Creating Fear: News and the Construction of Crisis.* (New York: Aldine de Gruyter, 2002), 108.

18. K. Lowney, *Baring Our Souls: TV Talk Shows and the Religion of Recovery* (New York: Aldine de Gruyter, 1999), 40.

19. L. Grindstaff, *The Money Shot* (Chicago: The University of Chicago Press, 2002), 116.

20. S. Morgen and A. Bookman, *Women and the Politics of Empowerment* (Philadelphia: Temple University Press, 1988), 4.

21. Figures for *Good Housekeeping* and *Ladies' Home Journal* are based on reports ending June 30, 2002, as reported by the Audit Bureau of Circulations. Figures for the political magazines are for 2003 and are based on phone interviews with editors at the magazines.

22. E. Klein, J. Campbell, E. Soler, and M. Ghez, *Ending Domestic Violence* (Thousand Oaks, CA: Sage, 1999).

Chapter 6

Violent Video Games, Rape Myth Acceptance, and Negative Attitudes toward Women

Karen E. Dill

This chapter enters the growing debate about whether playing video games with antisocial themes can be harmful. My specific focus is gender stereotypes in gaming and whether the perpetuation of these stereotypes supports violence against women. If in the end, my answer is yes, violent video games based on sexist stereotypes do support male violence against women, I am less sure about the appropriate response. Censoring video game content, even for children, raises serious privacy concerns. Yet leaving the regulation of these games to parents is also problematic. The Associated Press reports that 35 percent of parents are gamers themselves. Unsurprisingly, two-thirds of these parents say it is not the government's role to protect children from violent video games. If we cannot rely on the government or parents to monitor game playing, what can we do? Before we can even debate this question intelligently, we need to map the terrain.

If you have no experience with video games or your experience is limited, say to *Mario* or *Minesweeper*, odds are that you would be surprised by many of today's top video games and the latest gaming trends. Did you know, for instance, that there are now "virtual communities" on the Internet, like the popular *Second Life* (http://www. SecondLife.com), where "residents" can go to concerts or board meetings, chat, or even have cybersex with other characters? Have you heard about the *Hot Coffee* scandal from the summer of 2005, when game developers denied and then confessed to including secret sex scenes in the game *Grand Theft Auto: San Andreas*? Were you aware that in *Grand Theft Auto*, male characters can buy the services of a prostitute and then kill her, or that in *BMX XXX*, a bike-racing game, there are live-action scenes featuring dancing strippers? Well, if you thought hot coffee came from Starbucks and *Grand Theft Auto* was all about joyriding, pull up a chair, and I will bring you up to speed on video games and the controversies they provoke.

INDUSTRY STATS

Since the mid-1990s, the video game industry has been more profitable than Hollywood. Total US video game revenues topped $21 billion in 2008, with video game software sales earning $32 billion worldwide, surpassing DVD sales for the first time (Magrino, 2009; Ortutay, 2009).[1,2] The majority of Americans over age six play video games. Among U.S. children, eleven- to fourteen-year-old boys play video games most often. On average, elementary school children play video games ten hours per week (roughly thirteen and one-half hours for boys and six hours for girls) and watch twenty-one hours per week of television.

GOOD NEWS, BAD NEWS

What kinds of games are popular today, and are these games bad for you, particularly due to their depiction of violence? The answer is not simple. There are many positive and entertaining games available. My son and I play the *Guitar Hero* games, for example, in which players have fun getting in touch with their inner rock stars. I also enjoy *Brain Age*, a game designed to improve memory, concentration, and thinking. Other positive video games include dancing and karaoke games (like the *Dance, Dance Revolution*, and the *Karaoke Revolution* series).

But there are also games with harmful content, including those containing violence and employing imagery that is overtly racist and/or sexist. In fact, studies have consistently shown that most of the top-selling video games are violent. The *Grand Theft Auto* series has consistently broken sales records and topped the charts of the games most highly rated by gamers. *Grand Theft Auto: Vice City* was the top seller in its day. When a sequel, *Grand Theft Auto: San Andreas*, came on the scene, it sold more than half a million units in two days, crushing all previous video game sales records. In *Grand Theft Auto: Vice City*, female characters include a porn star named Candy Sux, prostitutes, and a bevy of female characters clad in bikinis and roller skates. In *Grand Theft Auto*, after the male hero has sex with a prostitute in the backseat of a car, he can kill her in a number of ways, including beating her to death with a golf club, kicking her in the crotch until she bleeds to death, or shooting her. If he does any of these things, he gets back the money he gave the prostitute, thus earning a reward for his violence. Positive reinforcement, anyone?

In *Grand Theft Auto: Vice City*, if you walk up to a female character dressed like a prostitute and hit her, she says things like, "I like it rough." The men who programmed this game may have thought this statement was just a humorous throwaway line. But it is critically important to a psychologist like myself. Research tells us that whenever females say they like sexualized violence, men are more likely to be violent toward women. In a classic study, psychologists Edward Donnerstein and Leonard Berkowitz angered some men by giving them electric shocks, while others were not shocked.[3] Then the men watched either a neutral film, an erotic film, a rape scene where the victim responded positively, or a rape scene where the victim responded negatively. Results showed that the angered men were more likely to be aggressive than those who were not angered. Interestingly, of the men who were not angered, only those who had seen the rape scene that showed a positive response from the victim were subsequently aggressive toward a real woman. Thus we learn that when media perpetuate what is called a "rape myth"—for example, the idea that women like sexual force—they encourage violence against women. In a very real way, this type of characterization sends the message to men that rape and abuse are secretly desirable to women. So, when a provocatively dressed woman in a video game tells a man that she "likes it rough," there is reason to be justifiably concerned about the harmful message sent to young men playing the game, and the consequences to the women around them.

Consider another bit of dialogue from *Grand Theft Auto: Vice City*. As the prostitute and the male hero have sex, the prostitute makes sarcastic quips like, "Oh, yeah, great," "You in me yet?," and "You're so big." The man returns the sarcasm and disrespect with comments such as, "That was okay," and refers to the prostitute as "sweetheart." What effect might playing this video game have on young men's views about sexual relationships? Comments that sexually demean men and women, that degrade sex, and that portray females as insulting and sexually unresponsive have the potential to damage real relationships. As youth grow and develop, they become more curious about sexual relationships. Young people are motivated to understand these relationships more and more as they move toward their first experiences with romance and sex. Just as a toddler watching dad or big brother drive a car may pay attention and imitate what he sees, a teenager pays special attention to information about how sexual relationships are supposed to work, about what he can expect from a partner, and about what the partner expects from him. Just as you may have learned something about sex and relationships by reading a coming-of-age novel like *The Catcher in the Rye*, your child may learn about them by playing a video game. And it is possible that embedding these messages in games in which children are actively engaged has a more powerful impact than the relatively passive experience of simply watching shows with similar themes.

SHOULD MEDIA PSYCHOLOGISTS REALLY JUST LIGHTEN UP?

I've repeatedly heard arguments that video games do not change how we act, think, or feel. One version of this argument is that those who are prone to violence will be more likely to enjoy violent video games but won't be changed by the experience. Another version is that no matter how violent or tasteless, video games are simply harmless entertainment, and psychologists who say otherwise are just trying to scare us. Furthermore, some add, we media experts are hopelessly naïve about the real world, where violence is commonplace among gamers and non-gamers alike. What we don't get is that games are only games—a break from school, family, church, and other settings where we get the values and cues that shape how we behave. If only this were true.

I've already suggested how much time Americans spend plugged into media. American children spend, on average, forty-five hours per week staring at electronic screens, including TVs, video games, cell phones, and computers. This is half again as many hours as they spend in school, even if we assume they sit in class year-round. And it is much more time than they spend interacting with their parents in any meaningful way. Of course, children attend school and interact with their parents for a host of reasons, including the fact that they have no other choice. But we do have a choice when it comes to media. So if media take up virtually all of our free time, there must be something compelling going on, something that is meaningful to us, even if we're not always aware what that meaning is. Saying it's "just" entertaining begs the question about what it is that makes it "fun?" We are *absolutely* affected by what we see on these screens, but most of us don't even know it. Actually, that's putting it mildly. Many of us passionately deny that we are, or that we even *could be* changed by what we watch and play. A related point was dramatized in two recent films, *Pleasantville* (Ross, 1998) and *The Truman Show* (Weir, 1998), in which the main characters are stunningly naïve about the extent to which their world is artificially constructed by the media.

HOW WHAT WE WATCH CHANGES US

Controversial from the beginning, mass media has always inspired both criticism and admiration. In the 1920s and 1930s, concern over the effects of movies on children motivated a series of investigations called the Payne Fund studies. Based on interviews with 3,000 people and summarized in a popular book as *Our Movie Made Children*, the study concluded, "the amount that average children carry away (from movies) is astonishing." Supported by feminists and more conservative movements to protect families against cultural pollution, results from these studies continue to inspire writing and debate. To date, psychologists and other media experts have produced volumes of research documenting media effects. A few of these studies should illustrate the scope of research on the variety of ways media change us. After looking at *Playboy* centerfolds, men said they were less in love with their wives than men who had not seen the centerfolds; after college men watched *Charlie's Angels* in a dorm, they thought normal college women were less attractive than did men who had not watched the show; and after seeing a promiscuous woman on *The Jerry Springer Show*, young men and women thought that a victim of sexual harassment was more responsible for the incident and less traumatized by the event than those who had seen a woman on the same show who was not promiscuous.[4,5] When children watch movies where the stars smoke cigarettes, they are more likely to start smoking. Coca-Cola paid $20 million for a product placement on *American Idol* because they understand that seeing a product in a popular show will increase sales. Not everyone imitates what they see. But enough do to make the effects significant.

What do we know about the influence of video games specifically? A few research findings must suffice. When college students played a car-racing video game where they were rewarded for killing pedestrians and other drivers, they more often attacked an opponent in another task than those who played a version of the same video game where aggression was punished. In another study, students were divided into a group that played a violent video game and a group that played a nonviolent game. Then both groups watched videos of real-life violence that included a news scene in which one prisoner stabbed another. Importantly, the students who had played the violent video game were less responsive to real-life violence than those who played the nonviolent game. And this showed up in their physical reactions: their heart rates and their galvanic skin responses (a measure of physiological desensitization) were lower than those not exposed to the violent video game. In this study, the physical desensitization caused by exposure to violent imagery could be traced to changes in the brain that led to a breakdown in the motivational system that normally inhibits aggression. At least in the laboratory, violent video game players who showed these brain responses also behaved more aggressively when provoked.[6] Not every effect demonstrated in a lab is replicated in real life. But this evidence is more than merely suggestive; the content of our media diet—whether TV, movies, magazines, or video games—matters.

I'm Okay, You've Got Problems

If media images and messages can change our feelings, thoughts, and actions, why aren't we more aware of their power over us? One reason is a well-documented research finding called the "third-person effect." People believe that media affect others, but that they themselves are immune to its effects. This may be because of what psychologists call "cognitive dissonance." Cognitive dissonance means that when we feel uncomfortable about something we are doing—particularly if it meets some need or is pleasurable in another respect—instead of inhibiting our behavior, we are motivated to rationalize our choices. If I am a teenager who is spends a lot of my free time playing violent video games, I am motivated to think they are not harmful. Years ago, when we started to learn that smoking had negative health consequences, many smokers denied that smoking was unhealthy for the same reasons. This dissonance is compounded by the developmental belief held by most teens that they are invincible; therefore, video game violence could not harm them. Furthermore, young people identify with their media choices (for example, liking hip-hop music or playing violent video games) in no small part because it is a powerful component in their relationships with their peers. Questioning their media choices can feel like questioning their very identity as well as their social standing. In combination, these factors create a situation whereby heavy media users, and therefore those who are potentially most affected by negative media content, become defenders of the very companies that profit from their ignorance.

Fantasy, Myth, and Reality

When it comes to media violence effects, there are a number of myths that hinder public understanding. For one thing, people expect media violence effects to be drastic and immediate. Interestingly, one of the intriguing findings in the Payne Fund studies was that a week after going to a disturbing film, children were actually better able to recall details of the movie than they were immediately afterward. Another false belief might be termed the "myth of misplaced specificity." As a media expert who speaks about the effects of media in a number of venues, I am often confronted with someone who tells me, "I play lots of violent video games and I have never shot anyone." Violent video game effects are more varied than this sentiment implies. They build up over time and reinforce or evoke any of a number of aggressive outcomes that extend from such everyday aggressive behaviors as name-calling, manipulation, hostility, and backstabbing to sexual assault, dating violence, and domestic violence.

Another argument, perhaps the most important because it has some academic cachet, involves the harmless nature of even the most offensive content. "Adults and older kids know the difference between fantasy and reality," I am told, "and are therefore totally unaffected by what's on a TV or video game screen. It's just harmless entertainment." Decades of painstaking psychological research refute this claim. In case the research I have described so far about the physiological and attitudinal changes induced by viewing violent content is not convincing on this score, let me give some additional examples. Countless studies have shown that watching a violent movie makes people more aggressive and that even something as seemingly insignificant as watching an episode of *Charlie's Angels* or flipping through an adult magazine can change a man's feelings toward his wife or partner. Knowing *Charlie's Angels* is not real does not prevent it from having a real effect. The same show that makes men feel more aggressive can make women feel unattractive and guilty (again, based on research, this is not just my opinion). Stories produced for the screen send messages about how the world could be or should be, how I should act, and what I should believe. No point in this chapter is more important than this: fantasy has a pervasive effect on our realities in deep and meaningful ways.

Why Media Sexism Matters

Now let's turn more specifically to sexist portrayals in the media. Why are demeaning, sexist portrayals damaging? Scientists believe that aggression and violence toward women is motivated by a desire for men to coerce, control, and dominate women. When women are consistently shown as sex objects rather than agents, consistently depicted in demeaning and degrading ways, and consistently shown as submissive, the result is to condone and support violence against women, the coercion of women, and anti-woman attitudes. Perhaps none of this would matter if we did not live in a society where violence against women was so widespread and where persistent sexual inequalities made women vulnerable to being harassed, abused, or dominated by men. These demeaning portrayals also both *cause* and *are caused by* a social structure where men are dominant and women submissive.[7]

A group of Italian researchers showed that when college men perceived their masculinity was threatened, they responded by being more likely to sexually harass a young woman by sending her unwanted pornographic images.[8] This was especially true for young men who identified with stereotypically masculine roles. Furthermore, young men were more likely to sexually harass a young woman if she simply expressed belief in the equality of men and women. In other words harassment, here putting women "in their place," was seen as a just punishment for fighting for equal rights and desiring a good career. Why? Presumably because fighting for equality challenges male dominance and the privileges that go with it.

We know those who are exposed to more violence in general, and more violence against women specifically, become more accepting of violence against women. For example, Martha Burt asked nearly 600 male and female college students about their attitudes toward rape. She found that those who held attitudes supportive of rape were likely to also hold traditional gender role beliefs, to distrust the opposite sex, and to be more accepting of violence against women.[9]

When it comes to teaching gender roles, video games are particularly blatant. My colleagues and I studied how male and female video game characters are portrayed. We found that female characters are much more likely than male characters to be sexualized (60 percent for females versus less than 1 percent of the time for males).[10] Male characters are overwhelmingly represented as aggressive and violent (more than 80 percent of the time). Female characters, in contrast, are quite often presented as scantily clad visions of beauty. So male video game characters are dominant and aggressive and female video game characters are sex objects. This is particularly troubling in light of research on hypermasculinity. Hypermasculine (also known as "macho") males have been found to be more accepting than non-macho males of callous sexual interaction and of coercive sex. Furthermore, the confluence model of sexual aggression proposes that hostile masculinity is an important predictor of sexual aggression. Hostile masculinity includes (1) a hostile/distrustful attitude—especially toward women, and (2) "sexual gratification from controlling or dominating women."

Teenagers were asked to describe typical male and typical female video game characters. The teens described male characters as strong, muscular, violent, mean, and cocky. They described female characters as provocatively dressed, as skinny with "big boobs," and with negative sexual terms such as "slutty" and "hooker." Interestingly, we also identified an emerging trend for female characters to be portrayed simultaneously as sex objects and as aggressors. While past research had shown the most typical portrayal of female video game characters to be as damsels in distress, the images we studied told a different story. Perhaps the game developers intended the portrayals of women as aggressive, in part, as a message of equality to the male characters and as a way of enticing more female players by giving them characters with which to identify. Or perhaps the gamers were neutralizing the belief among some male players that real women (those who fit the stereotype of damsels) should not be hit. The mix of objectification and aggression, though, potentially generates ambivalence and hostility toward women, which are both linked to real-life harm to women.

The view of women in video games is changing and not generally for the better. National Institute on Media and the Family (http://www.mediafamily.org) psychologist David Walsh and his colleagues reported that, "the best-selling games of the past year glorify and reward extreme violence, particularly toward women" and that top games "degrade women and reinforce dangerous stereotypes by treating them as sexual objects."[11] Moreover, observers are beginning to recognize the consequences of sexism in games on females as well as on the males whose aggression is encouraged. The American Psychological Association's 2007 Task Force on the Sexualization of Girls found that exposure to images of females who are degraded and portrayed as sex objects can elicit depression, low self-esteem, eating disorders, and sexuality issues in females. Other research extends these concerns by showing, for example, that men's exposure to ads in which women are sex objects cause them to have more rape-supportive attitudes. Furthermore, across sixteen nations, the more pronounced the macho "bad but bold" male stereotype in a culture, the lower the gender equality in that culture (for example, women had lower literacy rates, purchasing power, and job prestige). Furthermore, anti-woman attitudes such as rape myth acceptance, acceptance of interpersonal violence against women, and hostility toward women have been shown to predict both sexual and nonsexual violence against women.

RESEARCH STUDY ON VIOLENT VIDEO GAME PLAYING, RAPE MYTHS, AND ATTITUDES TOWARD WOMEN

To add to our understanding of the negative effects of exposure to media violence, I conducted a study in which I hypothesized that violent game playing would be related to negative attitudes toward women and greater acceptance of rape myths.

Rape Statistics

Consider statistics on the prevalence of rape in our society. Most studies show that a woman has a 15 to 25 percent chance of being raped in her lifetime. Girls and women ages fourteen to eighteen are at higher risk for rape, with incidence rates declining after age eighteen. Fifty-seven percent of reported rapes are acquaintance rapes, also known as date rapes. Many rape victims experience posttraumatic stress disorder, with the initial reaction to the trauma often lasting a year or more. Three of four women who reported being raped and/or assaulted said the perpetrator was their spouse, partner, or date. As we've seen repeatedly, a hypermasculine personality that emphasizes power, control, and macho characteristics predisposes men to rape, particularly when this is coupled with hostility toward women that includes disdain for traditionally feminine behaviors and traits.

Study Details

One hundred and sixty (ninety-five female, sixty-five male) college students completed four surveys, described below. Participants were students in general psychology classes.

The Surveys

Video game playing habits. Anderson and Dill's Video Game Questionnaire (VGQ) was used to assess participants' degree of exposure to violent video games. The VGQ asks participants to report their favorite video games and to rate how often they play each game and how violent the game is in content and graphics. Each participant earns an overall video game violence exposure (VGVE) score by multiplying time spent playing each game by the total amount of violence (content and graphics) reported for that game. Additionally, participants classify each of their favorite games by category. For the purposes of this study, three categories (education, sports, and skill) were considered non-aggressive, and three categories (fighting with hands, fighting with weapons, and fantasy) were considered aggressive.

Rape beliefs. Participants responded to a short form of the Rape Myth Acceptance Scale that measures the degree to which they endorse rape myths, including the ideas that women want to be raped, secretly enjoy rape, and do things to "deserve rape," such as dressing provocatively.[12] An example from the survey is "A woman who goes to the home or apartment of a man on their first date implies that she is willing to have sex." I predicted that those who played more violent video games would show greater acceptance of rape myths. Therefore, I expected a positive correlation between these variables.

Negative attitudes toward women. Participants completed a twenty-five-item short form of the Attitudes Toward Women Scale, which measures the conventionality of attitudes held toward women, including the ideas that women are intellectually inferior to men, that women "have their place" in the home, and that there are different rules of sexual behavior for men and women.[13] Sample items include, "The intellectual leadership of a community should be largely in the hands of men," "A woman should not expect to go to exactly the same places or to have quite the same freedom of action as a man," and "Women should be encouraged not to become sexually intimate with anyone before marriage, even their fiancées." Scores vary inversely with the degree to which persons hold conventional attitudes, with higher scores meaning they are less conventional. I predicted that those who played more violent video games would show lower scores on this measure of negative attitudes toward women. Therefore, I expected a negative correlation between these variables.

Aggressive personality. The Caprara Irritability Scale (CIS) measures the degree to which a person is inclined to respond to perceived frustration or provocation with aggression.[14] Since Caprara and his colleagues found that irritable people are more likely to respond to provocation with aggression, we will refer to CIS scores as aggressive personality. Irritable individuals respond positively to items such as,

"When someone raises his voice I raise mine higher," and "It makes my blood boil to have somebody make fun of me." Participants responded to each item on a scale of 1 (disagree) to 7 (agree) with agreement indicating more irritability. Total scores were calculated such that a higher score indicated more irritability. Aggressive personality should predict greater rape myth acceptance (a positive correlation) and more negative attitudes toward women (a negative correlation).

RESEARCH FINDINGS

Findings

As predicted, video game violence exposure was positively correlated with rape myth acceptance ($r = .225$, $p < .002$). Those who played more violent video games showed greater rape myth acceptance. Also as predicted, video game violence exposure was negatively correlated with attitudes toward women ($r = -.308$, $p < .0001$). In other words, those who played more violent video games were less likely to express positive attitudes toward women and therefore more likely to express negative ("traditional") attitudes toward them. Note that the correlation is negative here because higher scores indicated less traditional, more egalitarian attitudes toward women. Aggressive personality was also correlated with rape myth acceptance ($r = .323$, $p < .0001$) and with attitudes toward women ($r = -.311$, $p < .0001$) and with video game violence exposure ($r = .271$, $p < .0001$). This means that those with aggressive personalities also had more negative attitudes toward women, were more likely to endorse rape myths, and showed higher exposure to video game violence. Additionally, as shown in previous studies, rape myth acceptance and attitudes toward women were correlated with each other ($r = -.489$, $p < .0001$). Thus, those who endorse rape myths also hold more negative attitudes toward women.

Deeper Analysis

What explains the association between media violence exposure and antisocial attitudes toward women? Is it how aggressive you are—your score on the Aggressive Personality Measure—that explains your anti-woman attitudes, or is it your video game violence exposure? Are you an aggressive person who happens to play violent games and have anti-woman attitudes, or does your exposure to these games make a real difference in your attitudes toward women and violence? We found that greater exposure to video game violence increased the likelihood of endorsing rape myths as well as having greater negative attitudes toward women independently of having an aggressive personality.[15]

Video Game Categories

When participants spent more time playing games they categorized as fighting or fantasy, they were more likely to endorse rape myths and show negative attitudes toward women than if they spent more time playing games they categorized as educational, skill, or sports games. And these differences were statistically significant, which meant they were real.

Interpreting the Research Findings

Our research supported the predictions we had made about the relationship between video game violence exposure and attitudes supporting violence against women. In our study, playing violent video games was linked to believing that women want to be raped and that they ask for and deserve rape—what we've called rape myths because they are obviously untrue. Participants who play more violent video games are more likely to believe that women report rape to call attention to themselves, that rape victims are promiscuous, and that women who get drunk at a party are "fair game" for men to have sex with even when the women refuse. Violent video game players are even more likely to believe that women who are "too good" to talk to men need to be "taught a lesson" in the form of rape.

As this summary suggests, our research showed a dose-specific effect. Those with a higher degree of exposure to violent video games are more likely to hold negative, antisocial attitudes toward women. Violent video game players are more likely to believe that "women should worry less about their rights and more about becoming good wives and mothers." Violent video game players are also more likely to believe that men should have more authority than women have over children, that husbands should have more legal right than wives have to marital money and property, and that men should be given preference over women in being hired for a job and being promoted. So, violent video game playing is associated with a range of beliefs about sexual inequality that fly in the face of women's gains since the 1960s.

If these attitudes weren't worrisome enough on their face, they are particularly troubling in light of new knowledge about the dynamics of abusive relationships. Sociologist Evan Stark suggests that domestic violence has been miscast as being *only* or even *primarily* about physical battering. He offers a conservative estimate that in 60 percent of the cases in which women seek outside assistance from police, hospitals, or shelters, for instance, the physical violence is part of a larger pattern of coercive control by men who seek to oppress women through restriction of their basic human liberties.[16] Tactics of coercion and control include controlling money, transportation, communication, and social contacts and target how women perform stereotypic roles associ-ated with their gender identity, such as child care, housekeeping, and cooking. If those exposed to violent, antisocial video games endorse attitudes consistent with the domination of men over women, we must ask ourselves about the wisdom of raising our children with antisocial media. Since American children spend an average of forty-five hours a week with media, media content and its influence on our culture, espe-cially on our young people, should be an important topic of ongoing focus. We are not born with sexist and pro-violence attitudes.

Exaggerated sex role stereotypes are the rule rather than the excep-tion for video game characters. Women are overwhelmingly portrayed in disrespectful ways, particularly as sex objects, whereas men are overwhelmingly portrayed as violent and belligerent. These media rep-resentations are both the cause and the effect of a culture that disem-powers women, thus encouraging their victimization and broadening the base of opposition to sexual equality. Also, since aggression and intelligence are negatively correlated, over time, men who rely too heavily on aggression to resolve conflicts are less likely than their non-violent counterparts to grow intellectually. Furthermore, those who hold more stereotypical attitudes about gender have sex earlier and are less effective with their contraceptive use.

So, how should we interpret these findings? Do they mean that ex-posure to antisocial content in video games causes antisocial behavior? The design of our research, by itself, does not allow us to make that statement definitively. What the research *does* tell us is that if you know that a person plays violent video games, you also know that they are more likely to hold pro-rape, anti-woman attitudes than one who does not play violent video games. Another thing we know is that those who play violent video games are willing to report, in the context of a research study, that they hold anti-women attitudes. That fact alone is provocative.

Is there evidence that the content of the video games causes anti-women attitudes? While the literature in this field is small, there is some evidence that suggests a cause-and-effect relationship between stereotypical gender representations in video games and attitudes sup-porting violence against women. My colleagues and I exposed some participants to gender-stereotypic video game characters (violent men and sexualized women), and others to non-stereotypic images of men and women (male and female professionals).[17] All participants read a woman's real-life account of being sexually harassed by her professor and then answered questions about sexual harassment. Results showed that, compared to all other groups in the study, men who saw the ster-eotypical video game characters said the perpetrator in the story was less guilty and deserved less punishment, that the victim was more to blame for the harassment, and that they felt less sorry for the victim, and that the professor's behavior was less damaging and should be taken less seriously.

A similar study about television violence showed that hypermasculine males exposed to television violence were less sympathetic than other males to a victim of date rape and rated the perpetrator as less guilty and as using less force.[18] Across cultures, when men are considered stereotypically masculine (for example, macho), and women are considered weak and subordinate, those beliefs translate into real gender inequality. Similarly, research has demonstrated that men exposed to advertisements featuring women portrayed as sex objects subsequently show greater rape-supportive attitudes.

CONCLUSIONS

The point of this chapter, hopefully convincing, is that what we see, hear, experience, and do vis à vis the media matters. Specifically, how men and women are portrayed in video games matters, particularly with respect to violent video games. Starting with how men view women, these depictions have psychological, behavioral, and social effects that are negative for both sexes, but particularly for females. These concerns bear on violence against women not merely directly, because they may cause players to be more violent, but because their effects, mediated through the tolerance of and insensitivity to violence against women, relate to the larger political climate in which women aspire to become full persons on an equal plane with males. And they bear on future generations, what our sons and daughters learn to do, expect, or tolerate.

Video game players and industry spokespeople take a pro-media stance, positioning themselves against scholars, advocates, and politicians who tend to voice media criticism. Game enthusiasts argue that exposure to violent, antisocial media is positive or neutral rather than negative. In one often-heard plaint, industry apologists insist that playing violent games channels aggressive urges by letting gamers "blow off steam." Others simply insist that we protest too much, that video game playing is just a harmless diversion. They also tend to characterize the "other side" as misguided, humorless alarmists who are creating a problem where none exists. For example, the enthusiast-oriented Web site GamePolitics.com recently hosted a discussion about a conference where video game experts presented their work. One enthusiast commented, "find someone from the real world, not an ivory tower, to talk about the true effects games have on real life, which—besides a little wasted time—is not much."[19] Another enthusiast openly derided the scholars, saying: "I REALLY want to see a transcript, so we can point out all the errors and laugh."[20,21] Media experts are sometimes lumped with the Puritanical right-wing—quite an uncomfortable and perplexing position for us, given that, like many college professors, most of us are liberals. This simplistic "us" versus "them" mentality serves those who are out to make money from the sale of video games. If they can keep gamers and parents in the dark, and stereotype scientists as right-wing alarmists, then people will keep buying these games.

For Americans, valuing personal liberty is in our DNA. We have to remember, though, that with great freedom comes great responsibility. The climate our children grow up in will be what we make it. I'm not a prude or a killjoy. My philosophy is *not* if it feels good, don't do it. My philosophy is that you should enjoy your freedom, but you should also make smart choices—choices that uplift us all rather than choices that drag any of us down.

NOTES

1. T. Magrino, Games eclipse DVD/Blu-ray sales. (2009).

2. B. Ortutay, Video game sales top $21 billion in 2008. msnbc.com. (2008).

3. E. Donnerstein and L. Berkowitz, "Victim Reactions in Aggressive Erotic Films as a Factor in Violence against Women," *Journal of Personality & Social Psychology* 41 (1981): 710.

4. S. Gutierres, D. T. Kenrick, and J. J. Partch, "Beauty, Dominance and the Mating Game: Contrast Effects in Self-Assessment Reflect Gender Differences in Mate Selection," *Personality & Social Psychology Bulletin* 25, no. 9 (1999): 1,126.

5. T. Ferguson, et al., "Variation in the Application of the 'Promiscuous Female' Stereotype and the Nature of the Application Domain: Influences on Sexual Harassment Judgments after Exposure to *The Jerry Springer Show*," *Sex Roles* 52 (2005): 477.

6. B. Bartholow, B. J. Bushman, and M. A. Sestir, "Chronic Violent Video Game Exposure and Desensitization to Violence: Behavioral and Event-Related Brain Potential Data," *Journal of Experimental Social Psychology* 42, no. 4 (2006): 532.

7. R. Connell, *Gender and Power* (Stanford, CA: Stanford University Press, 1987).

8. A. Maass, et al., "Sexual Harassment under Social Identity Threat: The Computer Harassment Paradigm," *Journal of Personality & Social Psychology* 85 (2003): 853.

9. M. Burt, "Cultural Myths and Supports for Rape," *Journal of Personality & Social Psychology* 38 (1980): 217.

10. K. E. Dill and K. P. Thill, "Video Game Characters and the Socialization of Gender Roles: Young People's Perceptions Mirror Sexist Media Depictions," *Sex Roles* 57, no. 851 (2007).

11. National Institute on Media and the Family, "Mediawise Video Game Report Card," 2002.

12. All four scales were found to meet conventional standards for reliable measures. Cronbach's Alphas were computed for each scale described in the text. Alpha levels, each based on 160 participants, are as follows: Video Game Violence Exposure, .785; Attitudes Toward Women, .820; Rape Myth Acceptance, .723; Aggressive Personality, .873.

13. C. A. Anderson and K. E. Dill, "Video Games and Aggressive Thoughts, Feelings, and Behavior in the Laboratory and in Life," *Journal of Personality & Social Psychology* 78 (2000): 772.

14. J. T. Spence, R. Helmreich, and J. Stapp, "A Short Version of the Attitudes Towards Women Scale (ATS)," *Bulletin of the Psychonomic Society* 2 (1973): 219.

15. G. V. Caprara, et al., "Indicators of Impulsive Aggression: Present Status of Research on Irritability and Emotional Susceptibility Scales," *Personality & Individual Differences* 6 (1985): 665.

16. I calculated partial correlations between VGVE and RMA and between VGVE and ATW using AP as a control variable. Results indicated that the relationship between VGVE and RMA remained significant, even when controlling for AP ($r = .153, p < .05$. Similarly, the relationship between VGVE and ATW remained significant, even when controlling for AP, AP, $r = -.244, p < .001$.

17. E. Stark, *Coercive Control: How Men Entrap Women in Personal Life* (New York: Oxford University Press, 2007).

18. K. E. Dill, B. P. Brown, and M. A. Collins, "Effects of Exposure to Sex-Stereotyped Video Game Characters on Tolerance of Sexual Harassment," *Journal of Experimental Social Psychology* (in press).

19. E. D. Beaver, S. R. Gold, and A. G. Prisco, "Priming Macho Attitudes and Emotions," *Journal of Interpersonal Violence* 7 (1992): 321–33.

20. http://GamePolitics.com. "National Video Game Summit Agenda Details." http://gamepolitics.com/2006/09/28/national-video-gamesummit-agenda-details/, Response 16.

21. http://GamePolitics.com. "National Video Game Summit," Response 14.

Chapter 7

Gangsta Rap and Violence against Women

Edward G. Armstrong

Through most of its recorded history, music in Western civilization has been a male domain, including classical symphonies and opera. Women and relationships to women have probably been the most common topic of music through the ages, and girls and women have always comprised a significant segment of the audiences for music, sacred or profane. Moreover, the proportion of female performers in most musical genres has increased dramatically over the last century. But those "in charge"—composers, lyricists, conductors, producers, and performers—remain overwhelmingly male. It comes as no surprise, therefore, that with some marked exceptions—the great blues singers Bessie Smith and Ma Rainey and occasional songs by country artist Loretta Lynn come to mind—popular music has been a vehicle for socializing its largely youthful audiences to stereotypic gender roles in which females are sexually subordinate to, controlled by, and dependent on males, regardless of whether men or women deliver its message. Rock subverted some of the musical conventions of its predecessors, whose songs were overwhelming designed for dancing. But it did little to challenge the sexist core of popular music.

In songs, as in popular culture generally, "love" was offered to women as compensation for their deference to men. But just behind this façade lay the specter of male violence, including violence against women, alternately glorified or excused by women's betrayal or by their deviation in some other respect from the norms of loyalty, beauty, and obedience identified with the "male code." Although hurt by, anger at, and violence against women have been constant undercurrents, popular music forms such as the blues, country, and rock have been relatively constrained in dealing with these themes at least compared to opera, which has never hesitated to litter its stages with female (and occasionally male) bodies. A limited number of Delta blues recordings offer the threat of physical aggression as a way to deal with a non-compliant partner. An insignificant proportion of country "cheating" songs depict men killing unfaithful wives. And only a small number of rock songs produced by an even smaller number of bands describe women being murdered, tortured, and raped. It was only with the advent of rap that misogyny and violence against women moved center stage.

These tendencies culminated with the emergence of gangsta rap in the late 1980s, the first commercially produced musical form in which violent misogyny is the defining element. As a social phenomenon, gangsta rap is particularly interesting because its roots are ostensibly in urban ghettoes and because its emergence coincided with a worldwide movement to criminalize violence against women in personal life, an expression of the dramatic gains in equality won by women since the 1960s. Ironically too, gangsta rap become popular at the same time that actual street violence was declining largely because of demographic changes beyond the scope of this chapter.

This chapter explores the violent and misogynist nature of gangsta rap by analyzing its lyrics, documenting the major thematic elements around which its thematic emphasis on violence against women is conceived, and identifying its major audiences and marketing appeal. In plain talk, misogyny means hatred of women. While it has variously been contrasted to misandry (hatred of men) and misanthropy (hatred of humanity), the view adapted here, made popular by feminists in the 1960s, is that it is different than these other noxious attitudes because of its role as cause and consequence of patriarchal social structures and the degree to which it is generated by sexual inequality. The lyrics cited here are not pleasant reading. To the initiated, the choices may seem exaggerating and most shocking. To the contrary, representative rather than exceptional examples are provided, a claim supported by identifying the proportions of songs with identical language or themes.

Debate continues about how literally we should take the violent content of gangsta rap and whether rap lyrics should be interpreted as reportage or art. Critics find that rappers mean what they say in their easily understood public venting of woman-hating. But other commentators challenge the literal interpretation of rap lyrics, alleging that rappers present their harsh depictions merely as fictional imagery and/or exaggerated boasts, using language playfully to demonstrate their verbal skills. Still other observers highlight the responsibility of those who produce and market the music, not its creators, or point to audience "demand" as the prime stimulus. An entirely separate line of inquiry concerns how the misogyny impacts listeners or whether it does so at all. But the starting point for these debates must be the *what*, *who*, and *how* of the music, my concerns here.

OVERVIEW

Background

Rap is a dominant force in global popular culture. Nearly every country in the world features some form or mutation of rap music. Throughout this decade, rap has been rated the favorite musical genre by American teenagers, though by 2007, its popularity had slipped to third behind rock and country in terms of nationwide sales.[1]

During the 1970s, rap was part of hip-hop culture. This culture originated in New York, specifically in the South Bronx. At the time, hip-hop had three equally essential parts: break dancing, graffiti, and rap music. Eventually, in part due to its commercial success, rap music became the defining element of hip-hop culture and the terms "rap" and "hip-hop" became synonymous. Over the past few years, the term "hip-hop" has once again been extended to mean an urban culture that, along with rap, includes art, fashion, language, and seemingly contradictory and incompatible features: a spirit of rebellion and a materalistic lifestyle. Further, music marketers have conjured up a distinction between hip-hop and rap. The hip-hop genre is the more inclusive of the two and includes rap along with other forms of popular music.

Rap music began as entertainment during outdoor street parties. The first rap song to reach the Top 40 charts, Sugar Hill Gang's 1979 hit, *Rapper's Delight*, was a typical rap party song.

New York continued to dominate rap during the 1980s. Russell Simmons, the "godfather of rap," owned Def Jam Records and served as the catalyst for the majority of the successful acts: Run-D.M.C., LL Cool J., the Beastie Boys, and Public Enemy. Public Enemy rejected the party theme, becoming the first successful political rap group. Its leader, Chuck D, promoted a vision of rap as the "CNN of black America."

The most famous rap artists are those who have taken the most extreme violent and misogynist viewpoints. The first controversial group was the Miami-based 2 Live Crew, led by Luther Campbell. In 1989, they released their most popular record, *As Nasty as They Wanna Be*. A year later, the content of the album led to their arrest and conviction for obscenity in Florida. Upon appeal, a jury overturned the initial verdict, though *As Nasty as They Wanna Be* remains the first, and only, record in history banned by a federal judge. The word "horny" in the most popular song from the album, "Me So Horny," disturbed many listeners. Besides this word, the song contained lyrics such as "I fuck all the girls and I make them cry," though literally violent acts were implied rather than explicit. The convergence of misogyny and violence continued throughout the album. "Put Her in the Buck," for example, has the rapper telling a young girl that he plans to "bust your pussy then break your backbone." Although far from being funny, the intent and tone of the presentations reflect an admittedly absurd degree of sexual bravado. Nevertheless, these lyrics were far more graphic than those previously available on commercially produced records. At the time, other, less popular rappers were moving beyond 2 Live Crew in terms of lurid and vivid renderings of violent misogyny.

Gangsta rap was born in the late 1980s in Southern California. Its emergence set off an East Coast–West Coast antagonism about the central themes and most important artists of the genre that also became the focus of popular lore and helped market the music. Unlike their East Coast rivals, gangsta rappers moved away from party songs to raps about violence and misogyny, and often violent misogyny. Gangsta rap quickly became the the music's most popular subgenre, redefining the rest of the field. Artists offering other kinds of rap were categorized as either "alternative" or part of the "non-gangsta wing of hip-hop."

The first popular gangsta rap was the 1987 release of Ice-T's *Rhyme Pays*. Ice-T is the "professionally known as" name of Tracy Marrow, who picked the "Ice" prefix as a tribute to Iceberg Slim, a notorious Chicago pimp, whose 1967 autobiography, *Pimp: The Story of My Life*, sold more than 1 million copies. Ice-T used the term "reality-based" to describe his songs because he rapped about situations that actually happened to him. In one of his first appearances before a nationwide television audience, Ice-T defended the words to his song, "The Iceberg," on *The Oprah Winfrey Show* (December 14, 1989). In his opinion, women should find the song "funny." In "The Iceberg," Ice-T describes Evil E, who "fucked the bitch with a flashlight, pulled it out and left the batteries in" and consequently, the "bitch's titties start blinkin' like tail lights." Almost immediately, however, other rappers articulated more plausible misogynist scenarios and in even more elaborate detail.

Gangsta rap advances the idea that women are little more than bitches and "hoes" (whores), disposable playthings that exist for male abuse. In effect, words like "bitch" and "ho" are used as synonyms for "woman." At another level, though, "bitch" and "ho" have been appropriated much in the way the "N-word," pronounced "nigga," has come to have a postive meaning proclaiming an authentic, streetwise, strong black person. "Bitch" and "ho" have become so commonplace that young women have used them to describe themselves. In fact, two female rap groups chose the names Bytches With Problems (BWP) and Hoes With Attitude (HWA). The ambiguity about these meanings surfaced dramatically in 2007 when the white, nationally syndicated radio host Don Imus called the Rutgers Unviersity women's basketball team "nappy-haired hoes" and was promptly removed from the air because of the outraged reaction, though he subsquently returned.

The Nature of Rap

Rap involves neither musical instruments nor the ability to play instruments. Originally, rappers took either of two roles. The DJ (disc jockey) played the recorded music and the MC (master of ceremonies/ microphone controller) talked in rhyme over the recorded music. Rap's harmonies are "simple," based on one tonality as defined by a simple bass line. Instead, the genre's central focus is lyric content, that is, the power of the word. Words are spoken, not sung. The late Ray Charles commented that rap is just "talk with music."[2] Public Enemy's Chuck D even declared that "rap is a vocal culture" and "is not music per se."[3] Snoop Dogg summarized the nature of his raps in these terms: "I just be conversatin'."[4] Eminem distinguished himself from other artists, saying that he, in particular, cared "about the words."[5] Eminem emphasized that to analyze his songs one must examine them "lyric for lyric."[6]

Rappers avoid word play. They communicate straightforward meaning. Nearly all raps are first-person narratives, retellings of what the artists (allegedly) have seen or done or of events that happened personally and specifically to them. By telling their tales in this manner, rappers appear to commit themselves to the violent and misogynist impulses and behaviors portrayed in their lyrics. The nature of rap facilitates its content analysis, the transcription and interpretation of lyrics. Content analysis is accomplished by classification and categorization. Here the concern is with a collection of songs manifesting violent misogynist lyrics. Content analysis is used to determine whether a song depicts violent misogyny and, if so, the nature of the violence portrayed. To begin, however, a specification of the two fundamental periods of the gangsta rap domain is needed.

History

Before dealing with the history of gangsta rap in some detail, a timeline of the important events in this history may be useful in offering a basic overview of the genre's development. Table 7.1 is arranged according to the date key albums were released. Albums appearing in the same year are also listed chronologically—in terms of the exact dates of their release. The sales figures were obtained from the Recording Industry Association of America's Web site (www.riaa.com, accessed March 21, 2008).

Gangsta rap's first historical and foundational period lasts from 1987 to 1993. Ice-T's "6 'N the Morning" (in *Rhyme Pays*) served as the blueprint for the gangsta rap style. But two groups, N.W.A (Niggaz Wit Attitude) and the Geto Boys, and the spin-off solo careers of their members, eclipsed Ice-T's success. The Compton, California–based

Table 7.1.
A Gangsta Rap Timeline

Date	Artist and Album	Significance
1987	Ice –T *Rhyme Pays*	This was the first "hardcore" (gangsta) album and also the first album that bore a warning label about lyric content. It sold over 500,000 copies.
1988	Too short *Life Is …* *Too Short*	Too short made Oakland, California a hotbed of West Coast gangsta rap. The album sold over 2 million copies even though Short had virtually no radio air play. The censored versions of his songs were basically a series of "beeps" interspersed with an occasional phrase.
1988	N.W.A *Straight Outta* *Compton*	Now an American cultural artifact, the album contained the controversial "Fuck Tha Police" which indicted law enforcement for racial profiling and brutality. Subsequent events such as the video taped police beating of Rodney King gave the group credence as ethnographers of law enforcement's treatment of minorities. Eazy-E founded the group. Dr. Dre, N.W.A's non-rapping producer, coined the term "gangsta rap" to identify the music he produced. The album sold over 2 million copies.
1988	Eazy-E *Eazy-Duz-It*	The album sold over 2 million copies. It was produced by Dre.
1989	Ghetto Boys [Geto Boys] *Grip It On That* *Other Level*	Using the standard spelling of the word "ghetto" in the group's name, the album was locally released in Houston, Texas. It contained earlier versions of ten of the 12 songs on *The Geto Boys*, their next album.
1990	Geto Boys *The Geto Boys*	The Geto Boys self-titled album was the group's first major label release (on Def American Records) and was scheduled for distributorship by Geffen Records. But because of the album's lyrics, particularly those of the slightly re-written of "Mind of a Lunatic," the distributor dropped its deal with Def American delaying the album's release. But WEA (Warner Electra Asylum), at the time the leading record-distributor, agreed to do so.
1991	N.W.A *Efil4zaggin*	This was the first gangsta rap album to reach No.1 on the *Billboard* music charts. It sold over 1 million copies.

Year	Album	Description
1992	Body Count [Ice-T] *Body Count*	The album initially contained the song "Cop Killer." But Ice voluntarily recalled the album because of death threats made to employees of his label, Warner Brothers Records, and not because of criticisms made by major law enforcement organizations. *Body Count* was later reissued without the controversial song.
1992	Ice Cube *The Predator*	With over 2 million in sales, the album established Cube, a former member of N.W.A, as a major figure in the history of gangsta rap.
1992	Dr. Dre *The Chronic*	The album sold over 3 million copies. It introduced Snoop Dogg and offered criticisms of Eazy-E. The Chronic contained "Nuthin' But a 'G' Thang," a million-selling single that reached No. 2 on the *Billboard* Hot 100 chart.
1993	Eazy-E/ *It's On (Dr. Dre) 187um Killa*	This short form album sold over 2 million copies. The album was a response to and criticism of Dre.
1993	Snoop Doggy Dogg *Doggystyle*	Snoop Dogg, then using the middle name "Doggy," sold over 4 million albums. Dre produced the album. This was the first album by solo artist to reach No. 1 prior to its release.
1999	Eminem *The Slim Shady LP*	The album sold over 4 million copies. Dre was the executive producer.
2000	Eminem *The Marshall Mathers LP*	With sales over 9 million copies, it is the best-selling gangsta rap album. It was the third most popular album of 2000.
2002	Eminem *The Eminem Show*	The album sold 8 millions copies and is second only to Em's previous work in terms of gangsta rap sales. It was the No. 1 album of 2002.
2005	Eminem *Curtain Call—The Hits*	Basically a "greatest hits" compilation, it sold over 2 million copies. *Curtain Call* contains "Lose Yourself," the only song by a gangsta rapper to reach No. 1 on the *Billboard* Hot 100 chart. The song was originally included on the *8 Mile* soundtrack.

N.W.A, founded by the late Eazy-E, billed itself as "the World's Most Dangerous Group." Until Ice Cube left in early 1990, he served as its chief lyricist. (Ice Cube, born O'Shea Jackson, followed Ice-T's lead and renamed himself after Iceberg Skim.) MC Ren acted as the group's hardcore center. Dr. Dre, N.W.A's non-rapping producer, coined the term "gangsta rap" to refer to the albums he produced. In 1991, their *Efil4zaggin* (Niggaz4life spelled backwards) became the first gangsta rap album to reach No. 1 on the *Billboard* charts. In 1992, Dre's *The Chronic* became the most popular gangsta rap album. Only a year later, Snoop Dogg's *Doggystyle*, which Dre produced, surpassed *The Chronic*. Snoop's album was the first rap album by a solo artist to reach No. 1 prior to its release. Unlike N.W.A, members of Houston's Geto Boys had separate careers until they joined together in a business partnership. In 1990, their *Grip It! On That Other Level* sold nearly 500,000 copies without major-label sponsorship or radio air play. The Geto Boys spawned multiple solo successes: Bushwick Bill, Scarface, and Willie D. They also collaborated with the members of Too Much Trouble, a group that called themselves, "The Baby Geto Boys." Too short was another important artist. He single-handedly made Oakland, California, another center of West Coast rap.

In the mid-1990s, gangsta rap underwent major changes. In 1995, Ice-T ceased using the term "gangsta" to describe his music. A year later, Dre announced that the gangsta rap musical style was "over," that it had "run its course," and that it "is definitely a thing of the past."[7] In fact, a book published in December 1996 was entitled *Gangsta Rap Is Dead.*[8] By 1998, the common viewpoint was that gangsta rap was in ruins and that its reign had ended. But these assessments did not anticipate gangsta rap's reemergence, almost entirely because of the popularity of Eminem.

All of the artists in gangsta rap's foundational period were African Americans. But in the early 1990s, *Advertising Age* reported that Sound-Data, the company that provided the data for weekly album sales rankings, found that white teenagers purchased 75 percent of rap records.[9] In one of the first national articles about gangsta rap, expert testimonies were offered to explain more about this audience and its preference.[10] Basically, the relationship was clear: the more obscene and violent the lyrics were, the bigger their white audiences became. Market researchers took notice of the demand for harsher lyrics. An article on rap in the *Wall Street Journal* quoted a rap producer: "The sad truth is the harder the rapper's image, the more music they sell."[11] In addition, according to *Source* magazine, marketing experts agreed that a white rapper would be extraordinarily popular among gangsta rap's largest consumer base, white suburban kids. Dre decided "to make a white rapper the next heir to [his] gangsta legacy" and as everyone knows, Dre picked Eminem and produced Eminem's most popular albums.[12] Thus, although Eminem grew up in Detroit, he was linked to the West Coast style of rap. Since coining the term "gangsta rap" and producing the most renowned gangsta albums, Dre and his posse became rap royalty. His marketing skill partly determined his position of dominance in the rap hierarchy. Dre, in fact, became the prime motivating force behind gangsta rap's second period of prominence that lasted from 1999 to 2002.

Eminem won consecutive Grammy awards for best rap album. In 1999, *The Slim Shady LP* earned the honor, followed by his 2000 release, *The Marshall Mathers LP*. The latter became the fastest-selling rap album of all time, the fastest-selling album by a solo artist, and the second-fastest-selling album ever. ('N Sync's 2000 album, *No Strings Attached*, sold faster.) In 2000, Eminem joined luminary gangsta artists (for example, Dr. Dre, Snoop Dogg, and Ice Cube) as part of the "Up in Smoke" tour, the most successful rap tour in the short history of the genre. At the time, a concert industry trade publication correctly predicted the tour's outcome: "The timing absolutely could not have been better ... Eminem brings a huge cross-cultural appeal."[13] In other words, Eminem added even more white youth to the concert-going audience. Eminem's fame was such that the *New York Times* reported a rumor that *Time* magazine would name Eminem its "Man of the Year" for 2000.[14] In the summer of 2001, Eminem's group, D-12, saw its *Devil's Night* move to No. 1 on the charts upon its release. His film debut in the semiautobiographical *8 Mile* won him critical acclaim. *8 Mile* had the eighth-highest opening week gross of the 296 movies released in 2002. The same year, *The Eminem Show* and the *8 Mile* soundtrack moved directly to No. 1 upon their release. The former was the biggest-selling album of the year. Journalists proclaimed 2002 "the Year of Eminem."[15] As of March 2008, Eminem is the second-leading rap artist of all time. His 27 million units sold trails only 2Pac's (Tupac Shakur) 36.5 million total.

Eminem's success drew attention to his lyrics. In June 2001, for the first time ever, the Federal Communications Commission (FCC) fined a radio station for playing a "clean" version of a song. The focus of attention was Eminem's "The Real Slim Shady." In the FCC's opinion, "The edited version of the song contains unmistakable offensive sexual references in conjunction with sexual expletives that appear intended to pander and shock."[16] However, in January 2002, the FCC reversed its opinion and decided that the material broadcast was not patently offensive, and thus not actionably indecent. Apparently, the FCC thought that a word in "The Real Slim Shady" was "jerkin'," and referred to masturbation. But further investigation determined that the word in question was "Jergens," the brand name of a lotion.

It was not until November 2004 that Eminem released another studio album, *Encore*, which sold less than one-half of total of 9 million

albums reached by *The Eminem Show*. As one *Encore* reviewer concluded, Eminem has "past his allotted time."[17] More to the point, after
2002, gangsta rap "fell out of vogue" and was replaced by music characterized as "playa/pimp/balla/high-roller" rap.[18] The new emphasis
was on street-oriented manhood roles rather than criminal conduct per
se.[19] Nevertheless, Eminem's *Curtain Call: The Hits*, a greatest-hits com-
pilation, entered 2006 as the No. 1 selling album and was the No. 6
selling album of 2006. Perhaps stating the obvious, Eminem's Web site
(http://www.eminem.com) opens with an animated advertisement for
Curtain Call that features him appearing at a "Hip-Hop Heroes of Yes-
terday" concert (accessed March 15, 2008).

RAP'S VIOLENT MISOGYNY: 1987 TO 1993

To explore the frequency and nature of misogynist themes in gangsta rap, lyrics were gathered from 490 songs produced by thirteen
artists from 1987 to 1993 and then classified by the type of violence
involved.[20] Violent acts run the gamut in terms of the severity of harm
intended or caused, extending from threats designed to frighten someone into submission to assaults aimed to harm, maim, or kill. Here, the
focus is only on the most serious instances of criminal violence directed
toward women: assault, forcible rape, and murder, sometimes termed
femicide. Since these categories are not mutually exclusive, included is
the combination of rape and murder. Analysis of lyric content shows
that 22 percent (n = 107) of the 490 gangsta rap songs had violent misogynist lyrics. Assault was the most frequently occurring criminal
offense, portrayed in half (50 percent) of the violent misogynist songs;
murder was next in frequency, occurring in almost one-third of the lyrics (31 percent); and rape was least frequent, occurring in just over one
in 10 of the violent gangsta rap songs (11 percent).

Identifying the frequency of violent acts provides very limited information about the context in which these crimes are described. A passing reference to killing a woman who has betrayed a lover is less
revealing or salient than a detailed account of the person to be killed,
how specifically the act will be carried out, and why, that is, in
response to what behavior. The following section describes how these
crimes are depicted or enacted and the context in which these depictions and enactments occur.

Assault. The assault category is divided into nine subcategories, beginning with violence that results from something a woman says because
that's where gangsta rap begins its portrayals of violence against women.
The other categories are bad attitude, bad decisions, crime, intimate
relationships, pimp-prostitute relationships, personal characteristics,
pimp-prostitute relationships, sex, and finally, instances in which the
rappers don't offer an explanation for their violence against women.

Talk. Ice-T's "6 'N the Mornin'" (1987) and Eazy-E's and N.W.A's "Boyz-N-the-Hood" (1988) anticipated and affected gangsta rap's matter-of-fact depictions of violence against women. These songs concerned assault and signaled the coming age of gender-based conflict as a staple of the genre. In "6 'N the Mornin'," Ice-T batters a woman, heretofore a stranger, because she called him a name. "Boyz-N-the-Hood" suggests physical punishment for women who "talk shit." Dr. Dre presents the identical message in "Nuthin' but a 'G' Thang," a song often considered the No. 1 rap song of all time. Ice-T (in "My Word Is Bond") and Too short (in "Invasion of the Flat Booty Bitches" and "Way Too Real") react violently if women talk back. MC Ren (in "Right up My Alley") believes that women who complain should be hit with a shoe. Too short (in "All My Bitches Are Gone") hits a woman in the jaw because she yelled at him, then hurls into a tirade about breaking body parts. The Geto Boys (in "Talkin' Loud Ain't Saying Nothin'") physically punish a woman who simply talks to another man. They plan "to bust" her in her "goddamn mouth."

Bad Attitude. For N.W.A (in "Findum, Fuckum and Flee"), violence is the way to respond if women "diss," that is, show disrespect to them. Their suggestion is to "smack the bitch up." In another N.W.A song, "A Bitch Iz a Bitch," money-hungry or stuck-up women are dealt with in the same way: "Slam her ass in a ditch." Too short slaps women who act "shitty" (in "Freaky Tales") or bold (in "I Ain't Nothin' but a Dog"). Responses to mental slowness are equally harsh. In "Don't Come to Big," Bushwick Bill kicks a woman's ass if her "brain don't click."

Bad Decisions. If women choose the wrong friends, Willie D (in "Pass da Piote") says that they'll "need stitches" and Ice-T (in "Depths of Hell") will drop-kick them. For Eazy-E (in "Only If You Want It"), rejecting a sexual proposition provokes a physical attack.

Crime. Violence and criminality are linked. In "Trigga Happy Nigga," the Geto Boys kick a female employee for not quickly complying with their commands during a robbery. Ice-T (in "6 'N the Morning'") raps about a homeboy who broke his girlfriend's jaw "for smokin' cane." The desire for drugs even destroys a parent-child relationship. Snoop Dogg (in "Lodi Dodi") meets a woman who wants to take over her daughter's source of drugs, which happens to be Snoop himself. The mother hits her child "in the face" and punches her "in the eye" and "in the belly." N.W.A, in both versions of "Dope Man," tell of a woman who "got a black eye cause the dope man hit her."

Intimate Relationships. Marriage is depicted in violent misogynist terms. Consider "Bitches 2," where Ice-T mentions a friend who regularly "kicks his wife's ass." Domestic relationships are potentially problematic. Too short's (in "Step Daddy") domestic sexual encounters begin when he whips "ass like a world champ." Bushwick Bill, in his autobiographical "Ever So Clear," went "looking for somebody to take my pain out on" and traveled to the home of the women "closest" to him. Upon arriving, he "provoked her, punched her, kicked, and choked her." After trying to throw her baby out of a window, he's accidently shot in the eye. (Until the releases of Eminem's " '97 Bonnie & Clyde," in *The Slim Shady LP* and "Kim," in *The Marshall Mathers LP*, this was gangsta rap's only mention of killing children.) Tardy breakfasts are hard to handle. In Too Much Trouble's "Mother Fuckin' Thugs," violence accompanies the command to put some "eggs in the goddamn skillet."

Personal Characteristics. In "Punk Bitch," Too short expresses his desire to slap all bald-headed women. Ice-T (in "Lifestyles of the Rich and Infamous") pushes a woman to the floor because "she looked like Godzilla." Because a woman had "more crabs than a seafood platter," Eazy-E (in "Still Talkin'") "slapped the ho" and proudly proclaimed himself a "woman-beater." The Geto Boys (in "This Dick's for You") punished an "unsanitary bitch" by throwing her into a ditch.

Pimp-Prostitute Relations. Here, hurting women is part of the "work" men do to become men. The violence alternates between using women as sex objects and defending traditional womanhood against degradation identified with prostitution. Pimp-prostitute associations are a common locale for violence against women. In documentary fashion, Too Much Trouble depict themselves as pandering pimps in seven selections from their album, *Players Choice*. In five of these songs ("Best Little Whorehouse in Texas," "Break Yourself Bitch," "Bring It On," "Pimpin' Ain't Dead," and "Pleasin' My Pimp"), workers get "smacked" if they fail to meet their financial quotas. In "Who's the Mack," Ice Cube recommends similar actions: "Come short of the money, get your ass kicked." Alternatively, in "Little Hooker," Willie D beats a young girl *because* she became a prostitute.

Sex. Violent misogyny also takes the form of overly aggressive and rough sex. Scarface (in "The Pimp") brags that "bitches walk out of the crib with a limp," while Ice Cube (in "Dirty Mack") nearly breaks "that thing in half" during sex with a new partner. Too Much Trouble (in "If You Ain't Suckin'") say that after oral sex, they "leave some stretch marks" on a woman's jaw. Of course, another example of this is Ice-T's (in "The Iceberg") previously mentioned use of a flashlight as a sexual device.

Identifying a rapper as the father of one's unborn child generates a harsh response. In "You Can't Fade Me," Ice Cube plans to end a pregnancy by kicking the woman carrying his child "in the tummy" and by looking in a closet "for the hanger," by which he implies using a coat hanger for an abortion. The Geto Boys (in both versions of "Gangster of Love") handle a false accusation of paternity by trying to break the woman's neck. Too short (in "Way Too Real") deals with a similar situation by surprising the woman "like a mack" and then dropping "her ass off at Kaiser [hospital]."

No Apparent Reason. Without offering any excuse, Too Much Trouble (in "How Much Ghetto Can You Take") mentions only that "a bitch is just like glass—easy to break."

In the following songs, women are attacked but the reasons for the attacks remain unknown:

- —hit (in Ice Cube's "Make it Rough, Make it Smooth");
- —kicked (in Too short's "short Dog's In the House");
- —slapped (in Too short's "Cusswords" and "Rap Like Me");
- —smacked (in Too Much Trouble's "Jack Mission" and Too short's "Playboy Short II");
- —thrown into a trunk (in Too short's "In the Trunk");
- —tossed (in Eazy-E's "Ruthless Villain").

Rape

Willie D (in "Fuck Me Now") and Too short (in "Just Another Day") advocate raping women who do not submit to their sexual advances. In "Short Side," another of Too short's rape narratives, he beats his victim's "ass with a billy-club." In "She Swallowed It," N.W.A recommends specific procedures for attacking a fourteen-year-old by punching her, throwing her to the ground, and forcing her to have oral sex.

Ice-T (in Body Count's "KKK Bitch") proposes sex "with Tipper Gore's two twelve-year-old nieces." This is a clear case of seeking revenge against one of the founders of the Parents' Music Resource Center (PMRC). Founded in 1985, the PMRC succeeded in having the Recording Industry Association of America (RIAA) voluntarily label albums that contained explicit sex, violence, or substance abuse with the words, "Parental Advisory: Explicit Lyrics." ("KKK Bitch" was released in 1992. Later that year, Albert Gore, Tipper's husband, was elected vice president of the United States.)

As horrible as are the images conjured up by the criminal category of rape, the substance of the rapes in gangsta rap is more vicious still. Eazy-E (in "Nobody Move"), Snoop Dogg (in "Ain't No Fun"), and Too short (in "Punk Bitch") casually mention gang rapes. MC Ren (in "Behind the Scenes") tells of "ten niggas" who rape a child and then violate her with a broomstick. In Ice Cube's "Givin' Up the Nappy Dug Out," "fourteen niggas" line up to take turns placing themselves "two on top, one on the bottom" of an underage girl. Ice Cube claims that the victim enjoys the attack. When confronted by the girl's father, Ice Cube tells him that his daughter "is a slut" and mentions that he has already prepared a defense in case he gets in trouble with the law.

Apparently, Ice Cube didn't realize that he was guilty of statutory rape—sex with an underage partner is illegal regardless of whether the victim consented.

Too short conceives of an array of alternatives in his consideration of the pluses and minuses of statutory rape. In "She's a Bitch," he adapts a crude expression by implying that "if she can bleed then she can fuck." He recites similar words in "Hoes." But in "Little Girls," after an attempted rape fails, he rallies against sex with children.

Murder

Although the police targeted Too Much Trouble (in "Still on the Run"), they mistakenly shot and killed a "bitch." Other songs by Too Much Trouble have women dying in defense of personal possessions (in "Invasion") and their employers' property (in "Fugitives on the Run"). During another robbery, one "old bitch got her neck broke" (in "Wanted Dead or Alive"). MC Ren (in "Same Old Shit") tells about shooting a woman who set him up to be robbed. In "To Kill a Hooker," N.W.A drag a streetwalking prostitute into their car and kill her because she demanded money in exchange for sex.

Eazy-E (in "Neighborhood Sniper") murders a woman for choosing the wrong companion. The Geto Boys (in "Murder Avenue") kill a woman who asks too many questions. In "Gangsta Fairytale 2," Ice Cube feeds a girl to the wolves. Because "the little ho had no words ... the bitch got served."

Three other personal traits stimulate killing women: weight, poor hygiene, and style of grooming. In a song entitled, "Fat Girl," N.W.A try to kill a "fat girl" with an elephant gun. When that didn't work, they "grabbed a harpoon" and left the woman on the avenue "like a beached whale." MC Ren (in "You Wanna Fuck Her") mulls over shooting and burying a "bitch" whose "pussy really stinks" and who has "crabs on her pussy." In "Bald Headed Hoes," Willie D proposes "a bill on Capitol Hill to kill all bald-headed women at will."

Rappers plan murders to pay back women who, in their opinion, did something wrong. Transgressions include telling a lie (Scarface in "The Wall"), transmitting a venereal disease (in both versions of the Geto Boys' "Assassins" and N.W.A's "Just Don't Bite It"), and calling the cops (N.W.A's "The Dayz of Wayback"). Upon his release from jail, Eazy-E (in "Eazy-Duz-It") kills a woman who failed to make his bail.

Of course, a woman's unfaithfulness is a major issue. In "One Less Bitch," N.W.A's surprise discovery of a cheating mate propels them to dump the unfaithful partner, wearing cement shoes, into a river. Willie D (in "Trip Across from Mexico") and the Geto Boys (in "Cereal Killer") also kill cheaters. In the latter example, they report "nearly cuttin' the bitch in half."

In "Mack Attack" and "Ain't Nothin' but a Word to Me," Too short murders women but never offers a hint at what caused the killings. Bushwick Bill (in "Call Me Crazy") simply brags that he is the "neighborhood bitch slayer." In their two versions of "Let a Ho Be a Ho," the Geto Boys recommend putting "a ho in front of a trigger." Without supplying any explanation, N.W.A (in "Appetite for Destruction") say they took the life of a wife and daughter. N.W.A (in "Straight Outta Compton") also reminisce about "bitches" that they have shot and announce their plans to "smother" someone's mother. The Geto Boys kill a person's wife "for kicks" (in "It Ain't Shit") and pump anonymous women "full of lead" (in both versions of "Scarface"). In "Mr. Scarface," Scarface, a member of the Geto Boys, recounts the same senseless killings.

Songs combining murder and mutilation exemplify a harsh positioning of women as objects of violence. The Geto Boys (in "Chuckie") attack someone's nieces and cut the girls' heads into "eighty-eight pieces." Bushwick Bill recalls this incident in "Chuckwick," saying, "remember what happened to your motherfuckin' nieces." But Bushwick Bill adds cannibalism to the story. His breakfast menu includes "bacon and legs." Ice-T (in Body Count's "Momma's Gotta Die Tonight") sets his mother on fire, beats her to death with a baseball bat, and then disposes of her body. In both versions of the Geto Boys' "Assassins," the murder weapon of choice is a machete.

Rape and Murder

Too Much Trouble (in "Take the Pussy") kill an elderly rape victim whom they caught crawling for the telephone in order to dial 911. First, they hit her on the head with a hammer. The sound of a hammer hitting someone's head accompanies the lyrics. Then they beat her head with a phone as an operator's recorded message echoes in the background. In "One Less Bitch," N.W.A provide elaborate details of a rape-murder. In both versions of "Blow Job Betty," Too short slaps a young girl to force her to perform oral sex, after which the child dies by choking on sperm.

The Geto Boys produced two versions of their signature song and their only gold (selling more than 500,000 copies) single, "Mind of a Lunatic." Both begin by noting the identical initial actions of a Peeping Tom-turned rapist, blaming the victim's fate on the fact that she had her curtains opened. In the original rendition that appeared on *Grip It! On That Other Level*, she begs not to be killed, but her throat is slit. The revised version, in their self-titled album, heightens the macabre, noting that the Peeping Tom had sex with the corpse and drew on the walls with blood like Helter Skelter. (By using the term "Helter Skelter," the Geto Boys link themselves to Charles Manson, who used the expression to describe the mass murders carried out by his followers.

Interestingly, Manson took the words "Helter Skelter" from the title of a song on the Beatles' *White Album*. Consequently, we have confirmation that life imitates art and art imitates life.) In "Skitzo," Bushwick Bill, another member of the Geto Boys, recites the same lyrics. In "Murder Avenue," the Geto Boys depict a similar rape and murder, only this time they slit the woman's "fuckin' stomach and watched her squeal like a pig."

RAP'S VIOLENT MISOGYNY: 1999–2002

Eminem stands alone in his prominence and in his pervasive purveying of violent misogyny. Once again, criminal categories are used to classify the lyrics.

Of the forty-three Eminem songs analyzed, 56 percent had a violent misogynist content.[21] Of these, murder (50 percent) was the dominant category. Rapes and murders (38 percent) were second. Assault was the only violent act in 13 percent of these songs. No song dealt with a rape that did not also include a killing. But Eminem's work adds a bit of complexity to this basic categorization. Many of the songs dealing with murder and rape-murder present distinct instances of criminal behavior. A song categorized as dealing with murder may have more than one murder portrayed. The rape-murder songs possibly present different instances of victimization. In fact, a tabulation of the number of specific criminal acts against women reveals the following: twenty-nine murders; thirteen rapes; and four assaults.

Assault

Compared to what follows, Eminem's assault songs are comparative calm. There are three songs in which assault is the only crime mentioned: "Marshall Mathers," "The Real Slim Shady," and "White America." In "Amityville" and "Who Knew," an assault accompanies a distinctly different and more serious criminal act against women.

In "The Real Slim Shady," Eminem approvingly mentions a celebrity who threw his equally famous wife "over furniture" and "started whoppin' her ass." After all, Eminem (in "Who Knew") is proud that he treated with his own wife in the following way: "I beat her fuckin' ass every night." In "Marshall Mathers," Eminem alleges: "I don't need help ... to beat up two females." But the boast was framed by the equally misogynist and homophobic notion that rival rappers are like women, that is, "two little flaming faggots." In "Amityville," Eminem states: "I slap bitches," and the sound of someone getting slapped immediately follows. Finally, in "White America," Eminem complains that he is unfairly singled out for criticism even though he is not the first rapper "to smack a bitch."

Murder and Rape-Murder

One of the summary devices the FBI uses to catalog homicides in the United States is to classify them by the weapon used. I examined Eminem's weapons of choice.

Firearms. In "Remember Me," Eminem appears to have beaten a woman to death. He hit her and immediately her "whole head split up." But he adds that he also shot her: "Hollow tips is the lead, the .45 threw." In "Soldier," Eminem threatens "bitches" will "get shot, whether it's your [*sic*] fault or not." In "Kill You," Eminem assures a "bitch" that he "ain't gonna" shoot her. Instead, he plans to put a bullet right through her. In "I'm Shady," he instructs others on how to use a Glock pistol to "murder a girl." In "Bitch Please II," Eminem shoots up a club with a .44. That at least one "bitch" and one "girl" were in attendance had been previously established.

Sound effects accompany the shootings in two songs. In "Guilty Conscience," a cheating woman and her partner are confronted. At first, Eminem offers a recommendation: "cut this bitch's head off." But, on second thought, he suggests shooting her and her lover. The song includes the sounds of gunshots. Another scenario from "Guilty Conscience" has Eminem telling a potential liquor store robber to kill the female clerk, saying, "shoot that bitch." But whether the thief actually followed his suggestion is left to the listeners' speculation. "Criminal" concerns a bank robbery during which a woman teller begs: "Don't kill me. Please don't kill me." Eminem tells her, "I'm not gonna fuckin' kill you." But he does. After the sound of the shot, Eminem politely says, "Thank you."

Knifes or Cutting Instruments. In "Just Don't Give a Fuck," Eminem plans to slit a bitch's throat. (Here, however, the term "bitch" may be referring to a man.) In "When the Music Stops," D-12's Kuniva joins Eminem and raps that he is going to "fuck a ho with a knife." Eminem (in "Role Model") claims he killed Nicole Brown Simpson. Although the weapon of choice is unspecified, everyone knows that a knife-wielding assailant murdered her. In "Kill You," the female victim of a machete attack is not named. Upon meeting a woman, Eminem (in "As the World Turns") laments that all he wanted to do was "rape the bitch." Later, however, he decides to "kill her." Because she survives being shot five times, he grabs a "pocket knife and sliced off her right nipple." Eventually, the "fat slut" dies. In "Under the Influence," Eminem looks for and finds someone to rape and then uses a knife to dismember his victim, leaving parts of her body "wrapped up in the blinds" and "hung from the drapes." In "Who Knew," he puts wives at risk with knives. In "Amityville," Eminem is joined by Bizarre, a member of D-12, who rhymes about slitting his mother's throat.

In "Kim," more sound effects are added. Kim, the name of the woman Eminem married and divorced twice and the mother of his child, has her throat slashed. The song concludes with the sound of a woman gagging and having her throat cut. Prior to Kim's demise, Eminem killed her new husband and his son. Although recorded earlier than "Kim," the temporally subsequent, "'97 Bonnie & Clyde," details the throat-cut victims' burial in a lake. In "Kill You," Eminem asserts that he "invented violence, you vile venomous volatile bitches" and then the sound of a chainsaw revving up is heard.

Blunt Objects. In "Role Model," Eminem reports that he murdered his mother by hitting her "over the head with a shovel."

Personal Weapons. In another example from "Role Model," Eminem has a confrontation with Hillary Clinton, after which he "ripped her fuckin' tonsils out." In "My Name Is," Eminem "got pissed off" and tore a woman's "tits off." The question of whether these victims lived or died is unanswered. But in both instances, it appears death would follow. In "Drips," a cheating ho has her "fuckin' neck" bent back. Before doing this, Eminem had planned to kick the pregnant "bitch" in the stomach.

Poison. In "Superman," Eminem is annoyed by a woman who tries to establish a relationship with him. Basically, he warns her that if she doesn't leave him alone, she might discover "anthrax on a Tampax." (Anthrax is an infectious disease that is fatal if left untreated. Tampax is a leading brand of tampon made by Proctor & Gamble.)

Narcotics. In "My Fault," Eminem presumes that a party-going woman "came to get laid." So he decides to rape her by forcing her to eat mushrooms: "Shut up slut! Chew up this mushroom." It turns out that she eats too much of the psychoactive substance, loses her mind, drinks Lysol, and dies.

Drowning. In "As the World Turns," it is likely that Eminem kills a woman by drowning. The song "Stan" concerns a crazed Eminem fan who ties up his girlfriend, puts her in the trunk of his car, drives off a bridge, and drowns her.

Strangulation. In "Kill You," two different instances of strangulation are specified. In one, Eminem recites the threat of silencing a woman's vocal cords. In the other example, he comments that he intends to choke a "fat bitch."

Other Weapons or Weapons Not Stated. In "I'm Shady," Eminem confesses that he murdered someone's girlfriend and then, as an aside, remarks, "I did!"

Rape

Eminem labels himself a rapist (in "As the World Turns" and "Criminal") and reveals that he is constantly motivated by a "criminal intent to sodomize women" (in "Kill You"). In general, he advises his audience to "rape sluts" (in "Who Knew"). Another song ("My Fault") simply mentions that a father raped his daughter. In "Just Don't Give a

Table 7.2.
Violent Misogynist Lyrics: Foundational Period and Eminem

Artists	Number of Songs	Number with VM Lyrics (% of Total Songs)	Lyric Portrayals of Assault (% of VM Songs)	Lyric Portrayals of Rape (% of VM Songs)	Lyric Portrayals of Murder (% of VM Songs)	Lyric Portrayals of Rape & Murder (% of VM Songs)
Early Gangsta Rap	490	107 (22%)	54 (50%)	12 (11%)	33 (31%)	8 (7%)
Eminem	43	24 (56%)	3 (13%)	0 (0%)	12 (50%)	9 (38%)
Percent Increase/ Decrease		+34%	−37%	−11%	+19%	+31%

* Rounding numbers affected percentages.

Fuck," Eminem remembers that when he was in the eighth grade, he "went to gym" and "raped the women's swim team." After rapping this absurdity, he claims that he's not joking, that he's "no comedian." Eminem (in "Kill You") brags about raping his mother after instructing her to "just bend over and take it like a slut, okay Ma?" In "Guilty Conscience," beside the previously mentioned murder, a rape also occurs. A fifteen-year-old girl has a date-rape drug slipped into her drink.

In "Amityville," Bizarre notes that ten boys took his little sister's virginity on her birthday. Bizarre also contributes to "Under the Influence" by adding a line about rape. He lets a rival know that he spent some time "fuckin' your bitch in the ass with a tire iron." Obviously, we can assume that the woman wasn't a willing participant in this encounter.

CONCLUSIONS

Eminem's lyrics are consistently more violent than those of the artists in gangsta rap's foundational period. Whereas the 22 percent of the earlier rapes involve misogynistic acts of violence, more than half of Eminem's do. Table 7.2 presents the comparison in greater detail.

Too Much Trouble (the Baby Geto Boys) was the early titleholder, with 48 percent of its songs having a violent misogynist content. This most violent group was far less commercially successful than other representatives of the foundational period. Eminem surpassed this group's violent misogynist score and was, alternatively, the most commercially successful gangsta rapper.[22]

At the beginning of the 1990s, a focal point in the foundational period, *Billboard* editorialized against gangsta rap because it purveyed a "gangsta ideology," an unabashed espousal of violence and misogyny.[23] A *New York Times* editorial did likewise.[24] The late C. DeLores Tucker, then chair of the National Political Congress of Black Women and the most famous opponent of gangsta rap, considered the genre a profane and obscene glorification of murder and rape. Tucker held that gangsta rap is "filthy music" that teaches children "it's cool to murder, it's cool to rape." Gangsta rap, according to Tucker, was more suitably called "gangsta porno rap."[25] Other commentators agreed, characterizing rap as the domain of "lethal lyrics" and the genre itself as "violent pornography." But other scholars challenged the notion that violent misogynist lyrics were central to the gangsta rap enterprise. Such interpretations were considered a mere "moral panic."[26] Here, condemnations of gangsta rap's violent misogyny were seen as misdirected. This alternative position found that gangsta rap offered only a "seeming" glorification of violence against women.[27] The point was that critics attacked the words used but did not consider the context in which they were spoken. Supposedly, criticisms of gangsta rap's violent misogyny unfairly removed the lyrics from their context.[28] The two positions of the debate are clear: either gangsta rap is a violent misogynist enterprise or it is not.

This research establishes the frequency and nature of gangsta rap's violent misogynist lyrics in its foundational period. An immediate consequence of the content analysis is a "both/and" resolution to the either/or debate: "only" 22 percent of the songs had violent misogynist lyrics. Further, assault, the least-serious of the specified criminal acts, is the modal category of the violent misogynist lyrics. In addition, Dr. Dre and Snoop Dogg, the two premier artists of the period, combined for only three of the 107 cases of violent misogynist lyrics.[29]

Mainstream defenders of Eminem are hard to find. Kurt Loder, MTV's prime commentator, said that Eminem's success represented "the decline of the whole p.c. [political correctness] regime."[30] But other critics were not so complimentary. The National Congress of Black Women continued to fight against lyrics that glorify violence and denigrate women. The organization noted that "even worse lyrics [were] typified by gangsta/porno rapper Eminem."[31] In September 2000, Lynne Cheney, wife of the then-vice presidential candidate and future Vice President Dick Cheney, recited some of Eminem's lyrics before a Senate hearing. In 2001, Lynne Cheney told CNN that, "Eminem is certainly, I think, the most extreme example of rock lyrics used to demean women [and] advocate violence against women."[32] With the majority of Eminem's songs containing violent misogynist lyrics, it appears that the critics are correct.

Early gangsta rappers' and Eminem's lyrics, in particular, are evidence of a commercially established "rape culture." A rape culture is a complex set of beliefs supporting a continuum of threatened violence against women that ranges from sexual remarks to rape itself. It is a "culture" in the sense that it establishes a framework for the way men and women are supposed to interact with one another. By using the terms "bitch" and "ho" to refer to women, gangsta rappers "oppress women as a group."[33] Their portrayals of crimes of violence against women say, in effect, that "women as a group" are suitable targets of such horrible acts. When members of the National Political Congress of Black Women held a protest outside of a store selling gangsta rap music, one of the marchers carried a sign with the slogan, "Gangsta Rap Is Rape."[34] Minimally, gangsta rap lyrics are rather dramatic examples of the male use of language as violence.

This chapter has described gangsta rap's two historical periods: 1987 to 1993 and 1999 to 2002. Once again, commentators have reported on the death of the genre. In 2007, the *Washington Post* had gangsta rap "dying in the streets" and the (New York) *Daily News* reported that the "final nail" has been hammered into gangsta rap's "coffin."[35] With the 2008 publication of Eminem's autobiography, *The Way I Am*, many of the debates surrounding violence against women in music resurfaced.

Whether the themes will resurface during the Obama presidency remains to be seen.

NOTES

1. P. Katel, "Debating Hip-Hop," *CQ Researcher Beta*, 17 (June 15, 2007): 4.

2. Ray Charles, quoted in M. Silver, "Still soulful after all these years," *U.S. News and World Report* (September 22, 1997): 76.

3. Chuck D, quoted in G. Chambers and J. Morgan, "Droppin' Knowledge: A Rap Roundtable," *Essence* (September 1992): 85.

4. Snoop Dogg, *Week in Rock*, MTV (September 12, 1993).

5. Eminem, quoted in Z. Smith, "The Zen of Eminem," *Vibe* (November 2002): 92.

6. Eminem, quoted in C. Weiner, *Eminem: In His Own Words* (London: Omnibus Press, 2001), 80.

7. Dr. Dre, *Week in Rock*, MTV (September 2, 1996); Dr. Dre, quoted in A. Samuels and D. Gates, "Last Tango in Compton," *Newsweek* (November 25, 1996): 74; and Dr. Dre, quoted in P. M. Reilly, "Has Gangsta Rap's Popularity Started to Slip," *The Wall Street Journal* (September 20, 1996): B2.

8. E. Osayande, *Gangsta Rap is Dead* (Philadelphia: Talking Drum Communications, 1996).

9. J. Whalen, "Rap Defies Traditional Marketing," *Advertising Age* (March 21, 1994): 12.

10. D. Samuels, "The Rap On Rap," *New Republic* (November 11, 1991): 24–29.

11. D. Dickerson, quoted in B. Pulley, "How a 'Nice Girl' Evolved into Boss, the Gangster Rapper," *The Wall Street Journal* (February 2, 1994): A1.

12. R. Morales, "Eminem Psycho 2000," *Source* 130 (July 2000): 186.

13. G. Bongiovanni, editor-in-chief of *Pollstar*, quoted in G. Boucher, "Cover Story: This Rap Tour is Really Smokin'," *Los Angeles Times* (June 15, 2000): F6.

14. N. Strauss, "The Pop Life: Seeking The Truth about Eminem," *New York Times* (December 21, 2000): E3.

15. B. McCollum, "Pop Music," *Detroit Free Press* (December 22, 2002). Retrieved December 23, 2002, from http://www.freep.com; and N. Strauss, "The Year that Pop Lost Popularity," *New York Times* (December 26, 2002): E1.

16. Quoted in Neal N. Travis, "FCC Turns Eminem Song into 'Fine' Art," *New York Post* (June 6, 2001): 3.

17. R. Christgau, "Heads, Future and Past," *Village Voice* (January 11, 2005). Retrieved December 22, 2007, from http://www.villagevoice.com.

18. M. A. Neal, *"Soul Babies—Black Popular Culture and the Post-Soul Aesthetic* (New York: Routledge, 2002): 189, quoted in William Oliver, " 'The Streets': An Alternative Black Male Socialization Institution," *Journal of Black Studies* 36 (July 2006): 926.

19. Eminem's songs in *Encore* and those of artist 50 Cent are better described as a "playa/pimp/balla/high-roller" rap, not gangsta rap. In *Encore*, violent misogyny is mentioned in three songs. In "My First Single," Eminem explains that his early use of expressions such as "slap a bitch and smack a ho" were intended as mere "catchy" little jingles. In "Crazy in Love" and "I Love You

More," he places violence against a partner as a reaction to provocation in what he calls, in the former, a "crazy" and in the latter, a "sad" and "sick" relationship. 50's (or "Fitty") *Get Rich or Die Tryin'*, his first major-label album, and *The Massacre*, were produced by Eminem and Dr. Dre. Both were the No. 1 albums of the year in 2003 and 2005, respectively. Both albums are filled with examples of misogyny and violence. Neither, however, has any violent misogynist content. The same is true for 50's 2007 release, *Curtis*. But this album reached only No. 37 in sales in 2007.

20. The artists and their albums: (1) Bushwick Bill, *Little Big Man*, 1992; (2) Dr. Dre, *The Chronic*, 1992; (3) Eazy-E, *Eazy-Duz-It*, 1988; *5150 Home 4 Tha Sick*, 1992; *It's On (Dr. Dre) 187mm Killa*, 1993; (4) The Geto Boys, *Making Trouble*, 1988; *Grip It! On That Other Level*, 1989; *The Geto Boys*, 1990; *We Can't Be Stopped*, 1991; *Till Death Do Us Part*, 1993; (5) Ice Cube, *Kill At Will*, 1990; *AmeriKKKa's Most Wanted*, 1990; *Death Certificate*, 1991; *The Predator*, 1991; *Lethal Injection*, 1993; (6) Ice-T, *Rhyme Pays*, 1987; *Power*, 1988; *The Iceberg/Freedom of Speech*, 1989; *O.G. Original Gangster*, 1991; Body Count [Ice-T], *Body Count*, 1992; *Home Invasion*, 1993; (7) MC Ren, *Kizz My Black Azz*, 1992; *Shock of the Hour*, 1993; (8) N.W.A, *Straight Outta Compton*, 1988; *N.W.A and the Posse*, 1989; *100 Miles and Runnin'*, 1990; *Efil4zaggin*, 1991; (9) Scarface, *Mr. Scarface*, 1991; *The World Is Yours*, 1993; (10) Snoop Dogg, *Doggystyle*, 1993; (11) Too Much Trouble, *Bringing Hell on Earth*, 1992; *Players Choice*, 1993; (12) Too short, *Raw, Uncut, and X-Rated*, 1987; *Life Is . . . Too Short*, 1988; *Born to Mack*, 1988; *short Dog's in the House*, 1990; *Shorty the Pimp*, 1992; *Get In Where You Fit In*, 1993; (13) Willie D, *Controversy*, 1989; and *I'm Goin' Out Lika Soldier*, 1992.

21. Eminem's albums: *The Slim Shady LP*, 1999; *The Marshall Mathers LP*, 2000; and *The Eminem Show*, 2002.

22. Among gangsta rappers, Eminem holds first and second place in terms of sales. First, *The Marshall Mathers LP*, sold 9 million copies. Second, *The Eminem Show*, sold 8 million copies. He also tied for third place. Both his *The Slim Shady LP* and Snoop Dogg's *Doggystyle* sold 4 million copies.

23. Editorial, *Billboard* (November 23, 1991): 8.

24. B. Staples, "Editorial Notebook: The Politics of Gangster Rap," *New York Times* (August 27, 1993): A27.

25. Quoted in K. J. Kelly, "Levin Gets Rapped," [New York] *Daily News* (May 16. 1997): 72.

26. R. Potter, *Spectacular Vernaculars: Hip-Hop and the Politics of Postmodernism* (Albany: State University of New York Press, 1995), 86.

27. G. Wahl, "I Fought the Law (and I Cold [*Sic*] Won): Hip-Hop in the Mainstream," *College Literature* 26 (Winter 1999): 98.

28. G. Yancy, "Consider the Context Before Attacking the Words," *Philadelphia Tribune* (March 18, 1997): 7A.

29. Among gangsta rap's best-selling albums, Snoop is tied for third place with Eminem (see Note 20.) Dre is next in line. His *The Chronic* sold 3 million copies. Only five other gangsta rap albums have been certified as having more than 2 million in sales: Eazy-E's *Eazy-Duz-It* and *It's On (Dr. Dre) 187mm Killa*, Ice Cube's *The Predator*, N.W.A's *Straight Outta Compton*, and Too short's *Life Is . . . Too Short*.

30. Quoted in "Chris Norris, Artist of the Year," *Spin* 17 (January 2001). Retrieved July 14, 2002, from http://www.spin.com.

31. NCBW2001, "Crusading Against Gangsta/Porno Rap," *The National Congress of Black Women* (2001). Retrieved July 4, 2002, from http://www.npcbw.org.

32. Quoted in C. Siemaszko, "Cheney's Wife Raps Eminem," [New York] *Daily News* (February 21, 2001): 6.

33. T. M. Adams and D. B. Fuller, "The Words have Changed but the Ideology Remains the Same: Misogynist Lyrics in Rap Music," *Journal of Black Studies* 36 (July 2006): 949.

34. G. Lacharite, "Gangsta Rap Protest Gets 5 Arrested," *Washington Times* (December 12, 1993): C3.

35. C. Milloy, "Gangsta Rap, Dying In The Streets," *Washington Post* (September 19, 2007): B1; and E. Louis, "How to Kill Gangsta Music," [New York] *Daily News* (October 4, 2007) at elouis@nydailynews.com (accessed January 31, 2009).

FURTHER READING

G. Chambers and J. Morgan, "Droppin' Knowledge: A Rap Roundtable," *Essence* (September 1992): 83–85, 117–118, 120.

M. A. Neal, *Soul Babies: Black Popular Culture and the Post-Soul Aesthetic* (New York: Routledge, 2002).

D. Samuels, "The Rap on Rap," *New Republic* (November 11, 1991): 24–29.

C. Weiner, *Eminem: In His Own Words* (London: Omnibus Press, 2001).

Chapter 8

Troubling Violence through Performance

Elaine J. Lawless

Hester: Won't you answer those cries?

Reverend: If he dont respond to that then he's a good-for-nothing dead-beat, and you report him to the authorities. They'll garnish his wages so at least you all wont starve. I have a motivational cassette which speaks to that very subject. I'll give it to you free of charge.[1]

As an academic, my initial response to violence against women was to work in the local shelter in my town and tape record the stories of battered women living there. I was aware that abuse and violence against women were global concerns and often brought the topic into my courses on women's folklore, religion, and social justice. But I had rarely thought about relationship violence as an issue in our own community, let alone discussed it with students or colleagues. My work in the shelter altered me, as well as the way I want to advocate for change. The experience was intense; while only a few blocks from my university office, at the shelter, I felt I had entered a totally different world, a landscape filled with confusion, fear, death, and pain. But is the shelter really so alien from the places where the rest of us live and work?

As I am troubled deeply by violence against women, so too do I now want my work to "trouble" others in ways that move us toward finding innovative ways to eradicate violence against women. Starting local, exposing the violence we can identify in our midst, and calling for no tolerance in our own communities lays the groundwork for global change.

BACKGROUND TO PERFORMANCE

After two years of ethnographic research in a battered women's shelter during the late 1990s, I have turned to the performance of stories as advocacy work in the effort to stop violence against women. In both, the focus of the work depends on the use of narrative for personal and political ends. Before beginning my ethnographic research at the shelter, I took the requisite forty hours of volunteer training to work in the main office and answer the hotline. In the context of the women's shelter, I heard women tell their stories as they arrived seeking safety, in the shelter's kitchen as we prepared meals, in the children's rooms as they watched their own and each other's children, in the smoking room as they sat and talked, in the backyard as we watched their children play behind twelve-foot fences that would shield them from detection, and in the weekly support group meetings that included residents as well as community members who were seeking help for their own situations.

In the office, at any given time, there might be two or three shelter staff and volunteers working and answering the hotline. Several women seeking assistance and/or shelter might also be in the office. Police officers and rape counselors were often in the room as well because they had been called to assist. This is a busy, noisy, "messy" scene. Women arriving for shelter often bring their belongings with them in large plastic bags and have their small children in tow. Sometimes the women and the children are crying, either because they are afraid of what will happen or in response to actual violence. When the noise level calms a bit, I could hear stories being related to whoever is seeking information—it might be a staff person doing "intake," another shelter worker, a volunteer, the police officer, the rape counselor, or another woman staying at the shelter.

LISTENING TO STORIES OF VIOLENCE

Obvious to anyone who has worked in a safe shelter, the stories I heard in this context were privileged and could not be used for anything I might want to write or publish. I pondered this dilemma for months before I put up signs in the shelter, asking the residents if they would share their stories on tape for a book I wanted to write about them and their experiences with violence. I feared none would come forward, but in the end many actually wanted to participate.

I located a neglected room at the rear of the shelter, a room full of boxes and Christmas ornaments, abandoned stuffed animals, and a few broken chairs. I set up my tape recorder and waited for the women to volunteer. I did not "interview" them in any traditional sense—that is, I did not have a list of preconceived questions I wanted answered.

Rather, my approach was totally open-ended, asking them to "tell me your story," trusting that their "life story" would include the accounts of abuse and violence that had brought them to the shelter. I also trusted in the coherence of the story they would tell me at that moment—that is, I wanted to hear how they constructed their life within the context of the violence they had experienced. I was as interested in the storytelling as a vehicle for revealing and assessing the content it revealed as I was in the facts about violence. I wanted to hear about their childhoods. I listened for how they developed their sense of self. I heard them recount their "mistakes" with the men whom they loved and cared for. I heard their concerns for their children and especially for their girls who might face the same challenges. And I heard about the violence they endured and the confusion it engendered because it came from those who claimed to love them. Sometimes, in the telling, words failed them—they simply could not articulate what had happened to their bodies and their minds. For them, telling their stories to a concerned and interested listener not connected with their legal cases or part of their own family or trying to salve their wounds in any obvious sense was itself an unusual opportunity. As they told me their stories, they would often add an aside to note, "I'd never noticed I did that before," or "Now that I tell it, I can see more of the logic in what happened," suggesting how the telling of their story gave them an opportunity to reflect on as well as recount what had happened and why. Several told me that they hoped their stories would help other women be "smarter" or learn more quickly how to deal with a partner who was violent. They all thanked me for listening when we were done, and I thanked them for sharing their stories with me. At that point, I did not know what form my research might take. They had entrusted me with their private stories in the hope that together we could make a difference. I guaranteed them anonymity; they gave me their permissions.

In 2001, I published a book about the narratives of these brave women.[2] I was pleased with the book, particularly because the publisher agreed to include several of the longer stories verbatim. My argument was that the women's stories merited inclusion because they constituted a record of their experiences that had a narrative integrity, a cohesion, and a logic that was distinct from whatever insight my own commentary might add. The stories followed a thread: living with violence, surviving it, moving out of dangerous situations, and seeking safety at the shelter. But they also deserve attention at many other levels; for instance, for what they reveal about the women's childhoods and their evolving sense of self. The stories show how and why women find themselves in violent relationships, often revealing in the telling how the assumptions they had made about men and marriage were often betrayed by jealousy, battering, condescension, mental abuse, and outright violence. Through this work, I recognized that abuse takes many forms, is never easy to detect, and strikes in homes both well-to-do and poor. I found that neither race nor religion were good markers for violence, and I was appalled to meet one woman whose husband taught at the same university campus as I.

The power and intensity of the women's stories is best evident in the verbatim transcripts. I offer three segments here. These are not meant to be representative, but rather are accounts that impressed me with their poignancy as well as because they illustrate the reflexive markers within their personal experiences. Elaine Scarry talks about how terrorizers can "unmake" a person's world in *The Body in Pain*, a book about war and torture.[3] Clearly, the women's words do a far better job of explaining this reality than any analysis I could provide of their narratives.

Account #1: My job? Well, I had to clean the morgue. Oh, this is really interesting. I had this belief, because I was with Dale at the time—and at home you could look around and there was always blood somewhere—I could clean up, but there was always blood somewhere on my walls or whatever, and I hated that. And I had to clean the morgue, that was part of my area. Well, there was the autopsy table with all the blood. And I had this belief that if I could get all the blood off of that autopsy table that the abuse in my home would stop. I don't know how I associated that. But the morgue was brick, painted brick, you know, it's got those little holes. I would go through with a toothbrush and a toothpick, a wooden toothpick, trying to get the blood out of the little holes. Now, when I look back at it, it was crazy, but the whole time I was working in the morgue, cleaning the blood, it was somebody else's blood I was cleaning, it wasn't mine. And my morgue was spotless. When I got transferred over to the other hospital in surgery, every now and then we'd get a woman who had just had been—just beat to hell. And they would have to go in and like remove her spleen, because she got beat so bad. It was weird seeing a dead body that got beat, and then a woman go through all that stuff in surgery from being beat. It was weird. When it was me going through all that pain and stuff, that was one thing, but to actually sit and watch these other women go through it—it was like that was never going to happen to me. But it did. I've got this really long scar here right underneath my chin here, see? He put a knife through my chin because he said the pork chops weren't cooked right; he tried to cut my tongue out so I couldn't back talk him anymore.

Account #2: He started being abusive. I think he was drugging me to make me do sexual activities with him and his friends. I ended up getting pregnant, but he made me go have an abortion because he didn't know for sure if it was his or if it was his partner's. He told me that if I didn't have an abortion, that he would kick me so hard he would kill the baby. But I really didn't want an abortion, so I continued getting ass-beatings and broken bones, dislocated shoulder, broken legs, black eyes, you name it—I've had it all. Check the emergency room records, you'll see. He ran over me once with the car; he once drug me by the car when I tried to get out; he once made me take off all my clothes in the dead of winter and walk back into town. We lived out in the country; he made me take off all my clothes, shoes, and everything. There was snow on the ground and there was ice and my kids were in the backseat. It was late and the kids were in the back bundled up in a blanket, and he forced me out of the car and took off without me. Out there. I couldn't even tell you how long I walked, hours and hours it seemed. I ended up at a farmhouse. I was so cold and so numb. This old farmer come to the door and he saw me. I had black eyes where he had beaten me out of the car, and this man hollered at his wife. He turned around immediately when he saw that I didn't have no clothes on, and he yelled to his wife and she had brought me a robe to cover myself up with and she called the sheriff's department and the sheriff's department came and got me and took me right straight to the emergency room. I was frostbit on my hands and feet and a few other things. So then I went to my mother's house. And he got off work and he came to my Mom's house and he said, "Tell her to come out here." And my mom said, "She's not here." And he told her, "Don't lie to me. I know she's in the house." Well, he ended up kicking the door in. I was hiding from him, and he dragged me out by my hair and told me that I was going to come home. So I made several attempts to leave him and every time I did he'd end up finding me and I'd get it twice as bad. So it got to the point where I was scared to leave anymore because I knew what he was going to do. They told me to get an ex parte. I got an ex parte—an order of protection, but it didn't work. They put me in protective custody; I went into a shelter. Didn't work. He'd end up coming to the shelter and kicking the door in coming after me.

Account #3: I got beat up by a Bigfoot Tonka Truck. One of those remote-controlled things. He beat me in the face with it so bad I had to have a metal plate put in my head. They shaved the whole side of my head and pulled my skin down and replaced all this area because he had shattered all my bones on that side of my face. I waited until I healed up and I stayed with my mom at the time, and then I told her I was going back because my kids were there. And my mom begged and she cried and she said, "Please don't. Don't go back. One of these times, he's going to kill you."

THE PERFORMANCE TROUPE

These stories, and others like them, refused to leave me. I realized that publishing this book was just one step in my own work to end violence against women. I had honored the women's experiences with the book, made them part of the public record, and had argued for the power of women's words as part of their struggle against violence in their homes. Yet there was so much more to do. But where could I go next?

In the fall of 2003, I met Heather Carver, a colleague in performance studies who had organized a theatrical troupe in Texas to present monologues from patients who had received diagnoses of HIV or AIDS. The student performers in the troupe had memorized the stories and performed them for various classes on campus and for different groups in the community. The intent was to let the patients' voices be heard by using their own words and, during the discussion following the performances, to encourage audience members to tell their own stories or to empathize with those told. This, it was hoped, would foster understanding and encourage efforts at justice for the patients and their families. Carver viewed this performance troupe as a great success. Audiences had responded in positive ways, new alliances had been formed, and funding was secured.

These discussions spawned the idea for The Troubling Violence Performance Project. I was intrigued not only by Carver's enthusiasm for the project, but by the notion that dramatic performances of actual stories could educate and mobilize new audiences who perhaps were not aware of, or had ignored, the violence against women in their own families and our community. She explained that this was a different kind of theater, one without a stage, props, or costumes. She imagined how powerful it might be to tell women's stories about violence in classrooms and in the community:

> Only a woman and her voice, her story. After the stories have been performed, we will regroup with the audience and discuss the stories and ask the audience how they responded. We will ask them what they want to talk about. Just like the HIV stories I worked with in Texas, these are "taboo" stories in our culture because the subject—domestic violence—like AIDS, is a taboo subject, particularly for women. We do not have forums for these topics. They are our dirty little secrets. We get the stories out, then we talk about them with the audience.[4]

Eagerly, we began to plan how we might form such a performance troupe. Our intent was to "trouble" the violence, to make the violence visible, to expose it in our own neighborhoods, to encourage everyone in the room to accept their complicity in ignoring the problem, to help women understand that their stories were both unique and very similar to those of other women, to let women living with violence know that they were not alone and had options, to offer hope, and to build community through awareness and action.

In this collaboration, Carver and I have been working together to identify the intersections of performance studies and ethnographic studies as they have emerged in the twenty-first century. Her training is based solidly on the Chicago school of performance studies that identifies closely with Dwight Conquergood's work, a performance approach that grew directly out of the oral interpretation of literature that has expanded into arenas of performances of the self and the other. Because both of us have worked within social activist camps over the years, we determined that our goals in this project were activist in nature rather than primarily academic. That is, we wanted to combine the ethnographic research done by me with the performance approaches embraced by Carver to develop a performance troupe that would present monologues of women living with or trying to escape from violence in their lives and homes with the express purpose of creating a safe space for discussions of the problem and its impact on audience members.

Before we initiated the performance troupe, one of our mutual students chose to perform a narrative from my book for her assigned personal experience story in Carver's performance studies class. This provided a kind of case study for our ideas. In her early twenties, this soft-spoken woman had chosen a story about a boyfriend who became insanely jealous every time he saw his girlfriend with other people, male or female. The selection she performed recounts an incident when he sees his girlfriend in a car with a man from her workplace; she tells him she was only giving him a lift home, but the boyfriend becomes irate, loses control, beats her car hood in with his fists, tries to break out her car windows, rants, and exposes a side of him that she had never seen before and that was very frightening. The girl eventually marries this man, but in her narrative she is reflective: "I should have seen it then," she says, "I should have known what kind of guy he really was. But I loved him and I thought this jealousy was really pretty neat; he cared so much. But then I learned that wasn't really love; it was something else." This first performance of a narrative from the book was encouraging. The audience in Carver's class appreciated the student's performance; her claim to the story was convincing and powerful.

In late 2003, we initiated our plan for presenting the Troubling Violence Performance Project on the University of Missouri campus and beyond into mid-Missouri communities. We invited students from both of our classes to participate as performers in the new troupe. Each of them initially selected at least one story from my book. The stories had already been transcribed without actual names, dates, and geographic locations, so it was relatively easy for the performers to choose a story or a portion of a story that could be performed for roughly five to eight minutes. The only requirement for participation was that the performers had to memorize the story and be prepared to tell it as their own whenever the troupe was scheduled to perform. The performances are easy to plan and execute; we require nothing in the way of staged space. Most often we have the use of a chair or two positioned at the front of the room. The performers sit in the audience until they emerge from their seats to claim the performance space and tell their story. No more than four or five performers participate in any given situation.

Carver introduces the troupe and I perform my own narrative about what it was like for me to work in the battered women's shelter, explaining how I asked the women there to share their stories with me on tape, noting that some of the stories the audience will hear came from that. In fact, during the first year of our work with the troupe, the three stories from the beginning of this chapter were included in the performances. The stories had haunted me, but hearing them told again in the context of the troupe made them come alive with potency and promise for helping our advocacy work. After the performances, all the performers join us at the front of the room; Carver introduces the student performers and we invite the audience to respond to the stories in any way they wish. We have realized our goal of creating a safe space for the discussion of a subject too long taboo in our culture.

PERFORMANCE AS COMMUNITY HEALING

Early on, we realized that our performers needed to tell their own stories. With their input, we began to recognize the cathartic nature of storytelling in this new, performative context. Similarly, after each performance, one or more audience members would approach us and offer her story for future troupe performances. We also heard portions of stories from audience members as they responded to the performances and drew on their own experiences in the discussion. With these new storytelling contexts, I recognized the same intent to make sense out of one's experience, to make it coherent, that I had witnessed in the stories I taped at the shelter. The telling of the stories became a significant aspect of the troupe's work for all of the participants, whether they were performers or audience members. I was reminded of how Arthur Frank had described the power of telling stories about sickness in his book, *The Wounded Storyteller*: "Serious illness," he had written, "is a loss of the 'destination and map' that had previously guided the ill person's life: ill people have to learn 'to think differently.' They learn by hearing themselves tell their stories."[5] I felt his words about sick people were also true for how battered women had lost their "destination and map" and how through telling their stories they could regain their confidence to survive and find new ways to live. Frank goes on to argue that through the telling of their illness stories, new maps are already taking shape as the teller discovers "new perceptions of [her] relationship to the world." In fact, Frank also notes that illness narratives "correlate with spiritual autobiographies, stories of 'becoming' a man or a woman, and survivor stories of inflicted traumas such as war, captivity, incest, and abuse."[6]

We now recognize the evolution of the troupe and the stories the performers were telling as a natural response to the work of the troupe and the power of telling our own stories. Boldly, the performers began to bring new stories that they wanted to incorporate into the troupe performances. Some of these new narratives were their own; some were those of family members and friends. One story was written by a male member of our troupe about growing up with an abusive father. He told of how he and his little sister would creep up the basement stairs to watch their father throwing plates at his mother, who was crouched in a corner of the kitchen. His narrative was about him now as well as what happened in the past. He spoke of how much he loved his father. His story revealed his own tendency toward anger and he pondered the question of whether or not he would eventually be the one throwing plates.

Within several months, most of the narratives from my book had been largely replaced by stories that were closer to the lives of the performers. The dynamics of the group changed radically as stories came to be "owned" by the performers in ways that could not occur with the anonymous stories from my ethnographic field research. Our work was expanding beyond the intention of creating a safe space for discussion of the problem. We were now providing a space where we could all tell and contemplate our own experiences through stories, some performed by the troupe members. The social activist goals of this work were growing exponentially: women's stories of battering and abuse were being told publicly; discussions of this taboo topic were a direct result of the telling of these stories; the storytelling and discussions were leading troupe members, as well as audience members, to acknowledge their own private situations, to tell their own stories, and to reflect upon their experiences as they attempted to relate to what others in the room might be facing.

After our first session, one woman in the group told us that she had gone home to visit and was telling her mother and her aunt about having to learn a story about domestic abuse for this performance troupe. Her aunt responded quickly, insisting she should tell her story, not perform a narrative from a book. The aunt then told her niece her story of abuse and offered it to her as an alternative for her performance. By the next rehearsal, this woman's story had been incorporated into our production. Later, this same performer incorporated another narrative into the troupe's repertoire, her own story about a boyfriend who stalked and raped her in college and how she was only now, as a thirty-year-old graduate student, beginning to feel somewhat safe again.

Another member of our troupe also announced that she had chosen not to perform one of the stories from the book. Instead, she was prepared to tell her own story. This forty-something graduate student, a seasoned performer and a theatrical director, had just written and produced an award-winning play about domestic abuse that had been playing on campus and had been performed in New York at a special venue. Throughout the entire run of her play, even during a "talk back" session that included the director of the local shelter and several shelter residents, she had never revealed that the play was based on her own life. Yet she was willing to tell her own story within the context of the work of the Troubling Violence Performance Project—in part because it would never be clear to her audience whether or not the story she was telling was actually her own. That is, the troupe performances gave her an opportunity to tell her story in a neutral setting without having to identify herself as the victim.

TROUBLING VIOLENCE

By "troubling violence," our troupe contests the conventional representations of the battered woman through a performance of reinvention. We need to hear these stories with new ears, noting both what is in these stories and what is missing. The face that materializes in the performance is the face of the woman performer who is telling the story of an actual woman who has been violated. But she is not bruised and battered; she is escaping or has escaped; and she is represented by another woman (sometimes) who tells her story but does not stand in for her. She retains her status indirectly through her story. That is part of the power of the narratives in the performance troupe.

Our directive is that every performance must be followed by an open discussion of the issue of violence against women or we do not accept an invitation to perform. We do not direct the discussions following the performances. The audience is generally quiet at first, a bit stunned by the honesty and the power of the narratives they have heard and witnessed. Often the discussion begins with questions about how the performers feel doing this work and why they do it. Sometimes the stories cause audience members to be defensive; sometimes the stories cause audience members to acknowledge that there is violence and abuse in their own homes, their neighbors' homes, their parents' homes, their friends' homes, their sisters' homes, and their daughters' homes. They want to know what we can do about it. They agree it is a horrendous fact of our lives in contemporary America. They want to know if historically this has always been the case, or whether or not this a new response to a world full of unease, terror, uncertainty, unemployment, poverty, and alcoholism. They ask, How many women are abused daily? They want statistics and facts. We can provide that in handouts; what we seek here is discussion.

Most often audience members ask why the women don't just leave, or why women often leave but go back to their abusive partners. We do not provide answers, but we do provide a safe place for asking questions and exploring the answers to those questions. At one performance for all the university athletic coaches on campus, one coach explained how adamant he felt about his own sister's violent marriage. He had tried to help her, he said, but recently he had "just told her" that he wouldn't listen to her anymore unless she left her abuser. His frustration, anger, and response to his sister's painful situation enabled us to talk openly about other alternatives to how he might help her. In this setting, we did not have to have the final say. A female coach in the audience turned to him and suggested that if he was the only person she was talking to, he had cut her off with no help at all. We talked about how his frustration with her inability to leave her home required more sensitivity and understanding on his part. In many of our performances, women in the audience explain why "just leaving" is not always possible or doesn't work because the violence continues. Members of the audience talk to one another as well as to us. Many women tell their stories in the discussion or talk to us after the discussion. Collectively, as a community, women and men in the audience ask, "What can we do?" One answer is doing what we do. Talking, telling stories. Listening. By doing the performances and having public discussions about this taboo topic, the performers and the audience members are cooperating in a kind of community transformation.

Importantly, in the dramatic work of the performance troupe, the marked face of the actual violated woman/women is also materialized/mirrored/reflected back from the faces of the audience members. The face is transposed from the performers to the women in the audience as they begin to relate the experiences of their mothers, sisters, aunts, friends, and themselves. The performance continues in the discussion as women tell their own stories within this newly created safe space. They have connected with the narratives of the performers. The stories have evoked new stories; this becomes a storytelling event within the context of contemporary women's lives. Women offer to tell us their stories on tape for future performances. In this way, their stories, added to the troupe narratives, live on through the next performances. Again, we turn to Frank, who identifies the "obvious social aspect" of storytelling because stories are told to someone, whether that other person is immediately present or not. Even messages in a bottle imply a potential reader. A less evident social aspect of stories is that people do not make up their stories by themselves. The shape of the telling is molded by all the rhetorical expectations that the storyteller has been internalizing ... as they figure out what counts as "the story others want to hear."[7] Furthermore, this social act of telling becomes a political act. While recounting stories of abuse and violence can most certainly be difficult for women who have encountered battering, there are many arguments that maintain that the telling becomes a first step toward healing. In addition to personal healing, speaking boldly about partnership violence "outs" the offenders and refutes the claim they have made on our lives. Audre Lorde, who eloquently used the metaphor of using the "master's tools" to dismantle the "master's house," believes we can assist ourselves through the act of telling our stories. She invites us to reclaim "that language which has been made to work against us."[8]

With the Troubling Violence Performance Project, we are outing violence against women through the use of narrative art, specifically drama, to expose and resist abuse and violence against all members of our community. We offer new faces of surviving women, new voices, to replace the stereotypical "victim." And we provide a safe place for the open, community discussion of domestic violence; we refuse to call it a "private matter" in the home "as a sacred space." The home should be a sacred space, but if abuse or violence reside there, the private must become public and the community should claim the responsibility for attending to the safety and well-being of all its members.

The Troubling Violence Performance Project has created a venue for sharing personal stories with the collected community. Telling local stories of abuse and violence within various contexts of the community affords us the opportunity to hear stories, tell our own stories, and identify the potential personal and political power of storytelling as a tool for social justice work. Unfortunately, there are always new stories of abuse and violence against women to hear and tell. When there are no new stories, we will know our work is done. Until then, we will continue to bring new student performers into the troupe as others graduate. Right now, this feels like the best thing we can do to keep the subject of violence against women in the open, recounted boldly, and challenging our neighbors and ourselves to be ever vigilant, never forgetting that women are abused, beaten, and violated every day, in our own community.

NOTES

1. S. Parks, "In the Blood," *The Red Letter Plays* (New York: Theatre Communications Group, 2000), 48 [spellings are presented as in the original text].

2. E. J. Lawless, *Women Escaping Violence: Empowerment Through Narrative* (Columbia: University of Missouri Press, 2001).

3. E. Scarry, *The Body in Pain: The Making and Unmaking of the World* (New York: Oxford University Press, 1985). Approximately 1,000 words from "The Body in Pain: The Making and Unmaking of the World" (1985) by Elaine Scarry. By permission of Oxford University Press, Inc.

4. M. Heather Carver and E. J. Lawless, *Troubling Violence, A Performance Project* (Jackson: University Press of Mississippi, forthcoming 2009).

5. A. Frank, *The Wounded Storyteller: Body, Illness, and Ethics* (Chicago: University of Chicago Press, 1995).

6. Ibid., 69.

7. Ibid., 3.

8. A. Lorde, *The Cancer Journals: Special Edition* (San Francisco: Aunt Lute Books: 2007), 22.

Chapter 9

Reshaping Attitudes toward Violence against Women

Michael Flood
Bob Pease
Natalie Taylor
Kim Webster

Since the early 1970s, when the grassroots women's movement mounted its challenge to rape and domestic violence, there has been a worldwide revolution in societal responses to violence against women. Among the changes, the best known are the proliferation of community-based services for victims and reforms in public policy, law, policing, and health care. What is less well-known is whether the revolution in societal intervention is reflected in how ordinary citizens think about violence against women. However important institutional reforms are in the short term, they are unlikely to be sustained unless the normative climate changes that supports violence against women.

How widespread is the belief that women "ask to be raped," that there are circumstances in which it is acceptable for a man to hit a woman, or that violence against women is acceptable? Do people feel empathy for women who are assaulted or raped, or do they blame the victim and excuse the perpetrator? Why do some family members, friends, and professionals respond to victims with support and sympathy, while others respond with indifference or blame? Why do some men use violence against women and others do not? Why do some victims feel self-blame, while others do not? We know that individual and community attitudes shape how women and men experience and understand violence against women. More than this, these attitudes influence the perpetration of this violence, community responses to violence against women, how victims respond to assault, and whether institutional reforms can be sustained.

This chapter provides an international perspective on attitudes toward violence against women. We begin by identifying the role attitudes play in shaping the problem. Next, we provide an international picture of existing attitudes and identify the key factors that shape them. Finally, we identify critical junctures where interventions to change violence-supportive attitudes can make a difference.

THE LINK BETWEEN ATTITUDES AND VIOLENCE AGAINST WOMEN

Attitudes are significant in shaping violence against women in three domains. They influence (1) community and institutional responses to violence against women; (2) the perpetration of violence against women; and (3) women's responses to this victimization.

Attitudes and Community Responses to Violence against Women

Attitudes play a role in how individuals other than the perpetrator or victim interpret and respond to violence against women. First, community attitudes shape informal responses. We know that women living with intimate partner violence are more likely to turn to friends and family than to the police or other professional networks. The existence of violence-supportive attitudes means that family members, friends, acquaintances, and bystanders respond with less empathy and support to victims of violence. For example, people who make negative attributions of victims also are less likely to say that they would report the incident to the police and more likely to recommend lenient or no penalties for the offender. U.S. college students who hold more violence-condoning attitudes are more likely to blame the victim, and among men, victim-blaming is associated with offering less helpful interventions.

Societal attitudes also shape the formal responses of professionals and institutions to the victims and perpetrators of violence against women, including police officers, judges, priests, social workers, doctors, and others. It has been reported that police officers who allocated greater blame to the victim of family violence also indicated that they would be less likely to charge the assailant. In turn, if the assailant is not arrested despite the victim's preference, the victim is less likely to report future domestic violence to the police. Among doctors, psychologists, social workers, nurses, and other health care professionals, those who have received education about child, spouse, or elder abuse are more likely than other clinicians to suspect abuse among their clients and to intervene in violence (by noting it in their charts, discussing it with the family and with other professionals, and reporting it to the relevant agency).

These formal and informal responses have effects on the victims themselves. How others respond to a victim's efforts to obtain assistance influences subsequent help-seeking, separation, and eventual recovery from the abuse. Further, the psychological well-being of victims and their ability to escape from abuse are shaped by the levels of material and emotional support they receive.

Attitudes and the Perpetration of Violence against Women

Attitudes and values supporting the use of violence have also been shown to have a fundamental and causal link to the perpetration of violence against women at both the individual and community levels. For example, men are more likely to commit sexual assault if they have hostile and negative sexual attitudes toward women and identify with traditional images of masculinity and male privilege. Boys and young men who endorse more rape-supportive beliefs are also more likely to have been sexually coercive. Men with more traditional, rigid, and misogynistic gender-role attitudes are more likely to practice marital violence.[1]

A meta-analysis is a sophisticated way to summarize the empirical research that bears on a particular problem. A recent meta-analysis aggregating data across all studies relating an aspect of masculine ideology to the incidence of sexual aggression found that all but one measure of masculine ideology in general, and holding sexist, patriarchal, and/or sexually hostile attitudes in particular, was significantly associated with sexual aggression and the use of violence against women.[2] Qualitative research has also found that men who have been violent to their female partners use popular discourses about uncontrollable male aggression, female provocation, and weakness to excuse, justify, and rationalize their violence. Further, overall rates of violence against women are higher in communities where there is widespread acceptance of violence-supportive norms.[3]

Attitudes thus play a crucial role in the perpetration of violence against women. At the same time, they are not the only causal factor at work, and violence against women is also shaped by other social, cultural, and institutional forces. We return to this in the conclusion.

Attitudes and Subjection to Violence

Women's responses to being subjected to violence are shaped by their attitudes and those of others around them. To the extent that individual women agree with violence-supportive understandings of domestic violence or sexual assault, they are more likely to blame themselves for the assault, less likely to report it to the police or other authorities, and more likely to experience long-term negative psychological and emotional effects. Various studies document that female rape victims' self-attributions of blame are associated with greater trauma and distress. Women are also less likely to report violence and abuse by their partners if they adhere to traditional gender-role attitudes. The recovery process has also been shown to be affected by attitudes. For instance, black women's recovery from rape is hindered if they adhere to the cultural stereotype that black women are "sexually loose."

Furthermore, stereotypical and narrow representations of violence inhibit women from even recognizing and identifying their experience as constituting violence and hence as abusive. One of the key reasons women do not report incidents that meet the legal definition of sexual assault is that these do not fit common stereotypes of "real rape"—they were not by a stranger, did not take place outside and with a weapon, and did not involve injuries. Women are more likely to perceive acts as criminal victimization if they "deprive victims of liberty, threaten their lives or physical integrity, or produce psychological harm." Victims also do not report violence because of their perception of *others'* attitudes: their fear that they will be blamed by family and friends, stigmatized, and that the criminal justice system will not provide redress.[4]

Despite compelling evidence that attitudes influence the perpetuation of violence and how violence is experienced and perceived, there is no evidence that attitudes play a causal role in women's risks of victimization in the first place, particularly with respect to rape. To emphasize this would be to blame the victim for her victimization.

VIOLENCE-SUPPORTIVE ATTITUDES

Gauging the extent to which violence-supportive attitudes exist within the community is crucial for understanding the work needed to change attitudes about violence against women. Violence-supportive attitudes are those that "support" violence through trivializing violence and its impacts, attributing blame to victims, denying that violence has occurred, or justifying or excusing violence. The last three decades have seen the steady development of scholarly tools with which to assess attitudes toward violence against women. For instance, at least eleven measures of beliefs and attitudes regarding sexual aggression have been developed, addressing such dimensions of sexual violence as the acceptance of rape myths or adversarial sexual beliefs, hostile or hypermasculinity, victim-blaming or victim empathy, and the likelihood of committing rape if one was assured of not being caught. Other instruments focus on attitudes toward other, specific forms of violence against women, from wife assault to sexual harassment and date rape. These quantitative survey tools are complemented by more qualitative methods, using interviews, focus groups, and other ways to explore people's understandings and experiences of violence against women. These tools have been used in a wide variety of countries and contexts, generating a wealth of information about attitudes.

Internationally, there are typical patterns regarding attitudes toward violence against women. A large number of studies have shown that:

- The degree to which behaviors are regarded as violence or an offense varies widely;
- The acceptability and perceived seriousness of violent behavior varies with sex, sociodemographic variables, and context;
- Males, on average, tend to hold more violence-supportive attitudes compared with females; and
- There are differences based on cultural background, tradition, and country of birth (possibly reflecting different cultural and background influences) in attitudes toward violence against women.

A recent telephone survey with a representative sample of 2,000 people conducted in one of Australia's eight states in 2006 provides a convenient example of such patterns.[5] The survey found that pushing and slapping, forcing a partner to have sex, throwing or smashing objects near a partner to frighten them, or trying to scare or control one's partner by threatening to hurt family members were more likely to be viewed as "always" domestic violence than behaviors such as yelling abuse at one's partner, repeatedly criticizing one's partner, controlling the social life of one's partner by denying them money, and harassing one's partner by phone or e-mail. Instead, these latter behaviors were more often regarded as "usually" or "sometimes" violence. The particular circumstances that surround these less physical and more emotionally controlling behaviors seem to determine when they are considered violence. People are less willing to classify behaviors as violent when the community discerns shades of gray.

Another typical pattern in many countries is that the general population does not subscribe to attitudes supporting the use of violence. For example, most respondents in the Australian survey believed that violence was serious (98 percent of women and 93 percent of men) and that both intimate partner violence and forced sexual contact in a relationship were crimes (with these statements attracting the support of 97 percent and 93 percent of respondents, respectively). Eighty-two percent disagreed that violence was a private matter to be handled in the family. Most classified physical acts of force, such as slapping and pushing, forcing one's partner to have sex, and throwing and smashing objects near one's partner to frighten or hurt then as serious and as violence.[6] Fewer than 4 percent believed that intimate partner violence could be justified in most scenarios put to them (for example, if a woman keeps nagging her partner, if she refuses to have sex with him, or, if following separation, she commences a new relationship).

Nevertheless, international research indicates that a sizeable minority of the population continues to have attitudes supporting the use of violence. For example, in the Australian survey, a substantial proportion of respondents held beliefs that have the effect of diminishing perpetrators' responsibility for their behavior. In contrast to the small percentage of respondents who believed that violence could be justified, 23 percent believed that it could be excused if it resulted from people "getting so angry they lost control" and 24 percent if the violent person "genuinely regretted" what they had done afterward. Thirty-eight percent of respondents believed that rape results from men not being able to "control their need for sex." Eight percent of respondents agreed that, "most women who are raped asked for it" and 15 percent agreed that, in relation to sex, "women often say no when they mean yes." Similarly, 23 percent disagreed that women rarely make false claims of being raped.

In some countries and contexts, violence is accepted by the majority of the population. A recent World Health Organization (WHO) study found that the proportion of women who agreed with one or more justifications for wife-beating (such as a wife's infidelity) varied from 6 percent in Serbia and Montenegro city to more than 68 percent in areas of Bangladesh, Ethiopia, and Peru and in Samoa, Thailand, and the United Republic of Tanzania. Given the gender gap in this area (see below), men's agreement in such contexts is likely to be higher still.

While there is very little international data with which to test this, it is possible that there has been a general improvement over time in community attitudes regarding violence against women. The past decade has seen substantial efforts by government and health authorities in various countries, as well as community-based initiatives, to publicize the seriousness of violence against women and to inform and educate the community about what violence is and that it is unacceptable. It might be expected that attitudes toward violence against women may have changed over time as a consequence of such heightened awareness campaigns. Improvements may also reflect the liberalization of gender norms and growing gender equality in heterosexual relationships and families, given that one of the most significant predictors of violence against women is male economic and decision-making dominance in families.[7]

The 2006 Australian survey does allow assessment of changes over time, as its findings can be compared with a similar, national survey conducted eleven years earlier. Higher proportions of the community

in 2006 than in 1995 classified most of the behaviors widely associated
with abuse as violence. Throwing and smashing objects to frighten
and repeatedly criticizing were also regarded as more serious compared with the 1995 survey.[8] However, there were also some troubling
trends. For example, slapping or pushing was significantly less likely
to be regarded as very serious in 2006. Although most people still view
men as the main perpetrators of domestic violence, a higher proportion
of the community in the 2006 survey believed that domestic violence is
perpetrated by men and women equally (20 percent in 2006 compared
with 9 percent in 1995), despite findings which consistently show that
men are the main perpetrators of domestic violence.[9] There were gender differences in response to this question. Men were more likely in
the main sample to believe that both men and women equally commit
domestic violence (24 percent) than women (17 percent), while this pattern was reversed in the culturally and linguistically diverse sample
(32 percent and 31 percent, respectively).

We now turn to the factors that shape violence-supportive attitudes.

FACTORS SHAPING ATTITUDES

It is useful to break down the factors that shape attitudes toward violence against women into two clusters: those having to do with gender, including gender attitudes, roles, and relations, and those having
to do with race, ethnicity, and other cultural factors. We begin with
these, and then outline further individual, organizational, community-
level, and societal factors that influence community attitudes. We
emphasize only those factors whose influence has been demonstrated
by empirical research.[10]

Gender and Gender Norms

One of the most consistent findings to emerge from studies of attitudes toward violence against women is the gender gap in attitudes. In
general, men are more likely than women to agree with myths and
beliefs supportive of violence against women, perceive a narrower
range of behaviors as violent, blame and show less empathy for the
victim, minimize the harms associated with physical and sexual
assault, and see behaviors constituting violence against women as less
serious, inappropriate, or damaging. Much of the research on attitudes
has been done among college and university samples, and the gender
gap is well-documented among these and other populations both in
the United States and elsewhere. The gender gap is also evident in attitudes toward particular forms of violence against women, whether sexual harassment, date rape, or wife assault. Moreover, cross-gender
differences in attitudes in many countries are stronger than differences

associated with other social divisions, such as socioeconomic status or education.

Most men and women share the belief that violence against women is unacceptable. Yet there is a gender contrast in their understandings of and attitudes toward violence against women. This does not reflect their biological sex, but their socialized gender orientations. There is a powerful association between attitudes toward violence against women and attitudes toward gender. Traditional gender-role attitudes are associated with greater acceptance of violence against women, particularly for men. Conversely, egalitarian gender-role attitudes are associated with less acceptance of violence against women. This was also corroborated by the recent Australian survey.

The relationship between adherence to conservative gender norms and tolerance for violence has been documented among men in a wide variety of communities and countries, both Western and non-Western, including ultra-Orthodox Jewish communities in Israel; men in Cape Town, South Africa; Arab men in Israel; and males ages twelve to twenty in Australia. This relationship holds among women as well. At the same time, the relationship between gender-typing and victim-blaming seems to be far weaker among women, perhaps because of their low levels of attributions of blame overall.

Attitudes to violence against women are grounded in wider attitudes toward women, gender, and sexuality. Globally, wife-beating is seen as justified in some circumstances by a majority of the population in various countries, most commonly in situations of actual or suspected infidelity by wives or their "disobedience" toward a husband or partner.

In the United States, women who dress less modestly and more suggestively are more likely to be seen as responsible for and deserving of sexual assault. Among U.S. undergraduates, women are seen as more likely to "provoke" sexual harassment if they are attractive, and to be more culpable for date rape if wearing a short rather than long skirt, while stereotypically attractive male perpetrators are judged as less harassing.

Female victims of domestic violence are judged more harshly where they are perceived to have "provoked" aggression, for example by being verbally aggressive or in situations that might inspire their husbands' jealousy. Assumptions about men's rights of sexual access in marriages and sexual relationships also shape judgments. When a man rapes his wife or girlfriend rather than a stranger, he is seen as less responsible, the behavior is viewed as less harmful, and it is less likely to be considered rape.

In fact, common norms regarding sexuality and intimacy can make sexual violence either invisible or "normal." Studies among adolescents in the United States, New Zealand, and Britain find that for many boys and girls, sexual harassment is pervasive, male aggression is normalized, there is constant pressure among boys to behave in sexually aggressive ways, girls are routinely objectified, a sexual double standard polices girls' sexual and intimate involvements, and girls are compelled to accommodate male "needs" and desires in negotiating their sexual relations.

Class, Race, Ethnicity, and Other Forms of Social Differences

There is some evidence that attitudes toward violence against women vary with socioeconomic variables such as labor market participation and socioeconomic status. The recent Australian survey found that the relationship between indicators of socioeconomic status—education, occupation (white collar or not), and employment—and violence-supportive attitudes was not as consistent or strong as those of sex and support for gender equality. However, they did predict agreement with certain beliefs. For instance, white-collar workers were more likely than members of other occupational groups to agree that "women rarely make false claims of being raped," and unemployed workers were likely to hold that "domestic violence can be excused if there is genuine regret afterward."[11] We will return to the issue of education under "Organizational Factors" below.

Attitudes toward violence against women vary across different classes and cultural groups and communities in any one country and from one culture to another. Various studies in the United States and Australia find ethnicity-related differences in attitudes. For example, Hispanic men have been reported to be more likely than African American, Asian, and Caucasian men and women or any other gender/ethnic combination to support the myth that women provoke violence toward them.

The recent Australian survey included a sample of 200 men and women from each of four countries: Greece, Italy, China, and Vietnam. On average, respondents in this sample were more likely to hold violence-supportive attitudes than those in the main sample, particularly men. There were significant associations between violence-supportive attitudes in this sample and being born overseas, speaking a language other than English at home, having arrived in Australia more recently (since 1980), and cultural background (Chinese and Vietnamese backgrounds).

Asian students in the United States and Canada have been found to be more likely than non-Asian students to believe that women are responsible for preventing rape, that sex is a motivation for rape, and that victims precipitate rape. This perhaps reflects Asian cultural attitudes emphasizing female chastity and framing rape as a sexual matter between individuals. However, significant interethnic differences in attitudes have been reported within Asian communities, pointing to the differential influence of particular cultural systems, patterns of immigration, and other factors.

Apparent differences in attitudes among ethnic groups may reflect other demographic contrasts between them. For example, in a U.S. study, apparent differences between white and African American people's attitudes toward victims of rape disappeared once differences in socioeconomic status and education were taken into account.

Attitudes toward violence against women are constructed in particular cultural contexts. In Beirut, Lebanon, perceptions of rape are structured by the centrality of marriageability in determining a women's status. Women seen to be unmarriageable, because they are separated, divorced, or disabled for example, are perceived to have "nothing to lose" and thus as legitimate targets of sexual predation. Notions of male "honor" and female purity and modesty can be used to justify and excuse violence against women. Honor cultures involve emphases on male honor and dominance, strong familialism, and norms of female chastity and male sexual freedom. It appears that men and women from honor cultures are more tolerant of men's violence toward female partners. For example, men's violent responses to infidelity may be seen as more excusable and less stigmatizing. In a very different context, in a Dayak community in West Borneo (Indonesia), the idea of forcing someone to have sex is almost inconceivable.

Thus, community attitudes regarding violence against women also vary from one nation to another. The associations between culture and attitudes toward violence against women are dynamic, however. On the one hand, people who move from a culture supporting the use of violence to a culture less tolerant of violence may subsequently change their attitudes, reflecting, for instance, a "Westernizing" influence on attitudes. On the other hand, violence-supportive attitudes can be "imported" from one cultural context to another.

Individual Factors

One of the key mechanisms of attitude formation in relation to violence against women is intergenerational transmission. There is strong evidence that children who either witness such violence or are subjected to violence themselves are more likely as adults to adhere to violence-supportive attitudes and to perpetrate violence. (See the chapter by Cares in Volume 2). Further, the effects of witnessing or experiencing violence are greater for males than females. In other words, boys who have seen or suffered violence themselves are more likely to grow up to tolerate and perpetrate violence against women.

These patterns reflect boys' social learning and the stunting of their behavioral control, adaptive social skills, and empathy. At the same time, other argue that there is no link between childhood victimization and the adolescent or adult perpetration of violence or young people's attitudes toward domestic violence. There are diverse pathways to sexual aggression, with some research reporting that the impact of parental violence and child abuse on boys may potentially be mediated by sexually hostile attitudes and emphases on sexual conquest and promiscuity.

Age, and its associated developmental processes and relations, appears to be another factor shaping individuals' attitudes toward violence against women. Studies in the United States and Australia find that younger adults (under fifty-five) are less likely to hold violence-supportive attitudes than older adults. For example, in the recent Australian survey, younger respondents were more likely than older respondents to see forcing a partner to have sex as domestic violence, and as very serious, and physical force against a current wife or partner as less justifiable.

However, among the youngest age groups, and males in particular, younger people have more regressive attitudes than their older counterparts. High school males in the United States, Finland, and Australia show stronger tolerance for sexual aggression and other forms of violence against women than do college males. The greater endorsement by younger men of violence against women may reflect their lack of exposure to the liberalizing influence of late secondary school and a university education. It may also reflect developmental shifts in attitudes, empathy, and moral awareness. Alternatively, it may reflect the greater influence of the peer culture on younger males and the ways in which both gender segregation and homophobia peak in early adolescence.

Organizational Factors

Another cluster of factors shown to influence community attitudes toward violence against women are organizational, namely the social relations, cultures, policies, and other characteristics of formal organizations and institutions. Associations between violence-supportive attitudes and formal organizations have been documented in four contexts: sports, university residences (fraternities), the military, and religious institutions.

Early work noted that male athletes report significantly greater agreement with rape-supportive statements than men in general. Contemporary research documents that violence-supportive norms and behaviors are spread unevenly across sports, can vary even within a particular sport, and are influenced by local and contextual factors. In American universities, rape-myth acceptance has been reported to be highest among male athletes, especially younger athletes and those playing a team-based sport.

Violence-supportive norms are particularly intense in certain residential or organizational contexts known for their emphasis on stereotypical masculine roles. College fraternities on U.S. campuses are particularly known for their support and perpetration of sexual violence. Fraternities may be characterized by gender segregation, sexism and hostility toward women, an ethic of male sexual conquest, high alcohol consumption, homophobia, and use of pornography.

Similar dynamics are evident in the military, an example of a peer culture involving norms of gender inequality, male bonding, aggression, and sexualized talk. In such contexts, violence-supportive attitudes are shaped by several mechanisms, including socialization into group norms, identification with and attachment to the group, and self-selection by men with preexisting violence-supportive attitudes. There is also evidence that participation in particular occupational, educational, or religious contexts can shape attitudes toward violence against women. Individuals who have received a university education or have higher levels of educational attainment tend to have more progressive attitudes than those who have not.[12] A recent Australian survey found that individuals with lower levels of education were more likely to believe that women make up claims of domestic violence in order to gain tactical advantage in contested child custody cases, although education was only a sporadic predictor of attitudes in general.

While we lack precise comparative information on particular occupational groups, it appears that some workplace and professional cultures encourage attitude shifts away from supporting the use of violence. For example, psychologists, social workers, nurses, and other mental health professionals undergo training that encourages intolerance of violence. By contrast, occupational cultures such as police may intensify violence-supportive norms. When it comes to religious participation, there may be a relationship between fundamentalist religious beliefs and narrower definitions of abuse and more victim-blaming.

Community Factors

Attitudes toward violence against women are also shaped by participation in informal peer groups and social circles, and these influences overlap with the influence of formal institutions and occupations. For example, participation and investment in homosocial male peer groups can intensify men's tolerance for violence against women. Male peer support for sexual assault, including young men's emotional ties to abusive peers and peers' informational support for assault (guidance and advice that influences men to assault their dating partners), may be associated with sexual and physical abuse of women. Similarly, men with male friends and acquaintances whom they perceive to condone, reward, or perpetrate violence against women are more likely to condone or commit it themselves.

Societal Factors

Mass media

There are also numerous societal factors that influence attitudes toward violence against women, including particular forms of media. We take as given that the media does not have simple and deterministic effects on community attitudes or indeed behaviors. Instead, there is a diverse range of responses to media portrayals. Personal and developmental factors influence the impact of exposure. In addition, the relationships between representations and attitudes and/or behaviors are complex.

Pornography

Exposure to pornography has been consistently linked to sexual aggression. These links are strongest for violent pornography, but have also been found for nonviolent pornography, particularly among frequent users. Several types of empirical examination demonstrate this relationship.

In experimental studies, adults show significant strengthening of attitudes supportive of sexual aggression following exposure to pornography. Exposure to sexually violent material increases male viewers' acceptance of rape myths, desensitizes them to sexual violence, and erodes their empathy for victims of violence. Adults also show an increase in behavioral aggression following exposure to pornography, again, especially violent pornography. Men who view hardcore, violent, or rape pornography in everyday life and men who are high-frequency users of pornography are significantly more likely than others to report that they would rape or harass a woman if they knew they could get away with it.

Television and Other Popular Media

Other media, such as television, music, and film are also effective teachers of violence-supportive attitudes. Children exposed to media violence consistently demonstrate greater rates of aggressive attitudes and behavior. Sexually violent, misogynist, and objectifying themes in music and music videos influence adolescents' and young people's acceptance of violence against women. (See the chapter in this volume by Armstrong.) While the issue is still being debated, there is growing evidence that playing violent electronic games is associated with lower empathy and stronger adherence to pro-violence attitudes. (See the chapters in this volume by Dill.) Other aspects of popular culture identified as reinforcing community tolerance for violence against women include advertising and language.

News Coverage

There is evidence that media coverage of and public controversy regarding high-profile incidents of violence against women can increase community awareness. (See the chapter in this volume by Post.) In the wake of the trial of O. J. Simpson for the murder of his ex-wife, Nicole Brown Simpson, media coverage of domestic violence dramatically increased. During a single year, the percentage of male survey respondents who rated domestic violence as an "extremely important social problem" climbed from 25 to 33 percent. (See the chapter in this volume by Thill and Dill.)

After the Anita Hill-Clarence Thomas sexual harassment hearings in 1991, women were more likely to label particular behaviors as harassment. At the same time, media coverage may encourage victim blaming, and commentators in various countries suggest that violence-supportive attitudes are perpetuated by news coverage.

Community Education and Social Marketing Campaigns

The media has also been deliberately used to change community attitudes through education and social marketing campaigns. Such efforts can produce positive change in the attitudes (and behaviors) associated with men's perpetration of violence against women.[13] Another, more localized form of deliberate education concerns face-to-face community education. Education programs in primary and secondary schools and universities—particularly those which are intensive, lengthy, and use a variety of pedagogical approaches—can have positive effects on people's attitudes toward and participation in violence against women.[14]

Criminal Justice Policies and Law Reform

There is little consensus on the impact of criminal justice policies on community attitudes. The legal system may have an important symbolic role in shaping what is perceived to be legitimate or illegitimate behavior. For example, legal sanctions have been found to impact attitudes toward violence against women in the United States. Criminal justice policies also may have a negative influence, for example when the criminal justice system fails to respond appropriately to the victims and perpetrators of violence against women.

Social Movements

The last form of influence on community attitudes toward violence against women is social movements. Public recognition of men's violence against women as a "social problem" has been a major achievement of the women's movement in particular. While it is difficult to document the impact of social movements on social norms, the women's movement and feminism have undoubtedly had a distinctive, and substantial, impact on community attitudes toward violence against women.

Other collective mobilizations with a potential influence include anti-feminist "men's rights" and "fathers' rights," pro-feminist men's, and conservative religious groups and networks. While evidence of a direct impact is lacking, in Australia, anti-feminist men's groups may have influenced increases in support for the notions that domestic violence is gender-equal and that women falsify claims of violence to gain an advantage in family law proceedings.

KEY POINTS FOR INTERVENTION

Our framework for intervention is guided by six assumptions.

First, the process of changing attitudes must be part of a larger project to challenge and change familial, organizational, community, and societal norms that support violence against women.

Second, interventions must address not only those attitudes that overtly condone violence against women, but the wider clusters of attitudes related to gender and sexuality that normalize and justify this violence. Given the close association between attitudes toward violence against women and attitudes about gender, especially males' adherence to patriarchal and hostile attitudes toward women, traditional gender role attitudes must be targeted in educational campaigns.

Third, efforts to address violence-supportive attitudes must also work to provide an alternative set of norms and values centered on nonviolence, gender equality, and social justice.

Fourth, however valuable are social marketing and community education campaigns aimed at the general population or at specific subpopulations, more intensive and local interventions within specific settings and among specific groups also are essential.

Fifth, violence-prevention interventions must be culturally appropriate. This means that they must include sensitivity not only to ethnic diversities but also to local gender cultures and to men's and women's levels of awareness about and willingness to take responsibility for the problem of violence against women.

Finally, interventions aimed at attitudinal change must be accompanied by adjustments in structural relations and social practices if violence against women is to be prevented.

The following discussion identifies targets for intervention to change attitudes.

Children Who Have Witnessed or Experienced Violence and Are in Families Affected by Violence against Women

Intervention in the intergenerational transmission of violence is vital. In the domestic-violence field, there is growing recognition that physical or sexual violence against adult women often is accompanied by violence against their children, and that whether children are witnesses to or direct victims of interpersonal violence, their experience can have profound and long-lasting effects on their health and well-being. To prevent the intergenerational transmission of community attitudes tolerant of violence against women, we must improve service responses to all family members affected by violence.

Youth

Violence-supportive attitudes are already well-established in adolescence. Younger males are particularly likely to endorse violence against women, and some gender norms among adolescents "normalize" sexual coercion. While the influences of education, maturation, and greater experience of cross-sex social and sexual relations lessen adolescent boys' endorsement of violence-supportive attitudes, substantial proportions of young men continue to endorse such attitudes. Children and youth therefore are a particularly important group for intervention.

Boys' Peer Cultures and Young Men at Risk of or Already Using Violence

Interventions among children and youth in general should be complemented by peer education and mentoring and other strategies that address the intensive forms of support for violence in the peer cultures and group norms of some boys and young men. When the trajectories of young men who are repeat assaulters are compared to those who have sexually coerced girls in the past but have ceased, the latter express more remorse, hold the girl(s) less responsible, and are less likely to describe the violent behavior as "exciting." Intervention with boys and young men identified as at risk of violence perpetration or who are already using violence therefore may be valuable in changing their potentially lifelong violent trajectories.

Local Contexts and Cultures

Some peer cultures and organizations are particularly dangerous for women. Intensive intervention in such contexts is necessary to address their violence-supportive local cultures. There are inspiring instances of such intervention in sporting contexts in Australia. The professional sporting codes of the National Rugby League (NRL) and the Australian

Football League (AFL) are developing education programs for their players, codes of conduct, and other measures in response to a series of alleged sexual assaults by players in 2004. Education programs should be adopted at both community and professional levels of sport, particularly in the male-dominated, team-based, contact sports. Similar and substantial initiatives in military institutions, universities, colleges, and workplaces also are desirable.

Religious Institutions and Leaders

While religious beliefs historically have been used to justify violence against women and church clergy at times have been complicit in this violence, religious institutions and leaders also have a potentially powerful role to play in encouraging an ethic of nonviolence. The spiritual and theological understandings of Christian, Jewish, Muslim, and other world religions each contain emphases and values which could serve to lessen community tolerance for violence against women. Spiritual and religious leaders should be encouraged to challenge violence against women and gender inequality, whether as practiced among their adherents or as defended in theological teachings, through public statements, sermons, teachings, and religious materials. Clergy and lay leaders also should receive training in responding appropriately to domestic or sexual violence within faith communities, and U.S. experience suggests that such initiatives have a positive impact on clergy attitudes and responses.

Mass Media

At least four kinds of intervention are relevant in relation to the media's influence on community attitudes toward violence against women: social marketing, better news reporting, improving media literacy, and regulation.

Social marketing is an obvious strategy to encourage community intolerance for violence against women. Experience in relation to other social problems such as drunk driving suggests that comprehensive communication strategies are an effective tool of attitudinal and even behavioral change. Second, interventions among media outlets and journalists should encourage appropriate portrayals of violence against women through news guidelines or codes of practice and other mechanisms. Such efforts can make a significant difference to news coverage. Third, we should be encouraging media literacy, especially among children and youth. Teaching critical viewing and thinking skills improves viewers' ability to ignore or resist antisocial messages and reduces the negative impact of portrayals of violence. Such skills can be integrated into school curricula, and could even include education to address harmful aspects of such media forms as pornography. Fourth, the regulation of media content should include initiatives addressing violence in children's television, children's exposure to Internet pornography, and other violence-supportive content.

Criminal Justice System

The criminal justice system responds to only a small proportion of domestic violence and sexual assault matters, as there are both low rates of reporting and attrition through the legal process. At the same time, strong legal sanctions encourage community intolerance for this violence. Therefore, strengthening legal responses to violence against women will have positive effects not only for the victims and survivors of this violence, but for community attitudes in general.

Medicine and Health Systems

The attitudes of doctors and other health care professionals toward violence against women have wider implications for the trajectories and recovery of the female victims of violence they see (as well as others involved in this violence, such as perpetrators and children). There is increasing awareness of the need to train health care personnel and improve their attitudes through strategies such as routine screening and other case-finding approaches. In relation to other professionals who respond to the women and men affected by violence against women, the need for attitudinal change and the development of intervention strategies are being addressed through the development of materials on violence against women in the curricula of professional training and university courses.

Community Development and Mobilization

One of the most powerful ways in which societal attitudes toward violence against women can be transformed is through direct participation in activities, groups, and networks aimed at challenging this violence. These represent powerful and effective ways in which to improve participants' attitudes toward violence against women and transform community norms. The disadvantage of their smaller scale is balanced by the advantage of their significant educational and social impact. Community-development strategies therefore should be central to violence-prevention efforts.

It is important to develop culturally sensitive messages appropriate to the cultural norms of each community. For example, "cultural context models" can be used to educate members of culturally diverse communities about privilege and oppression and build communities that support nonviolence. This model utilizes male sponsors from the community who support nonviolence to mentor men toward nonviolence and culture circles whereby extended members of the family become involved in challenging men's violence. Efforts to address violence against women in indigenous and First Nation communities must be community-driven, based on partnerships between and among community and government agencies, and based in holistic approaches to community violence. This is supported by evaluations of "good practice" initiatives documented in North America, New Zealand, and Canada. Similarly, efforts to address violence-supportive community attitudes should be attentive to diversities associated with geography (urban versus rural), class, and other variables.

Community-development strategies are complemented by strategies of community mobilization. We must not only educate men and women, but also organize them for collective action. In other words, attitudinal and behavioral changes also can be fostered by creating opportunities for individuals to mobilize their communities through events, networks, and campaigns. It is particularly important that we mobilize men through such work, because of many men's greater endorsement of violence-supportive attitudes, their roles as community leaders and gatekeepers, and their relative absence from efforts to end violence against women.

CONCLUSIONS

Attitudes toward violence against women are powerful influences on the perpetration of violence against women, women's responses to this victimization, and wider community and institutional responses. However, attitudes are not the whole story. Attitudinal orientations are just one aspect of an explanation of an individual's perpetration of violence against women. When a man physically assaults his wife or sexually harasses his female colleague, his behavior may also be shaped by his affective orientations and other aspects of his identity or subjectivity. For example, in a study of university undergraduates, men's sense of entitlement, both general and specifically sexual, mediated the relationship between masculine gender roles and sexually aggressive behavior and attitudes. "Entitlement" refers here to men feeling entitled to have their needs met by women and believing that their needs or desires take precedence over women's.

Focusing on sexual violence for a moment, different factors may be involved in varying forms of sexual aggression or for diverse types of sexually aggressive men, with attitudes playing lesser or greater roles depending on these. Some perpetrators may be highly aroused by sexual violence and likely to commit multiple acts of aggression with different victims, while others may be more influenced by cognitive motivations (such as rape myths) and more likely to commit assaults in situations where they perceive or can argue for some justification for their behavior.

Men's use of violence against women clearly is shaped by patriarchal, anti-woman, and "hypermasculine" ideologies. However, holding such attitudes may not be sufficient to perpetrate sexually aggressive behavior. Instead, such attitudes can combine with *situational* factors to predict violence against women. This includes the presence (or deliberate creation) of situations in which coercive sexual encounters can occur, heavy alcohol consumption, and peer pressure and peer support for perpetration.

Indeed, adherence to violence-supportive attitudes in some instances may not even be a necessary condition of violence perpetration. Some men who do not endorse rape myths report sexually aggressive behaviors. These men may become sexually aggressive after drinking or engaging in risky behaviors.

An exclusive focus on individual attitudes would neglect the cultural, collective, and institutional underpinnings of violence against women. Beyond individual attitudes and perceptions, violence against women is shaped by the social, cultural, economic, and political relations of particular contexts, communities, and cultures. While these collective social relations do have attitudinal dimensions, they are not reducible to them. Individual men may hold violence-supportive attitudes but not act on them because of wider social norms, social relations, and social structures that constrain violent behavior or encourage nonviolence. In turn, attitudes that are intolerant of violence may be only weakly held and may be "rendered situationally inoperative" or neutralized by situational variables.

Explanations of violence against women must be grounded not only in attitudes but in social relations and social structures. We must move beyond a strictly cultural emphasis in both explanation and intervention and recognize that "violence has much deeper roots in the structural foundations of interpersonal relationships (and societal arrangements in general)."[14] To stop violence against women, certainly we must change community attitudes. But we must also do more to address the structural conditions that perpetuate violence.

NOTES

1. L. L. Heise, "Violence Against Women: An Integrated, Ecological Framework," *Violence Against Women* 4(3) (1998): 262–290.

2. S. K. Murnen, C. Wright, and G. Kaluzny. "If 'Boys Will Be Boys,' then Girls will be Victims? A Meta-Analytic Review of the Research that Relates Masculine Ideology to Sexual Aggression," *Sex Roles* 46 (11/12) (2002): 359–375.

3. L. L. Heise, "Violence Against Women: An Integrated, Ecological Framework," 1998.

4. D. Lievore, *Non-Reporting and Hidden Reporting of Sexual Assault: An International Literature Review*, (Canberra: Australian Institute of Criminology, 2003): 8–28.

5. N. Taylor, and J. Mouzos, *Community Attitudes to Violence Against Women Survey 2006: A Full Technical Report* (Camberra: Australian Institute of Criminology, 2006); and VicHealth, *Two Steps Forward, One Step Back: Community Attitudes to Violence Against Women. Progress and Challenges in Creating Safe, Respectful, and Healthy Environments for Victorian Women—A Summary of Findings of the Violence Against Women Community Attitudes Project*. (Melbourne: Victorian Health Promotion Foundation, 2006).

6. N. Taylor, and J. Mouzos, *Community Attitudes to Violence Against Women Survey 2006: A Full Technical Report*, 2006.

7. L. L. Heise, "Violence Against Women: An Integrated, Ecological Framework," 1998.

8. N. Taylor, and J. Mouzos, *Community Attitudes to Violence Against Women Survey 2006: A Full Technical Report*, 2006.

9. J. Belknap and H. Melton, "Are Heterosexual Men also Victims of Intimate Partner Abuse?" VAWnet National Electronic Network on Violence Against Women, Applied Research Forum, March 2005.

10. This discussion condenses a much longer review of the literature. M. Flood and B. Pease, *The Factors Influencing Community Attitudes in Relation to Violence Against Women: A Critical Review of the Literature* (Melbourne: Victorian Health Promotion Foundation, 2006).

11. N. Taylor, and J. Mouzos, *Community Attitudes to Violence Against Women Survey 2006: A Full Technical Report*, 2006.

12. ANOP Research Services Pty Ltd., *Community Attitudes to Violence Against Women: Detailed Report* (Canberra: Office of the Status of Women, Department of the Prime Minister and Cabinet, 1995).

13. R. Donovan and R. Vlais. *VicHealth Review of Communication Components of Social Marketing/Public Education Campaigns Focused on Violence Against Women* (Melbourne: Victorian Health Promotion Foundation, 2005).

14. J. H. Michalski, "Making Sociological Sense out of Trends in Intimate Partners' Violence: The Social Structure of Violence Against Women," *Violence Against Women* 10(6) (2004): 653.

REFERENCES

ANOP Research Services Pty Ltd., *Community Attitudes to Violence Against Women: Detailed Report* (Canberra: Office of the Status of Women, Department of the Prime Minister and Cabinet, 1995).

J. Belknap, and H. Melton, "Are Heterosexual Men Also Victims of Intimate Partner Abuse?" (VAWnet National Electronic Network on Violence Against Women, Applied Research Forum, March 2005).

R. Donovan and R. Vlais, *Vichealth Review of Communication Components of Social Marketing/Public Education Campaigns Focused on Violence Against Women* (Melbourne: Victorian Health Promotion Foundation, 2005).

A. Godenzi, M. D. Schwartz, and W. S. Dekeseredy, "Toward a Gendered Social Bond/Male Peer Support Theory of University Woman Abuse," *Critical Criminology* 10(1) (2001): 1–16.

L. L. Heise, "Violence Against Women: An Integrated, Ecological Framework," *Violence Against Women* 4(3) (1998): 262–290.

M. J. Hird and S. Jackson, "Where 'Angels' and 'Wusses' Fear to Tread: Sexual Coercion in Adolescent Dating Relationships," *Journal of Sociology* 37(1) (2001): 27–43.

D. Lievore, *Non-Reporting and Hidden Reporting of Sexual Assault: An International Literature Review* (Canberra: Australian Institute of Criminology, 2003).

N. Malamuth, T. Addison, and M. Koss, "Pornography and Sexual Aggression: Are There Reliable Effects and Can We Understand Them?" *Annual Review of Sex Research* 11 (2000): 26–91.

J. H. Michalski, "Making Sociological Sense Out of Trends in Intimate Partner Violence: The Social Structure of Violence Against Women," *Violence Against Women* 10(6) (2004): 652–675.

S. K. Murnen, C. Wright, and G. Kaluzny, "If 'Boys Will Be Boys,' then Girls will be Victims? A Meta-Analytic Review of the Research that Relates Masculine Ideology to Sexual Aggression," *Sex Roles* 46(11/12) (2002): 359–375.

N. Taylor and J. Mouzos, *"Community Attitudes To Violence Against Women Survey 2006: A Full Technical Report,"* (Canberra: Australian Institute of Criminology, 2006).

VicHealth, *Two Steps Forward, One Step Back: Community Attitudes to Violence Against Women. Progress and Challenges in Creating Safe, Respectful, and Healthy Environments for Victorian Women—A Summary of Findings of the Violence Against Women Community Attitudes Project,* (Melbourne: Victorian Health Promotion Foundation, 2006).

D. J. Whitaker, et al., "A Critical Review of Interventions for the Primary Prevention of Perpetration of Partner Violence," *Aggression and Violent Behavior* 11(2) (2006): 151–166.

Index

About the Editors and Contributors

Evan Stark is professor at the Rutgers School of Public Affairs and Administration, Rutgers University-Newark, the Department of Women and Gender Studies, Rutgers University-New Brunswick, and the University of Medicine and Dentistry School of Public Health, where he chairs the Department of Urban Health Administration on the Newark campus. His most recent book is *Coercive Control: How Men Entrap Women in Personal Life* (Oxford University Press, 2007)

Eve S. Buzawa is professor and the chairperson of the Department of Criminal Justice at the University of Massachusetts-Lowell. She is the co-author of the best-selling *Domestic Violence: The Criminal Justice Response* (Sage, 2003) among other works.

Edward G. Armstrong received his PhD in sociology from Temple University. He teaches sociology at St. Cloud State University.

Nancy Berns is associate professor of sociology at Drake University. She received her BA from Doane College and her PhD from the University of Illinois at Urbana-Champaign. Her teaching and research interests are in the areas of violence, media, social justice, grief, death, and social constructionism. She is the author of *Framing the Victim: Domestic Violence, Media and Social Problems* (2004).

Karen Boyle is a senior lecturer in film and television studies at the University of Glasgow, Scotland. She has written extensively about different aspects of gendered violence in representation and is the author of *Media and Violence: Gendering the Debates* (2005).

Karen E. Dill is a social psychologist whose research focuses on mass media, especially media violence and gender and racial stereotyping. She has given expert testimony before the U.S. Congress twice and has spoken professionally in Europe, Asia, and South America. She is currently writing a book about the social psychology of the mass media. She is the author of *How Fantasy Becomes Reality: Seeing Through Media Influence* from Oxford University Press.

Michael Flood is a research fellow at La Trobe University in Melbourne, Australia, funded by the Victorian Health Promotion Foundation (VicHealth). Dr. Flood conducts research on violence prevention, men and gender, male heterosexuality, fathering, and sexual and reproductive health. In 2006, he received an NSW Violence Against Women Prevention Award for his role in raising community and professional awareness of violence prevention.

Elaine J. Lawless is Curators' Distinguished Professor of English and Folklore Studies at the University of Missouri. She also holds joint and adjunct appointments with women's and gender studies, religious studies, and anthropology. Lawless has published extensively on women in religious practice and the narratives of battered women. She is the producer of the "Troubling Violence Performance Project" with M. Heather Carver, the director.

Donileen R. Loseke is a professor of sociology at the University of South Florida. Her books include *The Battered Woman and Shelters: The Social Construction of Wife Abuse* and *Thinking About Social Problems: An Introduction to Constructionist Perspectives*. With Richard Gelles she is the editor of *Current Controversies on Family Violence*. Her current project is an attempt to integrate the topic of emotion into scholarly attention to narrative identity.

Emily M. Meyer is a postdoctoral fellow in the College of Human Medicine, Department of Epidemiology, at Michigan State University. She earned her master's and undergraduate degrees in family and child ecology and doctorate in media and information studies. Her research synthesizes family issues with communication technology, media, and public health applications.

Bob Pease is chair of social work at Deakin University in Melbourne, Australia. His main research interests are in the fields of critical masculinity studies and critical social work practice. His most recent book is *International Encyclopedia of Men and Masculinities* (coedited, 2007).

Lori A. Post is associate professor in the Yale School of Medicine, Emergency Medicine. Her research interests are injury prevention from a public health perspective. Specifically, she is interested in gendered violence and has researched violence against women for the past decade.

Patricia K. Smith, MS, RD, is the Violence Prevention Program coordinator for the Michigan Department of Community Health. She has worked in violence prevention at MDCH for the past fourteen years and was director of the department's Violence Against Women Prevention Program for eleven years. She is currently the program director for the department's suicide prevention program.

Natalie Taylor is a senior research analyst with the Australian Institute of Criminology (AIC) and manages the AIC's Justice and Crime Analysis Research Program. Natalie's primary research interests at the AIC relate to sexual assault and domestic and family violence.

Kathryn Phillips Thill is a 2006 graduate in psychology from Lenoir-Rhyne College, where she did research on gender stereotypes in various media, including video game magazines. She currently works closely with children with special needs and is planning on continuing her education in the field of counseling.

Kim Webster is the senior program adviser at the Victorian Health Promotion Foundation. She is a social work graduate with more than twenty-five years' experience in direct care, policy development, and project management positions in both the government and non-government sectors. Kim has a particular interest in strengthening the role of social and economic policy to address the social determinants of health, especially those affecting women and migrant and refugee communities.